Bed & Breakfast U.S.A.

S O U T H E A S T   1 9 9 6

B&Bs can be your home away from home! With hundreds of listings under $50 a night, this indispensable directory gives you the keys to America's best alternative to hotels and shows you why B&Bs are the *only* way to travel. For business or pleasure, this information-packed book is every traveler's constant companion.

◆

"A valuable source of information."

—*New York Times*

◆

PEGGY ACKERMAN and her husband, MICHAEL ACKERMAN, are co-directors of the national Tourist House Association, based in Greentown, Pennsylvania. Founded by Betty Rundback in 1976, the Association now has over 1,300 members, all carefully screened by the Association to ensure the best homestay experience for travelers.

Bed & Breakfast U.S.A.

Southeast 1996

PEGGY ACKERMAN

Tourist House Association of America

A PLUME BOOK

PLUME
Published by the Penguin Group
Penguin Books USA Inc., 375 Hudson Street, New York, New York 10014, U.S.A.
Penguin Books Ltd, 27 Wrights Lane, London W8 5TZ, England
Penguin Books Australia Ltd, Ringwood, Victoria, Australia
Penguin Books Canada Ltd, 10 Alcorn Avenue, Toronto, Ontario, Canada M4V 3B2
Penguin Books (N.Z.) Ltd, 182–190 Wairau Road, Auckland 10, New Zealand

Penguin Books Ltd, Registered Offices:
Harmondsworth, Middlesex, England

Published by Plume, an imprint of Dutton Signet,
a division of Penguin Books USA Inc.

First Printing, January, 1996

10 9 8 7 6 5 4 3 2 1

Permission to use photographs on the back cover is gratefully acknowledged to Pulpit & Palette Inn, Martinsburg, West Virginia *(top)*, and The Elizabeth Bed & Breakfast, Charlotte, North Carolina.

 REGISTERED TRADEMARK—MARCA REGISTRADA

LC card number: 86-649303

Printed in the United States of America

Set in Palatino and Optima
Designed by Stanley S. Drate/Folio Graphics Co. Inc.

BOOKS ARE AVAILABLE AT QUANTITY DISCOUNTS WHEN USED TO PROMOTE PRODUCTS OR SERVICES. FOR INFORMATION PLEASE WRITE TO PREMIUM MARKETING DIVISION, PENGUIN BOOKS USA INC., 375 HUDSON STREET, NEW YORK, NEW YORK 10014.

If you want to be listed in future editions of this guide, DO NOT WRITE TO PLUME OR PENGUIN. See page 241 for a membership application, or write to:
    Tourist House Association
    RD 1, Box 12A
    Greentown, PA 18426
Applications will be accepted until March 31, 1996.

The book you are holding is the result of one woman's hard work and big dreams. In 1974, my mother, Betty Revits Rundback, began thinking about how to celebrate the American Bicentennial in 1976. She decided to take her family of seven on a cross-country tour, but didn't like the idea of staying in motels night after night. She wanted her children to really see the country, and to get to know its people along the way. Remembering back to her own childhood, when the house down the road offered comfortable lodging and a bountiful breakfast to travelers, she set out to create a similar experience for us. She never expected to spend months at the New York Public Library doing it! But that's exactly what she did, going through every telephone directory in America to find listings of family-style guesthouses, contacting all the owners individually, and finally assembling them into a pamphlet in time for the Bicentennial. With the information Betty had gathered, she founded the Tourist House Association of America, which she ran enthusiastically and successfully until her death on July 4, 1990. My wife, Peggy, now continues her work of bringing together guests and hosts from around the world. We dedicate this book to her, in loving memory of her warmth, compassion, and spirit.

—Michael Ackerman

Contents

Reservation service organizations appear here in boldface type.

Reservation service organizations appear here in boldface type.

Reservation service organizations appear here in boldface type.

Reservation service organizations appear here in boldface type.

Reservation service organizations appear here in boldface type.

Reservation service organizations appear here in boldface type.

Reservation service organizations appear here in boldface type.

Reservation service organizations appear here in boldface type.

Preface

If you are familiar with earlier editions of *Bed & Breakfast U.S.A.*, you know that this book has always been a labor of love. It is personally gratifying to see how it has grown from the first sixteen-page edition, titled *Guide to Tourist Homes and Guest Houses*, which was published in 1975 and contained 40 individual listings. Twenty years later, the eighteenth revised edition listed 1,305 homes and 111 reservation agencies, giving travelers access to over 11,000 host homes. This spectacular success indicates how strongly the revived concept of the guest house has recaptured the fancy of both travelers and proprietors. In fact, the book has become so big that we've divided it into three separate books for 1996! We hope you like this new, easier-to-use format.

On the other hand, what was welcomed as a reasonably priced alternative to the plastic ambience of motel chains has, in some instances, lost its unique qualities. Our mailbox is crammed with letters from grand hotels, condominium rental agencies, campground compounds, and chic inns with nightly tariffs topping the $100 mark. All share a common theme—they all serve breakfast and they all want to be listed in *Bed & Breakfast U.S.A.* Who can blame them? Since 1976, over half a million people have bought this best-selling guide.

We also receive a substantial amount of mail from our readers and we have tailored our book to meet their needs. We have given a great deal of thought to what we feel a B&B should be and are again focusing on our original definition: an owner-occupied residence with breakfast included at a fair rate, where the visitor is made to feel more like a welcome guest than a paying customer.

Because of personal experience, and comments from our readers, *Bed & Breakfast U.S.A., Southeast* will go back to the basics. We will no longer accept bed & breakfasts over $85 (this does not include reservation services, suites, cottages, apartments, or qualified inns) or with rates exceeding $40 when there are five guests sharing one bath; or if they do not offer breakfast (when paying $35–$40, no one wants to go out to a restaurant for breakfast—no matter how close it may be, it's just not the same as breakfast "at home").

As a result of these new guidelines, we will regretfully have to delete a great number of listings that have been on our roster for years. This does not imply in any way that these B&Bs aren't nice; it simply means that, in our opinion, they do not fit the traditional

B&B experience. I'm sure we will be receiving hundreds of letters from irate members disputing our opinion and pointing out that rising operating expenses must be reflected in their charges. Newcomers to the business decry our stand and tell us of the high costs that must somehow be recouped. While we sympathize and fully understand their positions, we must, in all fairness, be firm.

This is not a project for which listings have been compiled just for the sake of putting a book together; bigger isn't necessarily better. *Bed & Breakfast U.S.A., Southeast* is a product of a membership organization whose credo is "Comfort, cleanliness, cordiality, and fairness of cost." We solicit and rely on the comments of our readers. For this purpose, we include a tear-out form on page 251. If we receive negative reports, that member is dropped from our roster. *Bed & Breakfast U.S.A., Southeast* is looking for B&Bs set up to accommodate disabled guests. See page 251 for more information. We genuinely appreciate comments from guests—negative if necessary, positive when warranted. We want to hear from you!

All of the B&Bs described in this book are members of the Tourist House Association of America, RD 1 Box 12A, Greentown, Pennsylvania 18426. THAA dues are $45 annually. We share ideas and experiences by way of our newsletter and sometimes arrange regional seminars and conferences. To order a list of B&Bs that joined after this edition went to press, use the form in the back of this book.

PEGGY ACKERMAN
Tourist House Association of America

January 1996

Even after careful editing and proofreading, errors occasionally occur. We regret any inconvenience to our readers and members.

Acknowledgments

A special thanks to all the travel writers and reporters who have brought us to the attention of their audiences.

To my family, Mike Ackerman, Travis Kali, and Justin Ackerman, the three men in my life—thank you for all the encouragement and support you have shown; to Mary Kristyak Donnelly, a superb mother, grandmother, and best friend—I admire you so; to Bill Donnelly, dad and joke teller; to the grandmothers, Ann Revits and Helen Kristyak.

A final note of thanks to my editor, Leslie Jay, for her deeply appreciated assistance. Never too much, always a smile.

1

Introduction

Bed and Breakfast is the popular lodging alternative to hotel high-rises and motel monotony. B&Bs are either private residences where the owners rent spare bedrooms to travelers, or small, family-operated inns offering a special kind of warm, personal hospitality. Whether large or small, B&Bs will make you feel more like a welcome guest than a paying customer.

The custom of opening one's home to travelers dates back to the earliest days of Colonial America. Hotels and inns were few and far between in those days, and wayfarers relied on the kindness of strangers to provide a bed for the night. Which is why, perhaps, there is hardly a Colonial-era home in the mid-Atlantic states that does not boast: "George Washington Slept Here!"

During the Depression, the tourist home provided an economic advantage to both the traveler and the host. Travelers always drove through the center of town; there were no superhighways to bypass local traffic. A house with a sign in the front yard reading "Tourists" or "Guests" indicated that a traveler could rent a room for the night and have a cup of coffee before leaving in the morning. The usual cost for this arrangement was $2. The money represented needed income for the proprietor as well as the opportunity to chat with an interesting visitor.

In the 1950s, the country guest house became a popular alternative to the costly hotels in resort areas. The host compensated for the lack of hotel amenities, such as private bathrooms, by providing comfortable bedrooms and bountiful breakfasts at a modest price. The visitors enjoyed the home-away-from-home atmosphere; the hosts were pleased to have paying houseguests.

The incredible growth in international travel that has occurred over the past 30 years has provided yet another stimulus. Millions of Americans now vacation annually in Europe, and travelers have become enchanted with the bed and breakfast concept so popular in England, Ireland, and other parts of the Continent. In fact, many well-traveled Americans are delighted to learn that we "finally" have B&Bs here. But, as you now know, they were always here—just a rose by another name.

Bed and breakfasts are for:

- **Parents of college kids:** Tuition is costly enough without the added expense of Parents' Weekends. Look for a B&B near campus.
- **Parents traveling with children:** A family living room, playroom, or backyard is preferable to the confines of a motel room.
- **"Parents" of pets:** Many proprietors will allow your well-behaved darling to come, too. This can cut down on the expense and trauma of kenneling Fido.
- **Business travelers:** Being "on the road" can be lonely and expensive. It's so nice, after a day's work, to return to a home-away-from-home.
- **Women traveling alone:** Friendship and conversation are the natural ingredients of a guest house.
- **Skiers:** Lift prices are lofty, so it helps to save some money on lodging. Many mountain homes include home-cooked meals in your room rate.
- **Students:** A visit with a family is a pleasant alternative to camping or the local "Y."
- **Visitors from abroad:** Cultural exchanges are often enhanced by a host who can speak your language.
- **Carless travelers:** If you plan to leave the auto at home, it's nice to know that many B&Bs are convenient to public transportation. Hosts will often arrange to meet your bus, plane, or train for a nominal fee.
- **Schoolteachers and retired persons:** Exploring out-of-the-way places is fun and will save you money.
- **History buffs:** Many B&Bs are located in areas important to our country's past. A number have the distinction of being listed on the National Register of Historic Places.
- **Sports fans:** Tickets to championship games are expensive. A stay at a B&B helps to defray the cost of attending out-of-town events.
- **Antique collectors:** Many hosts have lovely personal collections, and nearby towns are filled with undiscovered antique shops.
- **House hunters:** It's a practical way of trying out a neighborhood.
- **Relocating corporate executives:** It's more comfortable to stay in a real home while you look for a permanent residence. Hosts will often give more practical advice than professional realtors.
- **Relatives of hospitalized patients:** Many B&Bs are located near major hospitals. Hosts will offer tea and sympathy when visiting hours are over.
- **Convention and seminar attendees:** Staying at a nearby B&B is less expensive than checking into a hotel.

And everyone else who has had it up to here with plastic motel monotony!

What It Is Like to Be a Guest in a B&B

The B&B descriptions provided in this book will help you choose the places that have the greatest appeal to you. A firsthand insight into local culture awaits you; imagine the advantage of arriving in New York City or San Francisco and having an insider to help you sidestep the tourist traps and direct you to that special restaurant or discount store. Or explore the countryside, where fresh air and home-cooked meals beckon. Your choice is as wide as the U.S.A.

Each bed and breakfast listed offers personal contact, a real advantage in unfamiliar environments. You may not have a phone in your room or a TV on the dresser. You may even have to pad down the hall in robe and slippers to take a shower, but you'll discover that little things count.

- In Williamsburg, Virginia, a visitor from Germany opted to stay at a B&B to help improve her conversational English. When the hostess saw that she was having difficulty understanding directions, she personally escorted her on a tour of Old Williamsburg.
- In Pennsylvania, the guests mistakenly arrived a week prior to their stated reservation date and the B&B was full. The hostess made a call to a neighbor who accommodated the couple. (By the way, the neighbor has now become a B&B host!)
- In New York City, a guest was an Emmy Award nominee and arrived with his tuxedo in need of pressing. The hostess pressed it; when he claimed his award over nationwide TV, he looked well groomed!

Expect the unexpected, such as a pot of brewed coffee upon your arrival, or fresh flowers on a nightstand. At the very least, count on our required standard of cleanliness and comfort. Although we haven't personally visited all of the places listed, they have all been highly recommended by chambers of commerce or former guests. We have either spoken to or corresponded with all of the proprietors; they are a friendly group of people who enjoy having visitors. They will do all in their power to make your stay memorable.

Our goal is to enable the traveler to crisscross the country and stay only at B&Bs along the way. To achieve this, your help is vital. Please take a moment to write us of your experiences; we will follow up on every suggestion. Your comments will serve as the yardstick by which we can measure the quality of our accommodations. For your convenience, an evaluation form is included at the back of this book.

Cost of Accommodations

Bed and Breakfast, in the purest sense, is a private home, often referred to as a "homestay," where the owners rent their spare bedrooms to travelers. These are the backbone of this book.

However, American ingenuity has enhanced this simple idea to include more spectacular homes, mansions, small inns, and intimate hotels. With few exceptions, the proprietor is the host and lives on the premises.

There is a distinction between B&B homestays and B&B inns. Inns are generally defined as a business and depend upon revenue from guests to pay expenses. They usually have six or more guest rooms, and may have a restaurant that is open to the public. The tariff at inns is usually higher than at a homestay because the owners must pay the mortgage, running expenses, and staff, whether or not guests come.

Whether plain or fancy, all B&Bs are based on the concept that people are tired of the plastic monotony of motels and are disappointed that even the so-called budget motels can be quite expensive. Travelers crave the personal touch, and they sincerely enjoy "visiting" rather than just "staying."

Prices vary accordingly. There are places listed in this book where lovely lodging may be had for as low as $40 a night, and others that feature an overnight stay with a gourmet breakfast in a canopied bed for $95. Whatever the price, if you see the sign ✪ , it means that the B&B has guaranteed its rates through 1996 to holders of this book, so be sure to mention it when you call or write! (If there is a change in ownership, the guarantee may not apply. Please notify us in writing if any host fails to honor the guaranteed rate.)

Accommodations vary in price depending upon the locale and the season. Peak season usually refers to the availability of skiing in winter and water sports in summer; in the Sunbelt states, winter months are usually the peak season. Some B&Bs require a two-night weekend minimum during peak periods, and three nights on holiday weekends. Off-season rate schedules are usually reduced. Resorts and major cities are generally more expensive than out-of-the-way places. However, B&Bs are always less expensive than hotels and motels of equivalent caliber in the same area. A weekly rate is usually less expensive than a daily rate. Special reductions are sometimes given to families (occupying two rooms) or senior citizens. Whenever reduced rates are available, you will find this noted in the individual listings.

Meals

Breakfast: *Continental* refers to fruit or juice, rolls, and a hot beverage. Many hosts pride themselves on home-baked breads, homemade preserves, as well as imported teas and cakes, so their Continental breakfast may be quite deluxe. Several hosts have regular jobs outside the home, so you may have to adjust your schedule to theirs. A "full" breakfast includes fruit, cereal and/or eggs, breakfast meats, breads, and a hot beverage. The table is set family-style and is often the highlight of a B&B's hospitality. Either a Continental breakfast or full breakfast is included in the room rate unless otherwise specified.

Other Meals: If listed as "available," you can be assured that the host takes pride in his or her cooking skills. The prices for lunch or dinner are usually reasonable but are not included in the quoted room rate unless clearly specified as "included."

Making Reservations

- Reservations are a MUST or you may risk missing out on the accommodations of your choice. Reserve *early* and confirm with a deposit equal to one night's stay. If you call to inquire about reservations, please remember the difference in time zones. When dialing outside of your area, remember to dial the digit "1" before the area code.
- Many individual B&Bs now accept charge cards. This information is indicated in the listings by the symbols MC for Master-Card, AMEX for American Express, etc. A few have a surcharge for this service, so inquire as to the policy.
- Cash or traveler's checks are the accepted method of paying for your stay. Be sure to inquire whether or not tax is included in the rates quoted so that you will know exactly how much your lodging will cost.

- Rates are based on single or double occupancy of a room as quoted. Expect that an extra person(s) in the room will be charged a small additional fee. Inquire when making your reservation what the charge will be.
- If a listing indicates that children or pets are welcome, it is expected that they will be well behaved. All of our hosts take pride in their homes and it would be unfair to subject them to circumstances in which their possessions might be abused or the other houseguests disturbed by an unruly child or animal.
- Please note that many hosts have their own resident pets. If you are allergic or don't care to be around animals, inquire before making a reservation.
- In homes where smoking is permitted, do check to see if it is restricted in any of the rooms. Most hosts object to cigars.
- Where listings indicate that social drinking is permitted, it usually refers to your bringing your own beverages. Most hosts will provide ice; many will allow you to chill mixers in the refrigerator, and others offer complimentary wine and snacks. A few B&B inns have licenses to sell liquor. Any drinking should not be excessive.
- If Yes is indicated in the listings for airport/station pickup, it means that the host will meet your plane, bus, or train for a fee.
- Feel free to request brochures and local maps so that you can better plan for your visit.
- Do try to fit in with the host's house rules. You are on vacation; he or she isn't!
- A reservation form is included at the back of this book for your convenience; just tear it out and send it in to the B&B of your choice.

Cancellations

Cancellation policies vary from one B&B to another, so be sure to read the fine print on the reservation form. Many require a 15-day notice to refund the entire deposit, after which they will refund only if the room is rebooked. When a refund is due, most keep a processing fee and return the balance. A few keep the deposit and apply it to a future stay.

While these policies may seem harsh, please keep in mind that B&Bs are not hotels, which commonly overbook and where no-show guests can easily be replaced. Your host may have turned down a prospective guest, and may have bought special breakfast food in anticipation of your visit and should not be penalized. If you feel you've been unfairly treated in a cancellation situation, please do let us know.

B&B Reservation Services

There are many host families who prefer not to be individually listed in a book, and would rather have their houseguests referred by a coordinating agency. The organizations listed in this book are all members of the Tourist House Association. They all share our standards regarding the suitability of the host home as to cordiality, cleanliness, and comfort.

The majority do a marvelous job of matching host and guest according to age, interests, language, and any special requirements. To get the best match, it is practical to give them as much time as possible to find the host home best tailored to your needs.

Many have prepared descriptive pamphlets describing the homes on their rosters, the areas in which the homes are located, and information regarding special things to see and do. *Send a self-addressed, stamped, business-size envelope to receive a descriptive directory by return mail along with a reservation form for you to complete.* When returning the form, you will be asked to select the home or homes listed in the brochure that most appeal to you. (The homes are usually given a code number for reference.) The required deposit should accompany your reservation. Upon receipt, the coordinator will make the reservation and advise you of the name, address, telephone number, and travel instructions for your host.

A few agencies prepare a descriptive directory and *include* the host's name, address, and telephone number so that you can contact the host and make your arrangements directly. They charge anywhere from $2 to $11 for the directory.

Several agencies are *membership* organizations, charging guests an annual fee ranging from $5 to $25 per person. Their descriptive directories are free to members and a few of them maintain toll-free telephone numbers for reservations.

Most reservation services have a specific geographic focus. The coordinators are experts in the areas they represent. They can often make arrangements for car rentals, theater tickets, and touring suggestions, and offer information in planning a trip best suited to your interests.

Most work on a commission basis with the host, and that fee is included in the room rates quoted in each listing. Some make a surcharge for a one-night stay; others require a two- or three-night minimum stay for holiday periods or special events. Some will accept a credit card for the reservation, but the balance due must be paid to the host in cash or traveler's checks.

All of their host homes offer a Continental breakfast, and some may include a full breakfast.

Many reservation services in the larger cities have, in addition to the traditional B&Bs, a selection of apartments, condominiums, and houses *without hosts in residence*. This may be appealing to those travelers anticipating an extended stay in a particular area.

Statewide services are listed first in the section for each state. City or regionally based organizations are listed first under the heading for that area. For a complete description of their services, look them up under the city and state where they're based.

NOTE: When calling, do so during normal business hours (for that time zone), unless otherwise stated. Collect calls are not accepted.

2

How to Start Your Own B&B

What It's Like to Be a Host

Hosts are people who like the idea of accommodating travelers and sharing their home and the special features of their area with them. They are people who have houses too large for their personal needs and like the idea of supplementing their income by having people visit. For many, it's a marvelous way of meeting rising utility and maintenance costs. For young families, it is a way of buying and keeping that otherwise-too-large house, as well as a way of furnishing it, since many of the furnishings may be tax deductible. Another advantage is that many state and local governments have recognized the service that some host families perform. In browsing through this book you will note that some homes are listed on the National Historic Register. Some state governments allow owners of landmark and historical houses a special tax advantage if they are used for any business purpose. Check with the Historical Preservation Society in your state for details.

If you have bedrooms to spare, if you sincerely like having overnight guests, if your home is clean and comfortable, this is an opportunity to consider. It is a unique business because *you* set the time of the visit and the length of stay. (Guest houses are not boarding homes.) You invite the guests at *your* convenience, and the extras, such as meals, are entirely up to you. You can provide a cup of coffee, complete meals, or just a room and shared bath. Remember that your income may be erratic and should not be depended upon to pay for monthly bills. However, it can afford you some luxuries.

Although the majority of hosts are women, many couples are finding pleasure in this joint venture. The general profile of a typical host is a friendly, outgoing, flexible person who is proud of his or her home and hometown. The following information and suggestions represent a guideline to consider in deciding whether becoming a B&B host is really for you.

There are no set rules for the location, type, or style of a B&B. Apartments, condos, farmhouses, town houses, beach houses, vacation cottages, houseboats, mansions, as well as the traditional one-family dwelling are all appropriate. The important thing is for the host to be on the premises. The setting may be urban, rural, or suburban, near public transportation or in the hinterlands. Location is only important if you want to have guests every night. Areas where tourism is popular, such as resort areas or major cities, are often busier than out-of-the-way places. However, if a steady stream of visitors is not that important or even desirable, it doesn't matter where you are. People will contact you if your rates are reasonable and if there is something to see and do in your area, or if it is near a major transportation route.

Setting Rates

Consider carefully four key factors in setting your rates: location, private versus shared bath, type of breakfast, and your home itself.

Location: If you reside in a traditional resort or well-touristed area, near a major university or medical center, or in an urban hub or gateway city, your rates should be at least 40 percent lower than those of the area's major motels or hotels. If you live in an out-of-the-way location, your rates must be extremely reasonable. If your area has a "season"—snow sports in winter, water sports in summer—offer off-season rates when these attractions are not available. Reading through this book will help you to see what the going rate is in a situation similar to yours.

The Bath: You are entitled to charge more for a room with private bath. If the occupants of two rooms share one bath, the rate should be less. If more than five people must share one bathroom, you may have complaints, unless your rates are truly inexpensive.

The Breakfast: Figure the approximate cost of your ingredients, plus something for your time. Allow about $2 to $3 for a Continental breakfast, $4 to $5 for a full American breakfast, and then *include* it in the rate.

Your Home: Plan on charging a fair and reasonable rate for a typical B&B home, one that is warm and inviting, clean and comfortable. If your home is exceptionally luxurious, with king-size beds, Jacuzzi baths, tennis courts, or hot tubs, you will find guests who are willing to pay a premium. If your home is over 75 years old, well restored, with lots of antiques, you may also be able to charge a higher rate.

The Three Bs—Bed, Breakfast, and Bath

The Bedroom: The ideal situation for a prospective host is the possession of a house too large for current needs. The children may be away at college most of the year or may have left permanently, leaving behind their bedrooms and, in some cases, an extra bath. Refurbishing these rooms does not mean refurnishing; an extraordinary investment need not be contemplated for receiving guests. Take a long, hard look at the room. With a little imagination and a little monetary outlay, could it be changed into a bedroom *you'd* be pleased to spend the night in? Check it out *before* you go any further. Are the beds comfortable? Is the carpet clean? Are the walls attractive? Do the curtains or shades need attention? Are there sturdy hangers in the closet? Would emptying the closet and bureau be an impossible task? Is there a good light to read by? A writing table and comfortable chair? Peek under the bed to see if there are dust balls or old magazines tucked away. While relatives and friends would "understand" if things weren't perfect, a paying guest is entitled to cleanliness and comfort.

Equip the guest bureau or dresser with a good mirror, and provide a comfortable chair and good reading light. The clothes closet should be free of your family's clothing and storage items, and stocked with firm, plastic hangers, a few skirt hangers, and some hooks. Sachets hung on the rod will chase musty odors. Provide room-darkening shades or blinds on the windows. And, if your house is located on a busy street, it is wise to have your guest bedrooms in the rear. Paying guests are entitled to a good night's rest! If your tap water is not tasty, it is thoughtful to supply bottled water.

If the idea of sprucing up the room has you overwhelmed, forget the idea and continue to be a guest rather than a host! If, however, a little "spit and polish," replacement of lumpy mattresses, sagging springs, and freshening the room in general present no problem, continue!

Mattresses should be firm, covered with a mattress pad, attractive linens, and bedspread. Although seconds are OK, good-quality linens are a wise investment, since cheap sheets tend to pill. Offer a selection of pillows of various firmnesses—a choice of down or fiberfill is the ultimate in consideration! Twin beds are often preferred, since many people do not wish to share a bed. Sofa beds are really not comfortable and should be avoided. Is there a bedside lamp and night table on each side of the bed? Bulbs should be at least 75 watts for comfortable reading. A luggage rack is convenient for guests and keeps the bedspread clean. Provide a varied assortment of books, current magazines in a rack, a local newspaper, and some information on what's doing in your town along with a map. If yours is a shared-bath accommodation, do provide a well-lit mirror and convenient electric outlet for makeup and shaving purposes. It will take the pressure off the bathroom! A fresh thermos of ice water and drinking glasses placed on an attractive dresser tray is always appreciated. Put it in the room while the guest is out to dinner, right next to the dish of hard candy or fruit. A fancy candlestick is a pretty accessory and a useful object in case of a power failure. Dresser drawers should be clean and lined with fresh paper. A sachet, flashlight, and a pad and pencil are thoughtful touches. For safety's sake, prohibit smoking in the bedroom. Besides, the odor of tobacco clings forever. Always spray the bedroom with air freshener a few minutes before the guest arrives. On warm or humid days, turn on the air conditioner as well.

From time to time sleep in each guest room yourself. It's the best test.

The Breakfast: Breakfast time can be the most pleasant part of a guest's stay. It is at the breakfast table with you and the other guests that suggestions are made as to what to see and do, and exchanges of experiences are enjoyed. From a guest's point of view, the only expected offering is what is known as a Continental breakfast, which usually consists of juice, roll, and coffee or tea.

Breakfast fare is entirely up to you. If you are a morning person who whips out of bed at the crack of dawn with special recipes for muffins dancing in your head, muffins to be drenched with your homemade preserves followed by eggs Benedict, an assortment of imported coffees or exotic teas—hop to it! You will play to a most appreciative audience. If, however, morning represents an awful intrusion on sleep, and the idea of talking to anyone before noon is difficult, the least you should do is to prepare the breakfast table the night before with the necessary mugs, plates, and silverware. Fill the electric coffeepot and leave instructions that the first one up should plug it in; you can even hook it up to a timer so that it will brew automatically!

Most of us fall somewhere in between these two extremes. Remember that any breakfast at "home" is preferable to getting dressed, getting into a car, and driving to some coffee shop. Whether you decide upon a Continental breakfast or a full American breakfast, consisting of juice or fruit, cereal or eggs, possibly bacon or sausage, toast, rolls, and coffee or tea, is up to you. It is most important that whatever the fare, it be included in your room rate. It is most awkward, especially after getting to know and like your guests, to present an additional charge for breakfast.

With so many of us watching calories, caffeine, and cholesterol, be prepared to offer unsweetened and/or whole grain breads, oat-bran cereals and muffins, and brewed decaf coffee or tea. It is also thoughtful to inquire about your guests' dietary restrictions and allergies. Whatever you serve, do have your table attractively set.

Some Suggestions

- Don't have a messy kitchen. If you have pets, make sure their food dishes are removed after they've eaten. If you have cats, make sure they don't walk along the countertops, and be certain that litter boxes are cleaned without fail. Sparkling clean surroundings are far more important than the decor.
- Let guests know when breakfast will be served. Check to see if they have any allergies, diet restrictions, or dislikes. Vary the menu if guests are staying more than one night.
- Do offer one nonsweet bread for breakfast.
- Consider leaving a breakfast order sheet in each room with a request that it be returned before guests retire. It might read:

We serve breakfast between 7 AM and 10 AM. Please check your preference and note the time at which you plan to eat.

☐ Coffee ☐ Tea ☐ Decaf ☐ Milk ☐ Toast ☐ Muffins
☐ Sweet Rolls ☐ Orange Juice ☐ Tomato Juice ☐ Fruit Cup

The Bath: This really is the third B in B&B. If you are blessed with an extra bathroom for the exclusive use of a guest, that's super. If guests will have to share the facilities with others, that really presents no problem. If it's being shared with your family, the family must always be "last in line." Be sure that they are aware of the guest's importance; the guest, paying or otherwise, always comes first. No retainers, used Band-Aids, or topless toothpaste tubes are to be carelessly left on the sink. The tub, shower, floor, and toilet bowl are to be squeaky clean. The mirrors and chrome should sparkle, and a supply of toilet tissue, fresh soap, and unfrayed towels goes a long way in reflecting a high standard of cleanliness. Make sure that the grout between tiles is free of mildew and that the shower curtain is unstained; add nonskid tape to the tub. Cracked ceilings should be repaired. Paint should be free of chips, and if your bath is wallpapered, make certain no loose edges mar its beauty.

Although it is your responsibility to check out the bath at least twice a day, most guests realize that in a share-the-bath situation they should leave the room ready for the next person's use. It is a thoughtful reminder for you to leave tub cleanser, a cleaning towel or sponge, and bathroom deodorant handy for this purpose. A wastepaper basket, paper towels, and paper cups should be part of your supplies. Needless to say, your hot water and septic systems should be able to accommodate the number of guests you'll have without being overtaxed. Call the plumber to fix any clogged drains or dripping faucets. Make sure that there are enough towel bars and hooks to accommodate the towels of all guests. Extra bathroom touches:

- Use liquid soap dispensers in lieu of bar soap on the sink.
- Provide a place for guests' personal toilet articles; shelves add convenience and eliminate clutter.
- Give different colored towels to each guest.
- Supply each guest room with its own bath soap in a covered soap dish.
- Provide guests with one-size-fits-all terry robes.

The B&B Business

Money Matters: Before embarking upon any business, it's a good idea to discuss it with an accountant and possibly an attorney. Since you'll be using your home for a business enterprise there are things with which they are familiar that are important for you to know. For instance, you may want to incorporate, so find out what the pros and cons are. Ask about depreciation. Deductible business expenses may include refurbishing, furnishings, supplies, printing costs, postage, etc. An accountant will be able to guide you with a simple system of record keeping. Accurate records will help you analyze income and expense, and show if you are breaking even or operating at a profit or a loss.

Taxes: Contact your state department of taxation requesting specific written information regarding tax collection and payment schedules. Get a sales tax number from your county clerk. If you rent rooms less than 15 days a year, you need not report the B&B income on your federal return. Income after the fourteenth day is taxable, and you can take deductions and depreciation allowances against it. If the revenues from running the B&B are insignificant, you can call it "hobby income" and avoid taxes. However, you can't qualify as a business and may lose other tax advantages.

Record Keeping: Open a B&B checking account and use it to pay expenses and to deposit all income, including sales tax associated with the B&B. Write checks whenever possible for purchases; get dated receipts when you can. Estimate the cost of serving breakfast and multiply it by the number of guests you feed annually; keep track of extra expenses for household supplies and utilities.

The Case for Credit Cards: Many guests prefer to stay now and pay later; business travelers like the easy record keeping for their expense sheets. Even if you don't wish to accept them on a regular basis, credit cards give you the opportunity to take a deposit over the phone when there isn't time to receive one by mail. The cost is negligible, generally 4 percent.

If you do accept a last-minute reservation without a credit card number to guarantee it, make certain the caller understands that if they don't show up, and you have held the room for them, you will have lost a night's rent. You may also remind the caller that if they aren't there by a mutually agreed upon time, you may rent the room to someone else. Needless to say, it is equally important for you to remain at home to receive the guests or to be on hand for a phone call should they get lost en route to your home.

Insurance: It is important to call your insurance broker. Some homeowner policies have a clause covering "an occasional overnight paying guest." See if you will be protected under your existing coverage and, if not, what the additional premium would be.

Every home should be equipped with smoke detectors and fire extinguishers. All fire hazards should be eliminated; stairways and halls should be well lit and kept free of clutter. If you haven't already done so, immediately post prominently the emergency numbers for the fire department, police, and ambulance service.

Safety Reminders: Equip guest bedrooms and bathrooms with nightlights. Keep a flashlight (in working order!) in each bedroom, in case of power failure. Bathrooms should have nonslip surfaces in the tub and shower, and handholds should be installed in bathtubs. Keep a well-stocked first aid kit handy and know how to use it. Learn the Heimlich Maneuver and CPR (cardiopulmonary resuscitation). Periodically test smoke detectors and fire extinguishers to make certain they are in working order.

Regulations: If you have read this far and are still excited about the concept of running a B&B, there are several steps to take at this point. As of this writing, there don't seem to be any specific laws governing B&Bs. Since guests are generally received on an irregular basis, B&Bs do not come under the same laws governing hotels and motels. And since B&Bs aren't inns where emphasis is on food rather than on lodging, no comparison can really be made in that regard either. As the idea grows, laws and regulations will probably be passed. Refer to the back of *Bed & Breakfast U.S.A., Southeast* to write to your state's office of tourism for information. The address and phone number are listed for your convenience. You might even call or write to a few B&Bs in your state and ask the host about his or her experience in this regard. Most hosts will be happy to give you the benefit of their experience, but keep in mind that they are busy people and it would be wise to limit your intrusion upon their time.

If you live in a traditional, residential area and you are the first in your neighborhood to consider operating a B&B, it would be prudent to examine closely the character of houses nearby. Do physicians, attorneys, accountants, or psychologists maintain offices in their residences? Do dressmakers, photographers, cosmeticians, or architects receive clients in their homes? These professions are legally accepted in the most prestigious communities as "customary house occupations." Bed and breakfast has been tested in many communities where the question was actually brought to court. In towns from La Jolla, California, to Croton-on-Hudson, New York, bed and breakfast has been approved and accepted.

Zoning boards are not always aware of the wide acceptance of the B&B concept. Possibly the best evidence that you could present to them is a copy of *Bed & Breakfast U.S.A., Southeast,* which indicates that it is an accepted practice throughout the entire country. It illustrates the caliber of the neighborhoods, the beauty of the homes, and the fact that many professionals are also hosts. Reassure the zoning board that you will accept guests only by advance reservation. You will not display any exterior signs to attract attention to your home. You will keep your home and grounds properly maintained, attractive, and in no way detract from the integrity of your neighborhood. You will direct guests to proper parking facilities and do nothing to intrude upon the privacy of your neighbors.

After all, there is little difference between the visit of a family friend and a B&B guest, because that is the spirit and essence of a B&B. Just as a friend would make prior arrangements to be a houseguest, so will a B&B guest make a reservation in advance. Neither would just drop in for an overnight stay. We are happy to share letters from hosts attesting to the high caliber, honesty, and integrity of B&B guests that come as a result of reading about their accommodations in this book. There are over 12,000 B&Bs extending our kind of hospitality throughout the United States, and the number is increasing geometrically every day.

You should also bring along a copy of *Bed & Breakfast U.S.A., Southeast* when you go to visit the local chamber of commerce. Most of them are enthusiastic, because additional visitors mean extra business for local restaurants, shops, theaters, and businesses. This is a good time to inquire what it would cost to join the chamber of commerce.

The Name: The naming of your B&B is most important and will take some time and consideration because this is the moment when dreams become reality. It will be used on your brochures, stationery, and bills. (If you decide to incorporate, the corporation needs a name!) It should somehow be descriptive of the atmosphere you wish to convey.

Brochure: Once you have given a name to your house, design a brochure. The best ones include a reservation form and can be mailed to your prospective guests. The brochure should contain the name of your B&B, address, phone number, best time to call, your name, a brief description of your home, its ambience, a brief history of the house if it is old, the number of guest rooms, whether or not baths are shared, the type of breakfast served, rates, required deposit, minimum stay requirement if any, dates when you'll be closed, and your cancellation policy. Although widely used, the phrase "Rates subject to change without notice" should be avoided. Rather, state the specific dates when the rates will be valid. A deposit of one night's stay is acceptable, and the promise of a full refund if cancellation is received at least two weeks prior to arrival is typical. If you have reduced rates for a specific length of stay, for families, for senior citizens, etc., mention it.

The Rate Sheet should be a separate insert so that if rates change, the entire brochure need not be discarded. Mention your smoking policy. If you do allow smoking inside the house, do you reserve any bedrooms for nonsmokers? Don't forget to mention the ages of your children, and describe any pets in residence. If you don't accept a guest's pet, be prepared to supply the name, address, and phone number of a reliable local kennel.

If you can converse in a foreign language, say so, because many visitors from abroad seek out B&Bs; it's a marvelous plus to be able to chat in their native tongue. Include your policy regarding children, pets, or smokers, and whether you offer the convenience of a guest refrigerator or barbecue. It is helpful to include directions from a major route and a simple map for finding your home. It's a good idea to include a line or two about yourself and your interests, and do mention what there is to see and do in the area as well as proximity to any major university. A line drawing of your house is a good investment since the picture can be used not only on the brochure but on your stationery, postcards, and greeting cards as well. If you can't have this taken care of locally, write the Tourist House Association. We have a service that can handle it for you.

Take your ideas to a reliable printer for his professional guidance. Don't forget to keep the receipt for the printing bill since this is a business expense.

Confirmation Letter: Upon receipt of a paid reservation, do send out a letter confirming it. You can design a form letter and have it offset printed by a printer, since the cost of doing so is usually nominal. Include the dates of the stay; number of people expected; the rate, including tax; the cancellation policy; as well as explicit directions by car and, if applicable, by public transportation. A simple map reflecting the exact location of your home in relation to major streets and highways is most useful. It is a good idea to ask your guests to call you if they will be traveling and unavailable by phone for the week prior to their expected arrival. You might even want to include any of the house rules regarding smoking, pets, or whatever.

Successful Hosting

The Advantage of Hosting: The nicest part of being a B&B host is that you aren't required to take guests every day of the year. Should there be times when having guests would not be convenient, you can always say you're full and try to arrange an alternate date. But most important, keep whatever date you reserve. It is an excellent idea at the time reservations are accepted to ask for the name and telephone number of an emergency contact should you have to cancel unexpectedly. However, *never* have a guest come to a locked door. If an emergency arises and you cannot reach your prospective guests in time, do make arrangements for someone to greet them, and make alternate arrangements so that they can be accommodated.

House Rules: While you're in the thinking stage, give some thought to the rules you'd like your guests to adhere to. The last thing you want for you or your family is to feel uncomfortable in your own home. Make a list of House Rules concerning arrival and departure during the guests' stay, and specify when breakfast is served. If you don't want guests coming home too late, say so. Most hosts like to lock up at a certain hour at night, so arrange for an extra key for night owls. If that makes you uncomfortable, have a curfew on your House Rules list. If smoking disturbs you, confine the area where it's permitted.

Some guests bring a bottle of their favorite beverage and enjoy a drink before going out to dinner. Many hosts enjoy a cocktail hour too, and often provide cheese and crackers to share with guests. B&Bs cannot sell drinks to guests since this would require licensing. If you'd rather no drinks be consumed in your home, say so.

Many hosts don't mind accommodating a well-behaved pet. If you don't mind, or have pets of your own, discuss this with your guests before they pack Fido's suitcase. Your House Rules can even be included in your brochure. That way, both host and guest are aware of each other's likes and dislikes, and no hard feelings are made.

Entertaining: One of the most appealing features of being a guest at a B&B is the opportunity to visit in the evening with the hosts. After a day of sightseeing or business, it is most relaxing and pleasant to sit around the living room and chat. For many hosts, this is the most enjoyable part of having guests. However, if you are accommodating several people on a daily basis, entertaining can be tiring. Don't feel you'll be offending anyone by excusing yourself to attend to your own family or personal needs. The situation can be easily handled by having a room to which you can retreat, and offering your guests the living room, den, or other area for games, books, magazines, and perhaps the use of a television or bridge table. Most guests enjoy just talking to one another since this is the main idea of staying at a B&B.

The Telephone: This is a most important link between you and your prospective guests. As soon as possible, have your telephone number included under your B&B name in the white pages. It is a good idea to be listed in the appropriate section in your telephone directory yellow pages. If your home phone is used for a lot of personal calls, ask the local telephone company about call-waiting service, or think about installing a separate line for your B&B. If you are out a lot, give some thought to using a telephone answering device to explain your absence and time of return, and record the caller's message. There is nothing more frustrating to a prospective guest than to call and get a constant busy signal, or no answer at all. Request that the caller leave his or her name and address so that you can mail a reservation form. This will help eliminate the necessity of having to return long-distance calls. If the caller wants further information, he or she will call again at the time you said you'd be home.

B&B guests don't expect a phone in the guest room. However, there are times when they might want to use your phone for a long-distance call. In your House Rules list, suggest that any such calls be charged to their home telephone. Business travelers often have telephone charge cards for this purpose. In either case, you should keep a telephone record book and timer near your instrument. Ask the caller to enter the city called, telephone number, and length of call. Thus, you will have an accurate record should a charge be inadvertently added to your bill. Or, if you wish, you can add telephone charges to the guest bill. A telephone operator will quote the cost of the per-minute charge throughout the country for this purpose.

Maid Service: If you have several guest rooms and bathrooms, you may find yourself being a chambermaid as part of the business. Naturally, each guest gets fresh linens upon arrival. If a guest stays up to three days, it isn't expected that bed linen be changed every day. What is expected is that the room be freshened and the bath be cleaned and towels replaced every day. If you don't employ a full-time maid you may want to investigate the possibility of hiring a high school student on a part-time basis to give you a hand with the housekeeping. Many guests, noticing the absence of help, will voluntarily lend a hand, although they have the right to expect some degree of service, particularly if they are paying a premium rate.

Keys: A great many hosts are not constantly home during the day. Some do "hosting" on a part-time basis, while involved with regular jobs. There are times when even full-time hosts have to be away during the day. If guests are to have access to the house while you are not on the premises, make extra keys and attach them to an oversize key chain. It is also wise to take a key deposit of $50 simply to assure return of the key. Let me add that in the 16 years of my personal experience, as well as in the opinions of other hosts, B&B guests are the most honest people you can have. No one has ever had even a washcloth stolen, let alone the family treasures. In fact, it isn't unusual for the guest to leave a small gift after a particularly pleasant visit. On the other hand, guests are sometimes forgetful and leave belongings behind. For this reason it is important for you to have their names and addresses so that you can return their possessions. They will expect to reimburse you for the postage.

Registering Guests: You should keep a regular registration ledger for the guest to complete before checking in. The information should include the full name of each guest, home address, phone number, business address and telephone, and auto license number. It's a good idea to include the name and phone number of a friend or relative in case of an emergency. This information will serve you well for other contingencies, such as the guest leaving some important article behind, an unpaid long-distance phone call, or the rare instance of an unpaid bill. You may prefer to have this information on your guest bill, which should be designed as a two-part carbon form. You will then have a record and the guest has a ready receipt. (Receipts are very important to business travelers!)

Settling the Bill: The average stay in a B&B is two nights. A deposit equal to one night's lodging is the norm; when to collect the balance is up to you. Most guests pay upon leaving, but if they leave so early that the settling of the bill at that time is inconvenient, you can request the payment the previous night. You might want to consider the convenience of accepting a major credit card, but contact the sponsoring company first to see what percentage of your gross is expected for this service. If you find yourself entertaining more business visitors than vacationers, it might be something you should offer. Most travelers are aware that cash or traveler's checks are the accepted modes of payment. Accepting a personal check is rarely risky, but again, it's up to you. You might include your preference in your brochure.

Other Meals: B&B means that only breakfast is served. If you enjoy cooking and would like to offer other meals for a fee, make sure that you investigate the applicable health laws. If you have to install a commercial kitchen, the idea might be too expensive for current consideration. However, allowing guests to store fixings for a quick snack or to use your barbecue can be a very attractive feature for families traveling with children or for people watching their budget. If you can offer this convenience, be sure to mention it in your brochure. (And be sure to add a line to your House Rules that the guest is expected to clean up.) Some hosts keep an extra guest refrigerator on hand for this purpose.

It's an excellent idea to keep menus from your local restaurants on hand. Try to have a good sampling, ranging from moderately priced to expensive dining spots, and find out if reservations are required. Your guests will always rely heavily upon your advice and suggestions. After all, when it comes to your town, you're the authority! It's also a nice idea to keep informed of local happenings that might be of interest to your visitors. A special concert at the university or a local fair or church supper can add an extra dimension to their visit. If parents are visiting with young children they might want to have dinner out without them; try to have a list of available baby-sitters. A selection of guidebooks covering your area is also a nice feature.

The Guest Book: These are available in most stationery and department stores, and it is important that you buy one. It should contain designated space for the date, the name of the guest, home address, and a blank area for the guest's comments. They generally sign the guest book before checking out. The guest book is first of all a permanent record of who came and went. It will give you an idea of what times during the year you were busiest and which times were slow. Second, it is an easy way to keep a mailing list for your Christmas cards and future promotional mailings. You will also find that thumbing through it in years to come will recall some very pleasant people who were once strangers but now are friends.

Advertising: Periodically distribute your brochures to the local university, college, and hospital, since out-of-town visitors always need a place to stay. Let your local caterers know of your existence since wedding guests are often from out of town. If you have a major corporation in your area, drop off a brochure at the personnel office. Even visiting or relocating executives and salespeople enjoy B&Bs. Hotels and motels are sometimes overbooked; it wouldn't hurt to leave your brochure with the manager for times when there's no room for their last-minute guests. Local residents sometimes have to put up extra guests, so it's a good idea to take an ad out in your local school or church newspaper. The cost is usually minimal. Repeat this distribution process from time to time so that you can replenish the supply of brochures.

Check the back of this book for the address of your state tourist office. Write to them, requesting inclusion in any brochures listing B&Bs in the state.

The best advertising is being a member of the Tourist House Association since all member B&Bs are fully described in this book, which is available in bookstores, libraries, and B&Bs throughout the United States and Canada. In addition, it is natural for THAA members to recommend one another when guests inquire about similar accommodations in other areas. The most important reason for keeping your B&B clean, comfortable, and cordial is that we are all judged by what a guest experiences in any individual Tourist House Association home. The best publicity will come from your satisfied guests, who will recommend your B&B to their friends.

Additional Suggestions

Extra Earnings: You might want to consider a few ideas for earning extra money in connection with being a host. If guests consistently praise your muffins and preserves, you might sell attractively wrapped extras as take-home gifts. If you enjoy touring, you can plan and conduct a special outing, off the beaten tourist track, for a modest fee. In major cities, you can do such things as acquiring tickets for theater, concert, or sports events. A supply of *Bed & Breakfast U.S.A., Southeast* for sale to guests is both a source of income and gives every THAA member direct exposure to the B&B market. Think about offering the use of your washer and dryer. You may, if you wish, charge a modest fee to cover the service. Guests who have been traveling are thrilled to do their wash or have it done for them "at home" rather than wasting a couple of hours at the laundromat.

Several hosts tell me that a small gift shop is often a natural offshoot of a B&B. Items for sale might include handmade quilts, pillows, potholders, and knitted items. One host has turned his hobby of woodworking into extra income. He makes lovely picture frames, napkin rings, and footstools that many guests buy as souvenirs to take home. If you plan to do this, check with the Small Business Administration to inquire about such things as a resale license and tax collection; a chamber of commerce can advise in this regard.

Transportation: While the majority of B&B guests arrive by car, there are many who rely on public transportation. Some hosts, for a modest fee, are willing to meet arriving guests at airports, train depots, or bus stations. Do be knowledgeable about local transportation schedules in your area, and be prepared to give explicit directions for your visitors' comings and goings. Have phone numbers handy for taxi service, as well as information on car rentals.

Thoughtful Touches: Guests often write to tell us of their experiences at B&Bs as a result of learning about them through this book. These are some of the special touches that made their visit special: fresh flowers in the guest room; even a single flower in a bud vase is pretty. One hostess puts a foil-wrapped piece of candy on the pillow before the guest returns from dinner. A small decanter of wine and glasses, or a few pieces of fresh fruit in a pretty bowl on the dresser are lovely surprises. A small sewing kit in the bureau is handy. Offer guests the use of your iron and ironing board, rather than having them attempt to use the bed or dresser. Writing paper and envelopes in the desk invite the guest to send a quick note to the folks at home. If your house sketch is printed on it, it is marvelous free publicity. A pre-bed cup of tea for adults and cookies and milk for children are always appreciated.

By the way, keep a supply of guest-comment cards in the desk, both to attract compliments as well as to bring to your attention the flaws in your B&B that should be corrected.

Join the Tourist House Association: If you are convinced that you want to be a host, and have thoroughly discussed the pros and cons with your family and advisers, complete and return the membership application found at the back of this book. Our dues are $45 annually. The description of your B&B will be part of the next edition of *Bed & Breakfast U.S.A., Southeast,* as well as in the interim supplement between printings. Paid-up members receive complimentary copies of the three *Bed & Breakfast U.S.A.* regional guides: *Northeast, Southeast,* and *West and Midwest.* You will also receive the THAA's newsletter; regional seminars and conferences are held occasionally and you might enjoy attending. And, as an association, we will have clout should the time come when B&B becomes a recognized industry.

Affiliating with a B&B Reservation Agency: There are 111 agencies listed in our three *Bed & Breakfast U.S.A.* books. If you do not care to advertise your house directly to the public, consider joining one in your area. Membership and reservation fees, as well as the degree of professionalism, vary widely from agency to agency, so do check carefully.

Prediction of Success: Success should not be equated with money alone. If you thoroughly enjoy people, are well organized, enjoy sharing your tidy home without exhausting yourself, then the idea of receiving compensation for the use of an otherwise dormant bedroom will be a big plus. Your visitors will seek relaxing, wholesome surroundings, and unpretentious hosts who open their hearts as well as their homes. Being a B&B host or guest is an exciting, enriching experience.

3

B&B Recipes

The recipes that follow are B&B host originals. They've been chosen because of the raves they've received from satisfied B&B guests. The most important ingredient is the heartful of love that goes into each one.

We always have a good response to our request for favorite breakfast recipes. Although we could not publish them all this time, we will use most of them in future editions.

Hewick B&B Pecan Coffee Cake

¾ c. brown sugar
1 pkg. of vanilla pudding (not instant)
1 tbsp. cinnamon
6 tbsp. margarine

1 c. pecans
1 12-oz. package refrigerated,
   unbaked dinner rolls

Preheat the oven to 350°F. Mix together the sugar, pudding, and cinnamon and set aside. Grease a Bundt pan with some of the margarine then coat it with the pecans. Put the rolls in the pan and sprinkle the dry mix over them. Dot with the remaining margarine and let the cake stand covered overnight. Remove the cover and bake for 30 minutes.

Hewick B&B, Urbana, Virginia

Baked Apples New England

6 baking apples (Cortland or
   MacIntosh)
6 heaping tsp. sugar mixed with 1
   tsp. cinnamon

3 tbsp. butter
2 tbsp. water
½ cup raisins (optional)
2 tbsp. rum (optional)

Preheat the oven to 350°F. Core the apples and make a slit through the skin with a knife all the way around, stopping about a third of the way from the top; this keeps the apples from exploding. Place the apples in glass pie plate. Spoon a heaping teaspoon of the sugar-cinnamon mixture into the center of each apple and top with a dab of butter. Pour water into pie plate. Bake 1 hour, basting after 30 minutes. Add water if necessary. You may add raisins to center of apple or a tablespoon of dark rum to the water for a slightly different flavor.

The Captain Ezra Nye House, Sandwich, Massachusetts

Peach Stratta

6 oz. peach baby food, no water added
1½ c. fresh peaches, diced
1⅓ c. sugar
¼ tsp. nutmeg

¾ tsp. cinnamon
4 eggs
7 c. French bread, crusts removed
   and cubed

Preheat the oven to 350°F. Mix the first six ingredients together until well blended. Pour over the bread and stir gently. Pour the mixture into a 1-quart casserole dish that has been sprayed with vegetable cooking spray. Bake for 50 to 60 minutes.

Joyce's Blueberry Muffins

1¾ c. flour
⅓ c. sugar
1 tbsp. baking powder
¾ c. milk
⅓ c. oil
1 tsp. grated lemon peel

1 egg, slightly beaten
18 oz. pkg. cream cheese, cut into
   ½-inch cubes
¾ c. fresh or frozen blueberries
1 tbsp. lemon juice
3 tbsp. sugar

Preheat the oven to 400°F. Mix the flour, sugar, and baking powder in a large bowl and set aside. Add the milk, oil, and grated lemon peel to the egg. Add the egg mixture to the flour mixture, blending until just moistened. Fold in the cream cheese and blueberries. Spoon the batter into greased or lined muffin tins until two-thirds full. Bake for 20 minutes. Mix together the lemon juice and sugar and brush over the muffins. Makes 12 muffins.

Miller's of Montana B&B Inn, Bozeman, Montana

Eggs Benedict Caledonia

1 pkg. Hollandaise sauce mix
3 tbsp. lemon juice
2 English muffins
2 tbsp. butter or margarine

4 slices Canadian bacon or ham
4 eggs
Garnish of choice

Preheat the oven to 160°F. Prepare Hollandaise sauce according to package directions, replacing 3 tablespoons of water with lemon juice and set aside. Toast or broil muffin halves and spread with the butter. Top with slices of the Canadian bacon or ham and keep warm in the oven. Poach the eggs for 3½ minutes in cups sprayed with vegetable oil. When the whites are set but the yolks are still loose, invert the eggs onto muffins. Cover the eggs with the sauce. Garnish with fresh parsley, kiwi slice, strawberry half, or a favorite garnish of your choice. Makes 2 servings.

Caledonia Farm B&B, Flint Hill, Virginia

Banana Butter

4 large ripe bananas, peeled and sliced
3 tbsp. lemon juice

1 tsp. pumpkin pie spice
1½ c. sugar

Place the bananas and lemon juice in a blender and process until smooth. Transfer to a large saucepan and stir in the pumpkin pie spice and sugar. Bring the mixture to a boil, lower the heat and simmer for 15 minutes, stirring frequently. Pour into sterilized jars and store in tightly covered containers in the refrigerator. Makes 3 cups.

Bannick's Bed & Breakfast, Dimondale, Michigan

Mountain Top Bacon

½ c. flour
¼ c. brown sugar

1 tsp. black pepper
1 lb. bacon, sliced

Preheat the oven to 300°F. Mix the flour, brown sugar, and pepper in a plastic bag. Add bacon slices one at a time and shake to coat. Lay the slices out in a baking pan. Bake for 20 to 25 minutes, or until crisp. Serves 4.

Von-Bryan Inn, Sevierville, Tennessee

Health Cereal

5 c. old-fashioned oats
2 c. wheat germ
½ c. sesame seeds, ground
1 c. shredded coconut (optional)
1 c. almonds or other nuts, chopped
   finely

½ tsp. cinnamon
¼ tsp. ground cloves
½ tsp. salt
1 c. brown sugar, or to taste
1 c. corn oil, or to taste
1 c. raisins

Preheat the oven to 350°F. In a large bowl, mix together all the ingredients except the raisins. Pour the mixture into a shallow pan and bake 30 minutes, stirring occasionally. Remove from the oven and stir in the raisins. Serve warm or at room temperature.

Honeysuckle Hill B&B, Madison, Connecticut

Aunt Dolly's Almost in the Country Quiche

¾ c. all-purpose flour
½ c. whole wheat flour
Pinch of salt
6 tbsp. butter
4 to 5 tbsp. ice water
5 slices bacon
1 large onion, chopped
2 large potatoes, thinly sliced
2 eggs

⅔ c. heavy cream
1 tbsp. each chopped parsley and
   chives
½ tsp. salt
¼ tsp. black pepper
½ sweet red pepper, seeded and
   chopped
¾ c. grated cheddar cheese

Preheat the oven to 375°F. In a large bowl, combine the flours and the pinch of salt and cut in the butter until the mixture turns to fine crumbs. Add enough water to make a firm dough. Knead lightly. On a lightly floured surface, roll out the pastry to a 10-inch circle. Ease the pastry into a 9-inch quiche pan, pressing evenly around the side; trim the edge. Prick all over with a fork; refrigerate for 30 minutes, or until the dough is firm. Line with foil, fill with dried beans and bake until set, 12 to 15 minutes. Remove the foil and beans and return the pastry to the oven for another 5 minutes. In a large frying pan, cook the bacon until crisp; remove it with a slotted spoon, allow it to cool, and crumble it. Add the onion and potatoes to the bacon drippings and cook until browned. Drain and set aside. Beat the eggs and cream together. Stir in the parsley, chives, the ½ teaspoon salt, and the black pepper and set aside. Spoon the potatoes and onion into the pastry shell and sprinkle with the bacon and red pepper. Pour in the egg mixture and sprinkle with the cheese. Bake for 20 to 25 minutes. Serve hot or cold.

Aunt Dolly's Attic B&B, Austin, Texas

Garden Harvest Muffins

4 c. all-purpose flour
2½ c. sugar
4 tsp. baking soda
4 tsp. cinnamon
1 tsp. salt
2 c. grated carrots
2 c. grated zucchini
1 c. raisins

1 c. chopped pecans
1 c. coconut
2 tart apples, peeled and grated
6 large eggs
1 c. vegetable oil
1 c. buttermilk
2 tsp. vanilla

Preheat the oven to 375°F. In a large bowl, sift together the flour, sugar, baking soda, cinnamon, and salt. Stir in the carrots, zucchini, raisins, pecans, coconut, and apples. In another bowl, whisk together the remaining ingredients and add to the flour-vegetable mixture. Stir the batter until just blended. Spoon the batter into well-buttered muffin tins (or use paper liners). Bake on the middle rack for 25 to 30 minutes, or until the muffins are springy to the touch. Let the muffins cool in the tins for 5 minutes, then turn them out onto a rack. Makes about 30 muffins.

Leland House, Durango, Colorado

Sausage en Croute

1 sheet frozen Pepperidge Farm puff
   pastry
1 lb. pork sausage
½ c. chopped onion
½ c. chopped green pepper

6 large mushrooms, sliced
1 large tomato, diced
1 c. total shredded Swiss and
   Cheddar cheese
3 tbsp. chopped parsley

Preheat the oven to 425°F. Thaw the puff pastry about 20 minutes. Meanwhile, brown the sausage in a skillet, breaking it into bits. Add the onion, green pepper, and mushrooms and cook until tender. Remove from the heat and pour off the drippings. Add the tomato, cheese, and parsley. Unfold the pastry sheet and roll it out on a lightly floured board to a 13- × -10-inch rectangle. Transfer to a baking sheet lined with brown paper (a grocery bag works well). Spread the sausage mixture on pastry. Roll up from the long side, jelly-roll fashion, and pinch the edges to seal. Bake for 20 minutes, or until golden brown. Serves 6 to 8 guests.

Grand Avenue Inn, Carthage, Missouri

4

Wheelchair Accessible Listings

Although this chapter is small, within a few years *Bed & Breakfast U.S.A., Southeast* hopes to have listings from all fifty states and Canada. The requirements are fairly simple. To be listed in this section, all B&Bs must have easy-access entrances and exits. Doorways must be wide enough to admit a wheelchair—36 inches should be wide enough. Toilets and tubs must have reach bars. If the bathroom has a shower, reach bars and a built-in seat are preferable. Wheelchairs should be able to fit under the breakfast table; 26 inches is high enough. It's also a good idea to check to see what kind of activities are available. Many parks, restaurants, shopping areas, museums, beaches, etc. have wheelchair accessibility. If you or someone you know has a B&B that is wheelchair accessible, please turn to page 251 for further details.

Kern River Inn Bed & Breakfast ✪
P.O. BOX 1725, 119 KERN RIVER DRIVE, KERNVILLE, CALIFORNIA 93238

Tel: **(619) 376-6750; (800) 986-4382**	Open: **All year**
Best Time to Call: **8 AM–8 PM**	Reduced Rates: **Available**
Hosts: **Jack and Carita Prestwich**	Breakfast: **Full**
Location: **50 mi. NE of Bakersfield**	Credit Cards: **MC, VISA**
No. of Rooms: **1**	Pets: **No**
No. of Private Baths: **1**	Children: **Welcome**
Double/pb: **$89–$99**	Smoking: **No**
Single/pb: **$79–$89**	Social Drinking: **Permitted**

Stay in a charming riverfront B&B in a quaint western town within Sequoia National Forest. Jack and Carita specialize in romantic, relaxing getaways. Their accessible room has a queen bed and a Piute-style, wood-burning fireplace. (Your hosts provide the wood.) Native American pictures and macramé wall hangings accent the room's Southwestern color scheme of beige, mauve, and sage green. The bath has grab bars; the full-size, mirror-doored closet has shelving that can be reached from a wheelchair.

Little Valley Inn
183 BROOKS ROAD, MARIPOSA, CALIFORNIA 95338

Tel: **(209) 742-6204; (800) 889-5444**	Breakfast: **Continental**
Hosts: **Kay and Robert Hewitt**	Credit Cards: **AMEX, MC, VISA**
Location: **8 mi. S of Mariposa**	Pets: **No**
Suite: **$100**	Children: **Welcome**
Open: **All year**	Smoking: **No**
Reduced Rates: **Available**	Social Drinking: **Permitted**

Little Valley Inn's accommodations were designed with the help of a wheelchair-bound friend. This wheelchair-accessible suite has a full kitchen, ramp, grab bars, 36-inch interior door, bath seat, and low switch plates. Guests can enjoy panning for gold in a big cattle trough filled with water; your hosts provide the dirt. If you don't know how to pan, Kay and Robert will be happy to show you!

Redwood Reflections ✪
4600 SMITH GRADE, SANTA CRUZ, CALIFORNIA 95060

Tel: **(408) 423-7221**	Reduced Rates: **10% seniors, disabled**
Best Time to Call: **Evenings**	Breakfast: **Full**
Hosts: **Ed and Dory Strong**	Credit Cards: **MC, VISA**
Location: **70 mi. S of San Francisco**	Pets: **No**
No. of Rooms: **1**	Children: **Welcome, over 7**
No. of Private Baths: **1**	Smoking: **No**
Suites: **$85**	Social Drinking: **Permitted**
Open: **All year**	

Nestled on 10 private acres of giant redwoods, Redwood Reflections offers one wheelchair-accessible room with a private bath and patio. A romantic Roman tub for two has a transfer seat and adjustable shower head. Grab bars for toilet and tub, 36-inch doors, and a roll-in vanity provide accessibility and safety. Guests are invited to concoct favorite goodies and listen to old-time piano music in an ice cream parlor featuring 1920s collectibles and a 100-year-old potbelly stove. A full breakfast is served and dietary restrictions can be observed. Santa Cruz is a wheelchair-friendly town and offers an amusement park, wharf with fine restaurants and a 2-mile coastline sidewalk. The Monterey Bay Aquarium and two state parks are great accessible day excursions.

Ferncourt Bed and Breakfast
150 CENTRAL AVENUE, SAN MATEO, FLORIDA 32187

Tel: **(904) 329-9755**	Hosts: **Jack and Dee Morgan**
Best Time to Call: **Evenings**	Location: **25 mi. W of St. Augustine**

No. of Rooms: **1**	Pets: **No**
No. of Private Baths: **1**	Children: **No**
Double/pb: **$45–$65**	Smoking: **No**
Open: **All year**	Social Drinking: **Permitted**
Breakfast: **Full**	Station Pickup: **Yes**

Ferncourt is a restored 1800s farm home, located in a tiny historic hamlet just a few minutes' drive from St. Augustine and Daytona Beach. Guests have use of several rooms and the wraparound veranda. Close by, restaurants serve excellent food. Cookies and tea are offered in the evening. Jack does woodworking and upholstery and many examples of his craft are on display throughout the inn. Dee dabbles in painting and loves antiques and flea markets, but her real passion is food, evidenced by the gourmet breakfast she serves. Discover North Central Florida, then retire to all the charm and hospitality of the Victorian era with your hosts. There is a long concrete wheelchair ramp, and one room is set up for the disabled, with a private bath and handrails installed. For hearing impaired guests, a smoke alarm has been installed.

Amanda's B&B Reservation Service ❂
1428 PARK AVENUE, BALTIMORE, MARYLAND 21217

Tel: **(410) 225-0001; fax: 728-8957**	Descriptive Directory of B&Bs: **$5**
Best Time to Call: **8:30 AM–5:30 PM**	Rates (Double):
Mon.–Fri.	Modest: **$60**
Coordinator: **Betsy Grater**	Luxury: **$75–$125**
States/Regions Covered: **Annapolis,**	Credit Cards: **AMEX, DISC, MC, VISA**
Baltimore, Delaware, District of	
Columbia, Maryland, New Jersey,	
Pennsylvania, Virginia, West Virginia	

The roster of this reservation service includes eight sites designed for visitors with disabilities—five in downtown Baltimore, two in Annapolis, and one in Chesapeake City.

Bed & Breakfast Associates—Bay Colony, Ltd. ❂
P.O. BOX 57166, BABSON PARK, BOSTON,
MASSACHUSETTS 02157-0166

Tel: **(617) 449-5302; (800) 347-5088;**	States/Regions Covered:
fax: (617) 449-5958	**Massachusetts—Boston (Beacon Hill**
Best Time to Call: **9:30 AM–12:30 PM;**	**and Back Bay)**
1:30–5 PM Mon.–Fri.	Descriptive Directory of B&Bs: **Free**
Coordinators: **Arline Kardasis and**	Rates (Single/Double)
Marilyn Mitchell	Luxury: **$89–$135 $95–$135**
	Credit Cards: **AMEX, CB, DC, MC,**
	VISA

Arline and Marilyn offer five accommodations for disabled travelers. All have private baths. Some are convenient to major colleges and universities.

Blue Goose Inn ●
ROUTE 103B, P.O. BOX 2117, MT. SUNAPEE, NEW HAMPSHIRE 03255

Tel: **(603) 763-5519**
Best Time to Call: **Before noon**
Hosts: **Meryl and Ronald Caldwell**
Location: **10 mi. from I-89**
No. of Rooms: **1**
No. of Private Baths: **1**
Double/pb: **$50**
Open: **All year**

Breakfast: **Full**
Credit Cards: **MC, VISA**
Pets: **No**
Children: **Welcome**
Smoking: **Permitted**
Social Drinking: **Permitted**
Airport/Station Pickup: **Yes**

This cozy nineteenth-century Colonial farmhouse is located on scenic Lake Sunapee, at the base of Mt. Sunapee. Meryl and Ronald offer one wheelchair-accessible room adorned with handmade quilts and attractive antiques. Breakfast specialties—such as a maple-flavored biscuit stuffed with bacon, eggs, and cheese—are served on the enclosed porch. Each evening, you're invited to join your hosts on the porch, or by the fireplace in the living room, for wine, fruit, and cheese.

Jemez River Bed & Breakfast Inn ●
16445 HIGHWAY 4, JEMEZ SPRINGS, NEW MEXICO 87025

Tel: **(505) 820-3262**
Best Time to Call: **Evenings**
Hosts: **Larry and Roxe Ann Clutter**
Location: **40 mi. NW of Albuquerque**
No. of Rooms: **2**
No. of Private Baths: **2**
Double/pb: **$99–$109**
Open: **All year**
Reduced Rates: **10% seniors**

Breakfast: **Full**
Other Meals: **Available**
Credit Cards: **AMEX, CB, DC, DISC,
    MC, VISA**
Pets: **Sometimes**
Children: **Welcome**
Smoking: **No**
Social Drinking: **Permitted**

A new, adobe-style home completed in 1994, Jemez River Bed & Breakfast Inn is nestled on 3½ acres in a valley below the Jemez Mountains Virgin Mesa. At night, the murmuring of the Jemez River—located in the B&B's backyard—will lull you to sleep. As you enjoy a hearty breakfast, you'll feast your eyes on breathtaking mountain views through the grand kitchen windows. Authentic Indian pottery, rugs, paintings, arrowheads, and kachina dolls decorate the bedrooms, which have individual access to a spacious garden plaza; there, a spring-fed birdbath draws hummingbirds and other wildlife. Stone-lined trails follow the spring around cottonwood trees, large rocks and crevices to secluded riverside rest spots. Two rooms are completely accessible for wheelchair users.

Harborlight Guest House ✪
332 LIVE OAK DRIVE, CAPE CARTERET, NORTH CAROLINA 28584

Tel: (800) 624-VIEW [8439];
  (919) 393-6868
Best Time to Call: 12 noon–9:30 PM
Hosts: Bobby and Anita Gill
Location: 15 mi. from 70E, exit 24W
No. of Rooms: 1
No. of Private Baths: 1
Double/pb: $75
Single/pb: $60

Open: **All year**
Reduced Rates: **Available**
Breakfast: **Full**
Credit Cards: **AMEX, MC, VISA**
Pets: **No**
Children: **No**
Smoking: **No**
Social Drinking: **Permitted**
Minimum Stay: **2 nights weekends**

Located on a secluded waterfront on the North Carolina coast, Harbor-light Guest House offers one waterview room on the first floor that can accommodate wheelchair guests. The bed is queen-size and has a standard bed frame. The bath meets all state specifications, and the outside entrance has a ramp. The room also has a remote color TV and in-room coffee and tea service. In the morning enjoy a gourmet breakfast consisting of egg and cheese dishes, fresh fruits, and fresh breads. Afterwards, explore the waterfront villages of Beaufort and Swansboro, which offer unique gift shops and intimate restaurants. Later in the day, experience the waterfront sunset amidst graceful palms and the tranquility of Harborlight Guest House.

McGillivray's Log Home and Bed and Breakfast ✪
88680 EVERS ROAD, ELMIRA, OREGON 97437

Tel: (503) 935-3564
Best Time to Call: 8 AM–8 PM
Host: Evelyn McGillivray
Location: 14 mi. W of Eugene
No. of Rooms: 1
No. of Private Baths: 1
Double/pb: $60–$70
Single/pb: $50

Open: **All year**
Breakfast: **Full**
Credit Cards: **MC, VISA**
Pets: **No**
Children: **Welcome**
Smoking: **No**
Social Drinking: **Permitted**
Airport/Station Pickup: **Yes**

Fir trees cover the five-acre property surrounding this massive home built with six types of wood and featuring both a split-log staircase and an entry ramp. One room, decorated in a classic Americana motif, has a king-size bed and doorways wide enough for wheelchairs. In the bathroom, there is a six-inch step in the shower stall, which has two grab bars and an adjustable height stool; another grab bar is placed near the toilet. Evelyn usually prepares buttermilk pancakes on an antique griddle her mother used. She also offers fresh-squeezed juice, farm-grown apples and grapes, fresh bread, eggs, and all the breakfast trimmings. This B&B is located only three miles from a vineyard, while country roads and a reservoir for fishing and boating are nearby.

Bed & Breakfast—The Manor ✪

830 VILLAGE ROAD, P.O. BOX 416, LAMPETER, PENNSYLVANIA 17537

Tel: **(717) 464-9564; (800) 461-6BED [6233]**
Best Time to Call: **9 AM–9 PM**
Hosts: **Mary Lou Paolini and Jackie Curtis**
Location: **3 mi. SE of Lancaster**
No. of Rooms: **2**
No. of Private Baths: **1**
Double/pb: **$75**
Double/sb: **$65**

Open: **All year**
Reduced Rates: **Available**
Breakfast: **Full**
Other Meals: **Available**
Credit Cards: **MC, VISA**
Pets: **No**
Children: **Welcome**
Smoking: **No**
Social Drinking: **No**
Airport/Station Pickup: **Yes**

Set on 4½ acres of lush Amish farmland, this cozy farmhouse is just minutes away from Lancaster's historic sites and attractions. Guests delight in Mary Lou's delicious breakfasts, with specialties like eggs mornay, apple cobbler, and homemade breads and jams. This cozy inn features two ground-floor bedrooms decorated with country charm and antique beds. Both rooms are easily accessible to the parking area; no steps involved. Guests may join an Old Order Amish family for dinner. A conference room is available for groups. In summer a swim in the pool or a nap under one of the many shade trees is the perfect way to cap a day of touring.

The Cookie Jar B&B ✪

64 KINGSTOWN ROAD, ROUTE 138, WYOMING, RHODE ISLAND 02898

Tel: **(401) 539-2680; (800) 767-4262**
Best Time to Call: **After 5 PM**
Hosts: **Dick and Madelein Sohl**
Location: **7/10 mi. off I-95, exit 3A**
No. of Rooms: **2**
No. of Private Baths: **1**
Max. No. Sharing Bath: **4**
Double/pb: **$75**
Double/sb: **$65**

Single/sb: **$58.50**
Open: **All year**
Reduced Rates: **Available**
Breakfast: **Full**
Pets: **No**
Children: **Welcome**
Smoking: **No**
Social Drinking: **Permitted**

The heart of this house, the living room, was a blacksmith's shop built in 1732; the original ceiling, hand-hewn beams, and granite walls are still in use. Fittingly, Dick and Madelein have furnished their home with a mixture of antique, country, and contemporary pieces. You'll enjoy looking around their property, which includes a barn, flower garden, and lots of fruit trees, berry bushes, and grapevines. Two rooms, each with a sink, are ideal for visitors with disabilities. The bathroom has a wall-mounted grab bar at the toilet and a large shower stall (3 by 4 feet) with a built-in fiberglass seat. Despite the rural setting, it's only a short drive to the University of Rhode Island and cities like Mystic and Providence. All guest rooms have color TV and air-conditioning.

Selby House Bed & Breakfast ☉
226 PRINCESS ANNE STREET, FREDERICKSBURG, VIRGINIA 22401

Tel: (703) 373-7037	Reduced Rates: Available
Hosts: Jerry and Virginia Selby	Breakfast: Full
Location: 54 mi. S of Washington, D.C.	Credit Cards: MC, VISA
No of Rooms: 4	Pets: No
No. of Private Baths: 4	Children: Welcome
Double/pb: $75	Smoking: No
Single/pb: $65	Social Drinking: Permitted
Open: All year	Station Pickup: Yes

Selby House has two barrier-free, ground-level rooms. In 1986, Jerry designed and built this annex to fulfill his dream of extending hospitality to physically challenged guests. All doorways are 36 inches wide. The bedrooms have large baths with grab bars and other necessary adaptations. Both guest rooms connect to a large community area as well as the dining room, and their cement patios provide easy access to all inn facilities.

The Iris Inn ☉
191 CHINQUAPIN DRIVE, WAYNESBORO, VIRGINIA 22980

Tel: (540) 943-1991	Breakfast: Full
Best Time to Call: 10 AM–8 PM	Credit Cards: MC, VISA
Hosts: Wayne and Iris Karl	Pets: No
Location: 25 mi. W of Charlottesville	Children: Welcome, by arrangement
No. of Rooms: 1	Smoking: No
No. of Private Baths: 1	Social Drinking: Permitted
Double/pb: $75–$95	Minimum Stay: 2 nights weekends
Single/pb: $65	Airport Pickup: Yes
Open: All year	
Reduced Rates: Corporate, Sun.–Thurs.	

Southern charm and grace in a totally modern facility overlooking the historic Shenandoah Valley from the Blue Ridge Mountains' wooded western slope—that's what awaits you at the Iris Inn. It's ideal for a weekend retreat, a refreshing change for the business traveler, and a tranquil spot for tourists to spend a night or more. The wheelchair-accessible room is comfortably furnished and delightfully decorated with nature and wildlife motifs. The bathroom has a lavatory without a vanity, for easier use. There are grab bars at the toilet and on the sides of the shower, which also has a seat. A pocket door connects the bathroom and bedroom. For your convenience, a ramp leads from the parking lot level to the porch.

5
State-by-State Listings

ALABAMA

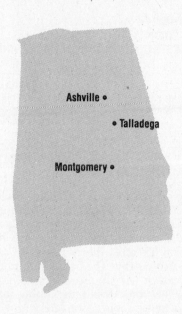

Ashville •

• Talladega

Montgomery •

Roses and Lace Country Inn ✪
P.O. BOX 852, FIFTH STREET AT NINTH AVENUE SOUTH, ASHVILLE, ALABAMA 35953

Tel: **(205) 594-4366, 594-4660**
Hosts: **Mark and Shirley Sparks**
Location: **40 mi. NE of Birmingham**
No. of Rooms: **4**
No. of Private Baths: **2**
Max. No. Sharing Bath: **4**
Double/pb: **$65**
Single/pb: **$55**
Double/sb: **$55**
Single/sb: **$45**

Suites: **$75**
Open: **All year**
Reduced Rates: **10% after 4 nights**
Breakfast: **Full**
Credit Cards: **MC, VISA**
Pets: **Sometimes**
Children: **Welcome**
Smoking: **No**
Social Drinking: **Permitted**

A friendly greeting awaits you at this handsome two-story Victorian with a wraparound porch and stained-glass windows. As you cross the threshold, your hosts Mark and Shirley will invite you to relax with a beverage and snack. Their home, lovingly restored over a two-year period by the entire family, contains fine woodwork and many antiques. Ask about other landmark buildings in the area; St. Clair County is an old, historic part of Alabama. For modern pleasures, visit Birmingham's thoroughbred racetrack, or take a day trip to the Huntsville Space and Rocket Center.

Red Bluff Cottage ✪

**551 CLAY STREET, MONTGOMERY, ALABAMA
(MAILING ADDRESS: P.O. BOX 1026, MONTGOMERY,
ALABAMA 36101)**

Tel: **(334) 264-0056**	Open: **All year**
Best Time to Call: **9 AM–10 PM**	Breakfast: **Full**
Hosts: **Anne and Mark Waldo**	Pets: **No**
No. of Rooms: **4**	Children: **Welcome (crib)**
No. of Private Baths: **4**	Smoking: **No**
Double/pb: **$65**	Social Drinking: **Permitted**
Single/pb: **$55**	Airport/Station Pickup: **Yes**
Suite: **$85**	

This raised cottage is high above the Alabama River in Montgomery's historic Cottage Hill District, close to the State Capitol, Dexter Avenue King Memorial Baptist Church, the First White House of the Confederacy, the Civil Rights Memorial, and Old Alabama Town. The Alabama Shakespeare Festival Theatre, the Museum of Fine Arts, and the expanded zoo are also nearby. The bedrooms are downstairs. Guests come upstairs to read or relax in the living rooms, to enjoy the front porch view, and to have breakfast in the dining room. Many interesting antiques and a music room, complete with harpsichord, add to the charm of this home.

Historic Oakwood Bed & Breakfast ✪

715 EAST NORTH STREET, TALLADEGA, ALABAMA 35160

Tel: **(205) 362-0662**	Suites: **$95**
Hosts: **Al and Naomi Kline**	Open: **All year**
Location: **45 mi. E of Birmingham**	Breakfast: **Full**
No. of Rooms: **3**	Pets: **No**
No. of Private Baths: **1**	Children: **Welcome, over 10, infants**
Max. No. Sharing Bath: **4**	Smoking: **No**
Double/pb: **$65**	Social Drinking: **Permitted**
Single/pb: **$55**	Airport/Station Pickup: **Yes, $5–$10**
Double/sb: **$55**	**fee**
Single/sb: **$50**	

This antebellum home, built in 1847, is listed on the National Register of Historic Places, and furnished with many heirloom antiques. The house was commissioned by Alexander Bowie, the first mayor of Talladega. Enjoy browsing through the antique stores in the area, visiting the International Motorsports Hall of Fame, or exploring DeSoto Caverns. The public golf course and tennis courts and beautiful Cheaha Mt. State Park are nearby. The hearty breakfast your hosts serve features homemade biscuits and Southern grits. Traveling business person or vacationer, enjoy a retreat into the quiet elegance of a bygone area.

For key to listings, see inside front or back cover.

⊙ This star means that rates are guaranteed through December 31, 1996, to any guest making a reservation as a result of reading about the B&B in *Bed & Breakfast U.S.A.*—1996 edition.

Important! To avoid misunderstandings, always ask about cancellation policies when booking.

Please enclose a self-addressed, stamped, business-size envelope when contacting reservation services.

For more details on what you can expect in a B&B, see Chapter 1.

Always mention *Bed & Breakfast U.S.A.* when making reservations!

If no B&B is listed in the area you'll be visiting, use the form on page 249 to order a copy of our "List of New B&Bs."

We want to hear from you! Use the form on page 251.

ARKANSAS

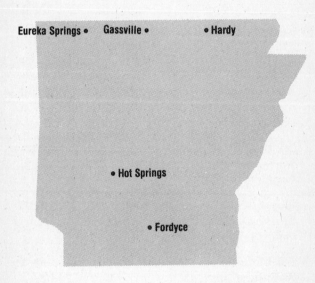

Eureka Springs •   Gassville •   • Hardy

• Hot Springs

• Fordyce

Bridgeford House B&B ✪
263 SPRING STREET, EUREKA SPRINGS, ARKANSAS 72632

Tel: **(501) 253-7853**
Best Time to Call: **10 AM–10 PM**
Hosts: **Denise and Michael McDonald**
No. of Rooms: **4**
No. of Private Baths: **4**
Double/pb: **$85–$95**
Open: **All year**
Reduced Rates: **10% less, Dec.–March**

Breakfast: **Full**
Credit Cards: **MC, VISA**
Pets: **No**
Children: **Welcome**
Smoking: **No**
Social Drinking: **Permitted**
Minimum Stay: **2 nights weekends, holidays**

A stay at the 1884 Bridgeford House is a step into the quiet elegance of yesterday. It is located in the historic district, where Victorian homes line charming streets, and old-fashioned trolleys carry guests to and fro. Denise and Michael will pamper you with coffee or tea in the afternoon or evening. Breakfast is a real eye-opener of fresh fruit, homemade cinnamon rolls, Ozark ham, and delicious egg casseroles.

Crescent Cottage Inn
211 SPRING STREET, EUREKA SPRINGS, ARKANSAS 72632

Tel: (501) 253-6022
Best Time to Call: 10 AM–8 PM
Hosts: Ralph and Phyllis Becker
Location: On Rte. 62B, Historic Loop
No. of Rooms: 4
No. of Private Baths: 4
Double/pb: $75–$115

Open: All year
Breakfast: Full
Credit Cards: DISC, MC, VISA
Pets: No
Children: Welcome, under 1, over 13
Smoking: No
Social Drinking: Permitted

Crescent Cottage Inn, built in 1881 for Arkansas' first post-Civil War governor, is listed on the National Register of Historic Places. This celebrated B&B has wonderful views of the mountains. All guest rooms are furnished with antiques; two have double Jacuzzi spas. Ralph and Phyllis serve a full breakfast each morning. Then you'll be ready for the short walk to historic downtown Eureka Springs on a route that leads past lovely springs, shade trees, and a trolley stop.

Harvest House ✪
104 WALL STREET, EUREKA SPRINGS, ARKANSAS 72632

Tel: (501) 253-9363
Best Time to Call: 9 AM–9 PM
Hosts: Bill and Patt Carmichael
No. of Rooms: 4
No. of Private Baths: 4
Double/pb: $75–$85
Open: All year

Breakfast: Full
Credit Cards: DISC, MC, VISA
Pets: Sometimes
Children: Welcome, over 12
Smoking: No
Social Drinking: Permitted

Located in the historic district of Eureka Springs, Harvest House is a step off the beaten path, yet close to the bustle of downtown. This turn-of-the-century Victorian house is filled with antiques, collectibles, and family favorites. All guest rooms have private entrances. Breakfast is served in the dining room or, weather permitting, in the screened-in gazebo overlooking pine and oak trees. Bill is a native Arkansan and knows all the hidden treasures of the area. Patt is a shopper with a particular interest in antiques and the local attractions.

Singleton House Bed and Breakfast ✪
11 SINGLETON, EUREKA SPRINGS, ARKANSAS 72632

Tel: **(501) 253-9111; (800) 833-3394**
Best Time to Call: **Anytime**
Host: **Barbara Gavron**
No. of Rooms: **5**
No. of Private Baths: **5**
Double/pb: **$65–$75**
Single/pb: **$55–$65**
Suites: **$75–$95**

Open: **All year**
Reduced Rates: **After 3rd night**
Breakfast: **Full**
Credit Cards: **AMEX, DISC, MC, VISA**
Pets: **No**
Children: **Welcome**
Smoking: **Restricted**
Social Drinking: **Permitted**

You'll find a hidden garden, winding stone paths, and more than fifty birdhouses on the grounds of this Victorian home in Eureka Springs' historic district. For help in identifying your various feathered friends, consult the titles in Singleton House's small nature library. Full breakfasts are served on the balcony overlooking the wildflower garden and lily-filled goldfish pond. After your meal, take a one-block stroll on the historic walking tour footpath to the city's shops, galleries, and cafes. If you prefer, there's an old-fashioned trolley that stops right at Singleton Street.

Wynne Phillips House ✪
412 WEST FOURTH STREET, FORDYCE, ARKANSAS 71742

Tel: **(501) 352-7202**
Best Time to Call: **Morning**
Hosts: **Colonel and Mrs. James H. Phillips**
Location: **60 mi. S of Little Rock**
No. of Rooms: **4**
No. of Private Baths: **4**
Double/pb: **$55**

Open: **All year**
Breakfast: **Full**
Credit Cards: **MC, VISA**
Pets: **No**
Children: **Yes**
Smoking: **No**
Social Drinking: **Permitted**

A gracious Colonial Revival mansion listed on the National Register of Historic Places, the Wynne Phillips House is filled with antiques and oriental rugs. Mrs. Phillips grew up here, and the bedrooms are furnished with family heirlooms. This is a place where you can enjoy old-fashioned pleasures, such as singing around the piano, or watching the sunset from the wraparound porch. A swimming pool is on the premises; tennis courts are nearby. The generous, Southern-style breakfasts feature fresh fruit, homemade biscuits, eggs, sausage, and grits.

Lithia Springs Bed & Breakfast Lodge ✪
RT. 1, BOX 77-A, HIGHWAY 126, GASSVILLE, ARKANSAS 72635

Tel: **(501) 435-6100**
Best Time to Call: **9 AM–9 PM**
Hosts: **Paul and Reita Johnson**
No. of Rooms: **5**

No. of Private Baths: **3**
Max. No. Sharing Bath: **4**
Double/pb: **$55**
Double/sb: **$50**

Open: **All year, Dec.–Jan. special reservation only**
Breakfast: **Full**

Pets: **No**
Children: **Welcome, over 7**
Smoking: **No**

This 100-year-old former health lodge has been lovingly restored with an additional gift shop featuring many of the hosts' own fine handcrafts. The rooms are furnished with many antiques and period furniture. Breakfast is served in the dining room or on the large screened front porch. Lithia Springs is on 39 acres of meadows and woods. It is near the White and Buffalo Rivers, famous for fishing and canoeing, and between Bull Shoals and Norfork Lakes. It's 10 minutes from Mountain Home and a scenic drive to Blanchard Spring Caverns and Mountain View Folk Center.

Olde Stonehouse Bed & Breakfast Inn ✪
511 MAIN STREET, HARDY, ARKANSAS 72542

Tel: **(501) 856-2983**
Best Time to Call: **10 AM–8 PM**
Hosts: **David and Peggy Johnson**
No. of Rooms: **7**
No. of Private Baths: **7**
Double p/b: **$55–$65**
Single p/b: **$50–$60**
Suites: **$85**

Open: **All year**
Reduced Rates: **10% seniors**
Breakfast: **Full**
Credit Cards: **DISC, MC, VISA**
Pets: **No**
Children: **Welcome in suites, over 13 in main house**
Smoking: **No**

Social Drinking: **Permitted**
Minimum Stay: **2 nights, holiday
weekends and special events**

Station Pickup: **Yes**

Recapture the romance of times past at the Olde Stonehouse. Unwind in lovely air-conditioned rooms decorated with period antiques, quilts, and old lace, plus a ceiling fan and queen-size bed. Curl up in the large rocking chairs on the front porch or take a walk to Old Hardy Town's antique and crafts shops. Stroll along the river or join other guests for conversation and games. Awaken to the aroma of freshly-brewed coffee and bread baking. After breakfast, canoeing, golfing, shopping, and horseback riding are among the many activities to choose from.

The Gables Inn ✪
318 QUAPAW AVENUE, HOT SPRINGS, ARKANSAS 71901

Tel: **(501) 623-7576; (800) 625-7576**
Best Time to Call: **9 AM–9 PM**
Hosts: **Larry and Shirley Robins**
Location: **50 mi. SW of Little Rock**
No. of Rooms: **4**
No. of Private Baths: **4**
Double/pb: **$50–$70**
Single/pb: **$45–$65**
Open: **All year**

Reduced Rates: **10% seniors**
Breakfast: **Full**
Credit Cards: **AMEX, MC, VISA**
Pets: **No**
Children: **Welcome, over 10**
Smoking: **No**
Social Drinking: **Permitted**
Minimum Stay: **2 nights weekends**

Located three blocks from the historic district and famous Bath House Row, The Gables Inn is a 1905 Victorian, personally restored by the innkeepers. Many special features have been returned to their former beauty, including mantels, light fixtures, and leaded and stained-glass windows. There are wood floors throughout. Upstairs are four guest rooms, all with private baths; furnishings include queen-size beds with handmade quilts and period pieces. Adjacent to the guest rooms is a cozy sitting area where early morning coffee is served, followed by a full breakfast in the turn-of-the-century dining room.

Stillmeadow Farm ✪
111 STILLMEADOW LANE, HOT SPRINGS, ARKANSAS 71913

Tel: **(501) 525-9994**
Hosts: **Gene and Jody Sparling**
Location: **4 mi. S of Hot Springs**
No. of Rooms: **4**
No. of Private Baths: **2**
Max. No. Sharing Bath: **4**
Double/pb: **$60**
Single/pb: **$50**

Suites: **$80**
Open: **All year**
Breakfast: **Full**
Pets: **No**
Children: **Welcome, over 12**
Smoking: **No**
Social Drinking: **Permitted**

Stillmeadow Farm is a reproduction of an 18th-century New England saltbox, set in 75 acres of pine forest with walking trails and an herb garden. The decor is of early country antiques. Your hosts provide homemade snacks and fruit in the guest rooms. For breakfast, freshly baked pastries and breads are served. Hot Springs National Park, Lake Hamilton, the Mid-America Museum, and a racetrack are nearby.

Vintage Comfort B&B Inn ✪
303 QUAPAW AVENUE, HOT SPRINGS, ARKANSAS 71901

Tel: **(501) 623-3258**	Breakfast: **Full**
Host: **Helen Bartlett**	Credit Cards: **AMEX, MC, VISA**
No. of Rooms: **4**	Pets: **No**
No. of Private Baths: **4**	Children: **Welcome, over 6**
Double/pb: **$65–$85**	Smoking: **No**
Single/pb: **$50–$70**	Social Drinking: **Permitted**
Open: **All year**	Airport/Station Pickup: **Yes**

This handsome turn-of-the-century Queen Anne–style home has been faithfully restored, attractively appointed, and air-conditioned. The theme here is comfort and Southern hospitality. Breakfast treats include biscuits and sausage gravy, grits, and regional hot breads. Afterwards, enjoy a short stroll to the famed Bath House Row or a brisk walk to the park, where miles of hiking trails will keep you in shape. Helen will be happy to direct you to the studios and shops of local artists and craftspeople. You are welcome to relax in the old-world sitting room and parlor or on the lovely veranda shaded by magnolia trees.

Williams House Bed & Breakfast Inn ✪
420 QUAPAW AVENUE, HOT SPRINGS, ARKANSAS 71901

Tel: **(501) 624-4275**	Open: **All year**
Hosts: **Mary and Gary Riley**	Breakfast: **Full**
Best Time to Call: **Evenings**	Credit Cards: **AMEX, MC, VISA**
Location: **50 mi. SW of Little Rock**	Pets: **No**
No. of Rooms: **5**	Smoking: **No**
No. of Private Baths: **5**	Social Drinking: **Permitted**
Double/pb: **$65–$85**	Minimum Stay: **2 nights weekends**
Single/pb: **$60–$75**	**Mar.–Apr.**
Suites: **$80–$90**	

This Victorian mansion, with its stained-glass and beveled-glass windows, is a nationally registered historical place. The atmosphere is friendly, and the marble fireplace and grand piano invite congeniality.

Breakfast menu may include quiche, toast amandine, or exotic egg dishes. Mary and Gary will spoil you with special iced tea, snacks, and mineral spring water. World health experts recognize the benefits of the hot mineral baths in Hot Springs National Park. The Inn is within walking distance of Bath House Row.

FLORIDA

Havana •

Pensacola •   • Seaside

Apalachicola •   San Mateo •   • St. Augustine

• Crescent City

• Ormond Beach

• New Smyrna Beach

Bushnell •   • Orlando

Tarpon Springs •   • Dade City

Palm Harbor •

Indian Shores • •   • Ruskin

St. Petersburg

Holmes Beach • • Madeira Beach   Jupiter •

• Arcadia

Palm Beach Gardens •   • West Palm

Fort Myers •   Beach

Key Biscayne •

• Islamorada

Big Pine Key •

Key West •   • Summerland Key

A & A Bed & Breakfast of Florida, Inc. ✪
P.O. BOX 1316, WINTER PARK, FLORIDA 32790

Tel: (407) 628-0322
Best Time to Call: 9 AM–6 PM
Coordinator: **Brunhilde (Bruni) Fehner**
States/Regions Covered: **Orlando
 area—Disney World, Epcot;
 Altamonte Springs, Cape Canaveral
 (Kennedy Space Center), Maitland,
 New Smyrna Beach, Sea World,**

**Winter Park, Delray Beach, Ft. Myers,
St. Augustine**
Rates (Single/Double):
 Modest: $35 / $40
 Average: $40 / $55
 Luxury: $65 / $125
Credit Cards: **No**
Minimum Stay: **2 nights**

You should allow several days to really savor all this area has to offer.
Bruni's hosts will suggest hints on getting the most out of the major
attractions, wonderful un-touristy restaurants, and tips on where to
shop for unique gifts to take home. All of her homes have a certain

"touch of class" to make you delighted with your visit. Rollins College is close by. There is a surcharge of $10 for one-night stays.

Alexander's VIP Reservations Service
P.O. BOX 4162, KEY WEST, FLORIDA 33041

Tel: (800) 503-4636; (305) 293-0277
Coordinator: **Alexander**
States/Regions Covered: **Florida Keys, Key West**

Rates (Single/Double):
Modest: **$65 / $85–$100**
Average: **$85–$150 / $120–$150**
Luxury: **$200–$225 / $275**

Key West is a tropical blend of gorgeous water, exotic foliage, wonderful restaurants and beautiful lodging facilities. History-enriched attractions and activities abound. Visitors immediately enjoy the Caribbean feel of this island nation called Conch Republic. Since its founding in 1822, Key West has gone through many phases, from housing pirates to poets. Today, it carries the creative touch of each former resident, such as Ernest Hemingway and Tennessee Williams. Tourists can view treasures from shipwrecks, discover the haunts of their literary heroes, and marvel at architecture and the dazzling gardens that bloom the entire year. From delicious cuisine to delightful shopping and spectacular events, Key West offers sun-drenched hospitality and entertainment. President Harry Truman once wrote, "I've a notion to move the capital to Key West and just stay."

Bed & Breakfast Co.—Tropical Florida
P.O. BOX 262, SOUTH MIAMI, FLORIDA 33243

Tel: (305) 661-3270
Best Time to Call: **9 AM–5 PM Mon.– Fri.**
Coordinator: **Marcella Schaible**
States/Regions Covered: **Statewide**

Rates (Single/Double):
Modest: **$35–$38 / $35–$40**
Average: **$38–$55 / $40–$60**
Luxury: **$55–$150 / $60–$170**
Credit Cards: **AMEX, MC, VISA**

Native Floridians, Marcella's hosts live in mansions on historic properties, in homes along the ocean and Gulf of Mexico, in woodland retreats, and on private residential islands. They exude Southern hospitality and want you to come stay in their accommodations that range from a charming cottage to a contemporary condo to unhosted accommodations. The decor may be simple or wildly extravagant. Hosts are ready to direct you to famous attractions or to an undiscovered special restaurant or shop that only a resident knows about. There is a $5 surcharge for each night stayed less than three.

Bed & Breakfast Scenic Florida
P.O. BOX 3385, TALLAHASSEE, FLORIDA 32315-3385

Tel: (904) 386-8196
Best Time to Call: **9 AM–6 PM Mon.– Fri.**

Coordinator: **Dianne C. Mahlert**
States/Regions Covered: **Gainesville,**

Gulf Beaches, Jacksonville, Orlando, St. Petersburg, Tallahassee
Descriptive Directory of B&Bs: **Free**

Rates (Single/Double):
Modest: **$35–$35**
Average: **$60–$65**
Luxury: **$125 / $125**
Credit Cards: **MC, VISA**

Bed & Breakfast Scenic Florida specializes in unique accommodations throughout North and Central Florida and beyond. This service's goal is to attract pleasure and business travelers to beautiful Florida and to help them select the best location to meet their needs and tastes. The people at Bed & Breakfast Scenic Florida inspect all locations and can answer very detailed questions about individual room decor and amenities. They are familiar with the cities and towns and can recommend things to do, where to eat, what to see. The service also provides written confirmation and directions to each accommodation.

Coombs House Inn ✪
80 SIXTH STREET, APALACHICOLA, FLORIDA 32320

Tel: **(904) 653-9199**
Best Time to Call: **Before noon, after 5 PM**
Hosts: **Marilyn and Charles Schubert**
Location: **75 mi. SW of Tallahassee**
No. of Rooms: **14**
No. of Private Baths: **14**
Double/pb: **$79–$89**
Single/pb: **$59–$69**

Suites: **$95**
Open: **All year**
Breakfast: **Continental**
Credit Cards: **AMEX, DISC, MC, VISA**
Pets: **Sometimes**
Children: **Welcome**
Smoking: **No**
Social Drinking: **Permitted**

Elegantly restored, this 1905 Victorian mansion welcomes those special guests who appreciate the charm and historical authenticity of another era and an intimate homey atmosphere. The three-story mansion features high ceilings and nine fireplaces. Inside you'll admire antique furniture of the period, paintings, historical photographs, imported English chintz draperies that frame the large bay windows, and oriental carpets. Each guest room has a private bath and cable TV. Located only minutes from fishing, boating, the Apalachicola River, and from the white beaches of St. George Island.

Historic Parker House ✪
427 WEST HICKORY STREET, ARCADIA, FLORIDA 33821

Tel: (941) 494-2499; (800) 969-2499	Single/sb: $60
Best Time to Call: 8 AM–10 PM	Open: All year
Hosts: Bob and Shelly Baumann	Reduced Rates: 10%
Location: 45 mi. E of Sarasota	Breakfast: Continental
No. of Rooms: 4	Credit Cards: AMEX, MC, VISA
No. of Private Baths: 2	Pets: No
Max. No. Sharing Bath: 4	Children: Welcome, over 10
Double/pb: $75	Smoking: No
Single/pb: $75	Social Drinking: Permitted
Double/sb: $60	

Once you step inside the Historic Parker House you become acquainted with a much grander, yet simpler life. The 6000-square-foot home is chock full of antiques, old clocks, and Florida's past. The original section of the home dates to the mid 1890s; a large addition was added in 1914 by the original owners, the Parkers, Florida cattle barons. Located in historic downtown Arcadia, recently named one of the one hundred best small towns in America, the home is close to antique and gift shopping and the Peace River for canoeing. Nearby are all of South Central Florida's attractions.

The Barnacle ✪
ROUTE 1, BOX 780A, LONG BEACH ROAD, BIG PINE KEY, FLORIDA 33043

Tel: (305) 872-3298	Open: All year
Best Time to Call: Before 9 PM	Breakfast: Full
Hosts: Wood and Joan Cornell	Pets: No
Location: Mile marker 33	Children: No
No. of Rooms: 4	Smoking: Permitted
No. of Private Baths: 4	Foreign Languages: French
Double/pb: $75–$110	

The ultimate in privacy is this self-contained cottage—a tropical tree house with stained-glass windows and private terrace. Rooms overlook the ocean or the atrium, with its hot tub and lush plants. One room has a private entrance and opens onto the beach. Every detail in and around their home reflects Wood and Joan's taste, attention to detail, and artistic flair. The structure was built to frame their eclectic collection of statuary, tapestries, and art. Their emphasis is on the sun and sea, with warm hospitality offered in abundance. You can snorkel or fish right off "your own" beach. Bahia Honda State Park and Key West are close by.

Bed & Breakfast-on-the-Ocean "Casa Grande" ✪
P.O. BOX 378, BIG PINE KEY, FLORIDA 33043

Tel: **(305) 872-2878**
Hosts: **Jon and Kathleen Threlkeld**
Location: **30 mi. E of Key West**
No. of Rooms: **3**
No. of Private Baths: **3**
Double/pb: **$85**

Open: **All year**
Breakfast: **Full**
Pets: **No**
Children: **No**
Smoking: **Permitted**
Social Drinking: **Permitted**

This spectacular Spanish-style home, facing the ocean, was custom-designed to suit the natural beauty of the Keys. The large landscaped garden patio, with panoramic beach views, is where you'll enjoy Jon and Kathleen's bountiful breakfast. It is also the site of the hot tub/Jacuzzi for relaxing by day or under a moonlit sky. The large and airy guest rooms are comfortably cooled by Bahama fans or air-conditioning. Key deer and birds abound. From the private beach, you'll enjoy swimming, fishing, snorkeling, bicycling, and jogging. There's a picnic table, gas grill, hammock, and Windsurfer for guests to use, compliments of the gracious hosts.

Canal Cottage Bed & Breakfast
P.O. BOX 430266, BIG PINE KEY, FLORIDA 33043

Tel: (305) 872-3881
Best Time to Call: **Evenings**
Hosts: **Dean and Patti Nickless**
Suites: **$85 for 2**
Open: **All year**
Breakfast: **Continental**

Pets: **No**
Children: **Welcome**
Smoking: **Permitted**
Social Drinking: **Permitted**
Minimum Stay: **2 nights**

Get away and relax! You can be self-sufficient in this unusual wood stilt house. Your accommodations are nestled in the trees and consist of a bedroom with a queen-size bed, a bathroom, a living room with sleeping space for two, and a kitchen stocked for your breakfast, which you can prepare at leisure and enjoy on the porch. Take advantage of local diving, snorkeling, and fishing charters, or bring your own boat to launch at the neighborhood ramp and tie it up at your backyard dock. There are bicycles for those so inclined, and a gas grill to cook your catch. You'll probably see a Key deer, too.

Deer Run ✪
LONG BEACH ROAD, P.O. BOX 431, BIG PINE KEY, FLORIDA 33043

Tel: (305) 872-2015, 872-2800
Best Time to Call: **Anytime before 10 PM**
Host: **Sue Abbott**
Location: **33 mi. E of Key West**
No. of Rooms: **3**
No. of Private Baths: **3**
Double/pb: **$85–$95**
Single/pb: **$75**

Open: **All year**
Breakfast: **Full**
Pets: **No**
Children: **No**
Smoking: **No**
Social Drinking: **Permitted**
Minimum Stay: **2 nights**
Airport/Station Pickup: **Yes**

Deer Run is a Florida Cracker-style home nestled among lush native trees on the ocean. The house is beautifully designed, with skylights, high ceilings, central air-conditioning, and Bahama fans. The decor boasts many paintings, artifacts, and antiques to compliment wicker and rattan furnishings. Upstairs each room has French doors that open onto a large veranda. Breakfast is served outside overlooking the ocean where you may spot Key deer walking along the beach. Looe Key Coral Reef, Bahia Honda State Park, and Key West are all within easy reach, or you can relax and soak up the rays in the free-form deep spa, where there's room for eight.

Florida Keys House ✪
P.O. BOX 431812, BIG PINE KEY, FLORIDA 33043

Tel: (800) 833-9857
Best Time to Call: **8 AM–8 PM**

Hosts: **Capt. Dave and Camille Wiley**
Location: **27 mi. E of Key West**

Suites: **$79–$125**
Open: **All year**
Breakfast: **Continental**
Pets: **No**
Children: **Welcome**

Smoking: **No**
Social Drinking: **Permitted**
Minimum Stay: **2 nights**
Foreign Languages: **French, Spanish**

Set among an abundance of coconut palm trees, your private guest quarters can accommodate up to four people and consist of one or two bedrooms, a bathroom, living room, and large kitchen stocked with breakfast selections which you may prepare at your convenience. Florida Keys House is canal front with a dock where you can fish, swim, barbecue or just relax in the hammock under the shade trees. Dave and Camille also offer snorkeling and diving trips to beautiful Looe Key Reef. Ask about their specialty, "backcountry flats fishing" for tarpon and bonefish, and permit for the Great White Heron Wildlife Refuge.

Vacation in Paradise ✪
ROUTE 1, BOX 641, BIG PINE KEY, FLORIDA 33043

Tel: **(305) 872-9009**
Host: **Joan Thoman**
Location: **30 mi. E of Key West**
Guest Cottage: **$85, for two**
Open: **All year**

Breakfast: **Continental**
Pets: **Sometimes**
Children: **Welcome**
Smoking: **Permitted**
Social Drinking: **Permitted**

True to its name, Vacation in Paradise is located six miles from Bahia Honda State Park (one of the best beaches in the country) and the famed Looe Key Reef. This spacious two-bedroom unit sleeps six and has a large kitchen and living room. Joan offers free dockage twenty feet from your door, a barbecue grill for cooking your dinner, and cable TV. Guests can enjoy fishing, scuba diving, snorkeling and the great nightlife in Key West.

Cypress House Bed and Breakfast ✪
8545 C.R. 476B, BUSHNELL, FLORIDA 33513

Tel: **(904) 568-0909**
Best Time to Call: **8 AM–10 PM**
Hosts: **Jan Fessler and Thelma Schaum**
Location: **50 mi. N of Tampa**
No. of Rooms: **6**
No. of Private Baths: **3**
Max. No. Sharing Bath: **4**
Double/pb: **$65**
Double/sb: **$45**

Suite: **$85**
Open: **All year**
Reduced Rates: **Seniors, 10%**
Breakfast: **Continental, buffet**
Other Meals: **Available**
Pets: **Horses ($10 per night)**
Children: **Welcome, over 5**
Smoking: **Restricted**
Social Drinking: **Permitted**

A new log home built in the gracious old Florida style, Cypress House is set on wooded farmland. From the oak rockers on the wide wraparound veranda, you can see oak trees draped with moss. The Webster Flea Market (Mondays only) and Brooksville's Christmas House are nearby, and Disney World and Busch Gardens are an hour away. You won't have to travel far to browse for antiques, fish, hike, or go canoeing. To bolster your energy, your hosts offer a generous breakfast buffet, plus coffee and snacks round the clock. Your hosts have five horses and offer one- to six-hour trail rides. There's a pool 15 × 40 feet, long enough for lap swimming.

Sprague House Inn & Restaurant ✪
125 CENTRAL AVENUE, CRESCENT CITY, FLORIDA 32012

Tel: **(904) 698-2430**	Breakfast: **Full**
Hosts: **Terry and Vena Moyer**	Other Meals: **Available**
Location: **75 mi. N of Orlando**	Credit Cards: **MC, VISA**
No. of Rooms: **5**	Pets: **No**
No. of Private Baths: **5**	Children: **No**
Double/pb: **$60**	Smoking: **No**
Suite: **$75–$125**	Social Drinking: **Permitted**
Open: **All year**	Airport/Station Pickup: **Yes**

A Steamboat Gothic inn, Sprague House Inn has been welcoming guests since 1905. The comfortably air-conditioned guest rooms are highlighted in antiques. Accents of stained glass and handsome woods are found throughout. The wraparound porches both upstairs and down boast rockers and swings from which you may enjoy the views of the lake. A public boat ramp and dock are a stone's throw away. You are welcome to borrow a cane fishing pole (no license required) or grab your net and try your luck at blue crabs. This one-stoplight town, unspoiled by plastic and neon, claims to be "the bass capital of the world." Terry is the gourmet cook for their on-premises restaurant.

Azalea House Bed & Breakfast ✪
37719 MERIDIAN AVENUE, DADE CITY, FLORIDA 33525

Tel: **(904) 523-1773**	Open: **All year**
Best Time to Call: **8 AM–10 PM**	Reduced Rates: **10% seniors**
Hosts: **Nancy and Grace Bryant**	Breakfast: **Continental**
Location: **40 mi. NE of Tampa**	Credit Cards: **AMEX, MC, VISA**
No. of Rooms: **3**	Pets: **No**
No. of Private Baths: **3**	Children: **Welcome, over 5**
Double/pb: **$65–$85**	Smoking: **No**
Single/pb: **$65–$75**	Social Drinking: **Permitted**
Suites: **$115, sleeps 4**	Station Pickup: **Yes**

Step back into time and enjoy true Southern hospitality. The Azalea House Bed & Breakfast is a beautifully restored, vintage 1906 home nestled in a setting of old oak trees, azaleas, hibiscus, and bamboo.

The interior is a harmonious blend of traditional, Oriental, and country decor. Wood floors, fireplaces, high ceilings, and soft colors create an enjoyable atmosphere of relaxation and comfort. Dade City has antique stores, specialty shops and the well-known restaurant, Lunch on Limoges.

Windsong Garden & Art Gallery ✪
5570–4 WOODROSE COURT, FORT MYERS, FLORIDA 33907

Tel: **(813) 936-6378**	Breakfast: **Continental**
Host: **Embe Burdick**	Pets: **No**
No. of Rooms: **2**	Children: **No**
No. of Private Baths: **2**	Smoking: **No**
Double/pb: **$55**	Social Drinking: **Permitted**
Suite: **$55**	Minimum Stay: **2 nights**
Open: **All year**	

This modern clear-shake-and-brick town house has a private courtyard and balcony for your enjoyment. The spacious combination bedroom-and-sitting room is most comfortable. Embe's varied interests include arts, crafts, music, and her household cats. It's close to Sanibel and Captiva Islands, Ft. Myers Beach, fine shopping, good restaurants, and the University of Florida. You are welcome to use the pool.

Gaver's Bed & Breakfast
301 EAST SIXTH AVENUE, HAVANA, FLORIDA 32333

Tel: **(904) 539-5611**	Breakfast: **Full**
Hosts: **Shirley and Bruce Gaver**	Pets: **No**
Location: **12 mi. N of Tallahassee**	Children: **Welcome, over 8**
No. of Rooms: **2**	Smoking: **No**
No. of Private Baths: **2**	Social Drinking: **Permitted**
Double/pb: **$65–$75**	Airport/Station Pickup: **Yes**
Open: **All year**	

This B&B, situated on a quiet residential street two blocks from the center of town, is a likely stop for collectors—at last count, Havana had thirty antique shops plus many related businesses. Tallahassee, the state capital and home of Florida State University, is only fifteen minutes away by car. A restored 1907 frame house, Gaver's has a large screened porch, and guests are welcome to watch cable TV in the common area. For breakfast, your hosts will design a menu to suit your preferences.

Harrington House B&B Inn ✪
5626 GULF DRIVE, HOLMES BEACH, FLORIDA 34217

Tel: **(813) 778-5444, 778-6335;**	Host: **Jo Davis**
fax: **(813) 778-0527**	Location: **40 mi. SW of Tampa**
Best Time to Call: **Noon–8 PM**	No. of Rooms: **12**

No. of Private Baths: **12**
Double/pb: **$89–$189**
Open: **All year**
Breakfast: **Full**
Credit Cards: **MC, VISA**
Pets: **No**

Children: **Welcome, over 12**
Smoking: **No**
Social Drinking: **Permitted**
Minimum Stay: **2 nights weekends, Feb.–Apr.**
Airport/Station Pickup: **Yes**

Surrounded by tropical foliage and the gulf's blue waters, this gracious Florida home, built in 1925, has the beach for its backyard. Each of the seven eclectically furnished guest rooms has its own charm and character. Relax by the pool, baste on the beach, take a moonlight stroll, or just let the sound of the surf lull you to sleep. Whatever your pleasure, the warm hospitality will ensure that your stay is a memorable one.

Meeks B&B on the Gulf Beaches ✪
19418 GULF BOULEVARD, #408, INDIAN SHORES, FLORIDA 34635

Tel: **(813) 596-5424; fax: (813) 593-0065**
Best Time to Call: **7 AM–10 PM**
Hosts: **Greta and Bob Meeks**
Location: **35 min. from Tampa Airport**
No. of Rooms: **4**
No. of Private Baths: **3**
Double/pb: **$50–$60**

Single/pb: **$45–$55**
Suites: **$75–$85**
Open: **All year**
Breakfast: **Full or Continental**
Pets: **No**
Children: **Welcome**
Smoking: **No**
Social Drinking: **Permitted**

Beach! Pool! Sunsets! Enjoy your stay in this beach condo overlooking the Gulf of Mexico. A beach cottage is sometimes available. Choose your breakfast, then bask in the sun, swim in the gulf, and catch spectacular sunsets from your balcony. Dine at nearby seafood restaurants and visit the local seabird sanctuary, sunken gardens, and the Dali Museum. Other nearby attractions are Busch Gardens in Tampa and sponge diving in Tarpon Springs. This B&B is located between Clearwater and St. Petersburg Beach, only two hours from Walt Disney World. Your hostess is a real estate broker.

Bed & Breakfast of Islamorada ✪
81175 OLD HIGHWAY, ISLAMORADA, FLORIDA 33036

Tel: **(305) 664-9321**
Host: **Dottie Saunders**
Location: **87 mi. S of Miami**
No. of Rooms: **2**
No. of Private Baths: **2**
Double/pb: **$50–$60**
Single/pb: **$45**
Open: **All year**

Reduced Rates: **Available**
Breakfast: **Full**
Credit Cards: **MC, VISA**
Pets: **Sometimes**
Children: **Welcome**
Smoking: **Permitted**
Social Drinking: **Permitted**

Make the most of the Florida Keys while staying in this one-story house. Bicycles and snorkeling gear are at your disposal, and sailing trips on a historic old boat can be arranged. John Pennecamp Coral Reef State Park, 40 minutes away, is a great place for snorkeling and diving, and the whole family can ride in the glass-bottomed boats. Your hostess has had a varied career, from cooking on a freighter to selling real estate; she enjoys waterfront activities, gardening, and photography.

Innisfail ✪
134 TIMBER LANE, JUPITER, FLORIDA 33458

Tel: (407) 744-5905	Reduced Rates: 10% weekly; 10% seniors
Best Time to Call: Evenings	
Hosts: Katherine and Luke Van Noorden	Breakfast: Continental
	Other Meals: Available
Location: 20 mi. N of Palm Beach	Pets: Welcome
No. of Rooms: 2	Children: Yes
Max. No. Sharing Bath: 4	Smoking: No
Double/sb: $51–$60	Social Drinking: Permitted
Open: All year	Airport/Station Pickup: Yes

A contemporary ranch framed by palm trees, Innisfail—Gaelic for "the abode of peace and harmony"—doubles as a gallery. The Van Noordens are sculptors, and guests are welcome to watch them work in their home studio. While you don't have to be an art lover to visit, it helps to be a pet lover; Katherine and Luke's four-footed family comprises three dogs and two cats. Jupiter has wonderful beaches, but you can get an equally good tan lounging by the Van Noordens' swimming pool. In the morning, a Continental breakfast of coffee or tea, fresh citrus fruit, and muffins or cereal is served.

Hibiscus House ✪
345 WEST ENID DRIVE, KEY BISCAYNE, FLORIDA 33149

Tel: (305) 361-2456	Open: All year
Best Time to Call: 9 AM–5 PM	Reduced Rates: May 1–Dec. 15
Hosts: Bernice and Earl Duffy	Breakfast: Full
Location: 10 mi. SE of Miami	Pets: No
No. of Rooms: 2	Children: No
No. of Private Baths: 2	Smoking: Permitted
Double/pb: $65	Social Drinking: Permitted
Single/pb: $60	Minimum Stay: 2 nights

Welcome to an island paradise only 15 minutes from downtown Miami and 20 minutes from Miami International Airport. Key Biscayne features two lushly landscaped parks, a championship golf course, and miles of white sandy beaches; your hosts offer private beach privileges. Tennis courts and bicycle paths are in plentiful supply.

Add to this the famous Miami Seaquarium and easy access to Greater Miami's many attractions and you have all of the ingredients for a very pleasant visit.

Center Court Historic Inn & Cottages ✪
916 CENTER STREET, KEY WEST, FLORIDA 33040

Tel: (305) 296-9292; (800) 797-8787
Best Time to Call: 9 AM–9 PM
Host: Naomi Van Steelandt
Location: 120 mi. S of Miami
No. of Rooms: 6
No. of Private Baths: 6
Double/pb: $128
Single/pb: $98
Guest Cottage: $148–$300, sleeps 2–6
Suites: $148
Open: All year

Reduced Rates: May 1–Dec. 15, 5% seniors
Breakfast: Continental, plus
Credit Cards: AMEX, DISC, MC, VISA
Pets: Sometimes
Children: Welcome in cottages, over 12 in main house
Smoking: No
Social Drinking: Permitted
Minimum Stay: 2 nights weekends, cottages

Center Court is located in the heart of Key West's Historic District, within walking distance to every major attraction. All rooms have been recently renovated with loving care and have lightweight comforters, feather pillows, hair dryers, TV, telephones, fans and air-conditioning. Amenities include private sundecks, an eight-person Jacuzzi, heated pool, exercise room and a private courtyard with outdoor dining and barbecue grills. In the morning, enjoy breakfast at your leisure.

Lighthouse Bed & Breakfast ✪
13355 2ND STREET, MADEIRA BEACH, FLORIDA 33708

Tel: (813) 391-0015; (800) 241-0334
Hosts: Joyce and John Dickinson
Location: 4 mi. W of St. Petersburg
No. of Rooms: 5
No. of Private Baths: 5
Double/pb: $45–$85
Open: All year

Breakfast: Full (Winter), Continental (Summer)
Credit Cards: MC, VISA
Pets: Sometimes
Children: Welcome, over 5
Smoking: Permitted
Social Drinking: Permitted

Lighthouse Bed & Breakfast is located only 50 steps from the Intracoastal Waterway and 300 steps from white sand on the Gulf of Mexico's beaches. Guests enjoy the comfort of the Key West–style surroundings with a palm-filled courtyard, a gazebo for dining or relaxing, and a sundeck atop the lighthouse—for lying in the sun or watching the sunrise or sunset. If you want to cook your own supper, there's a barbecue grill. It's an easy walk to the famous John's Pass Boardwalk and village where shopping, restaurants, jet skiing, parasailing, chartered fishing boats, and casino cruises are available. St. Petersburg Pier, Dali Museum and the Florida International Museum are within ten minutes. Busch Gardens in Tampa is approximately thirty minutes away. In 1995 St. Petersburg was awarded a major league baseball team. The Lighthouse is a quiet retreat from the city's traffic and commercial buildings, yet close enough to join in the rush if you want to. Breakfast specialties include pancakes, waffles and omelettes. For those flying in, airport door-to-door service is available.

Night Swan Intracoastal Bed & Breakfast ✪
512 SOUTH RIVERSIDE DRIVE, NEW SMYRNA BEACH, FLORIDA 32168

Tel: **(904) 423-4940**	Open: **All year**
Best Time to Call: **9 AM–9 PM**	Reduced Rates: **Available**
Hosts: **Martha and Charles**	Breakfast: **Continental, Full**
Nighswonger	Credit Cards: **AMEX, DISC, MC, VISA**
Location: **15 mi. S of Daytona Beach**	Pets: **No**
No. of Rooms: **8**	Children: **Welcome**
No. of Private Baths: **8**	Smoking: **No**
Double/pb: **$59–$79**	Social Drinking: **Permitted**
Suites: **$99–$129; sleeps 4**	Airport/Station Pickup: **Yes**

Come sit on Night Swan's wraparound porch or by its windows and watch pelicans, dolphins, sailboats, and yachts ply the Atlantic Intracoastal Waterway. Then enjoy the waterfront yourself: surf, swim, fish, drive, or bicycle along the bathing beach two miles to the east. This spacious three-story home in New Smyrna's historic district has a central fireplace and intricate, natural woodwork in every room, and some rooms overlook the Indian River. Breakfast is served in the dining room; low-cholesterol dishes are a house specialty.

PerriHouse Bed & Breakfast Inn
10417 STATE ROAD 535, ORLANDO, FLORIDA 32836

Tel: **(407) 876-4830; (800) 780-4830;**	Open: **All year**
Fax: **(407) 876-0241**	Reduced Rates: **Seniors, weekly**
Best Time to Call: **9 AM–9 PM**	Breakfast: **Continental**
Hosts: **Nick and Angi Perretti**	Credit Cards: **AMEX, DISC, MC, VISA**
Location: **3 mi. N of I-4 Exit 27, Lake**	Pets: **No**
Buena Vista, on SR 535N	Children: **Welcome (crib)**
No. of Rooms: **6**	Smoking: **No**
No. of Private Baths: **6**	Social Drinking: **Permitted**
Double/pb: **$69–$85**	Airport/Station Pickup: **Yes**
Single/pb: **$65**	

PerriHouse is a quiet, private country estate inn secluded on 20 acres of land adjacent to the Walt Disney World Resort complex. Because of its outstanding location, Disney Village and Pleasure Island are only 3 minutes away; EPCOT center is only 5 minutes. It's the perfect vacation setting for families who desire a unique travel experience with a comfortable, convenient home away from home. An upscale Continental breakfast awaits you each morning, and a refreshing pool relaxes you after a full day of activities. Each guest room features its own private bath, entrance, TV, telephone, ceiling fan, and central air/ heat. The PerriHouse grounds are being developed and landscaped to create a future bird sanctuary and wildlife preserve. Come bird-watch on the peaceful, tranquil grounds of the PerriHouse estate and wake up to bird songs outside your window. Your hosts, Nick and Angi, instinctively offer their guests a unique blend of cordial hospitality, comfort, and friendship!

Bed 'n Breakfast of Greater Daytona Beach
P.O. BOX 1081, ORMOND BEACH, FLORIDA 32175

Tel: (904) 673-2232
Coordinator: **Rusty Reed**
States/Regions Covered: **Daytona Beach, Ormond Beach, Pt. Orange, Wilbur-by-the-Sea**

Rates (Single/Double):
  Average: **$35–$75**
Credit Cards: **No**
Minimum Stay: **4 nights Speed/Bike weeks in Feb. and Mar.**

The host homes, each with its own special amenities and charm, are located throughout the greater Daytona area and pride themselves on catering to the needs of each guest. The Space Center and Disney World are within 60 miles. Closer to home, Daytona offers deep-sea fishing, golf, tennis, jai alai, dog racing, theater, and Halifax River cruises. A Daytona International Speedway tour and a drive on "the world's most famous beach" are a must. Yacht enthusiasts will be interested in the new 600-slip Halifax Marina, where they can dock, and then bed-and-breakfast nearby.

Heron Cay ✪
15106 PALMWOOD ROAD, PALM BEACH GARDENS, FLORIDA 33410

Tel: (407) 744-6315; fax (407) 744-6315
Best Time to Call: **10 AM–12 noon; after 7 PM**
Hosts: **Randy and Margie Salyer**
Location: **15 mi. N of Palm Beach International Airport**
No. of Rooms: **9**
No. of Private Baths: **7**
Max. No. Sharing Bath: **4**

Double/pb: **$85–$115**
Guest Yacht: **$175–$250, sleeps 2–6**
Suites: **$135–$185**
Open: **All year**
Reduced Rates: **Available**
Breakfast: **Full**
Pets: **No**
Smoking: **Restricted**
Social Drinking: **Permitted**

At Heron Cay you'll think you're in Key West. This island-style home is quietly nestled on two tropical acres overlooking the Intracoastal Waterway. Randy and Margie's private half-acre island is fun to explore—it protects their harbor that accommodates boats to 55 feet, plus a boat ramp for smaller water toys. All guest rooms open to a balcony leading to the sundeck and several patio areas for relaxation beside the 10-foot-deep pool or heated spa. Guests are provided with refrigerators in rooms and may use the recreation room and barbecue area poolside. Fine restaurants, major shopping, and miles of natural ocean beaches are just minutes away. Margie and Randy are avid boaters who regularly invite guests aboard their 48-foot sportsfisherman, *Waterfront Lady*, for Palm Beach area cruises.

Bed & Breakfast of Tampa Bay ⊘
126 OLD OAK CIRCLE, OAK TRAIL, PALM HARBOR, FLORIDA 34683

Tel: **(813) 785-2342**	Double/sb: **$45**
Best Time to Call: **7–9 AM; 6–10 PM**	Single/sb: **$30**
Hosts: **Vivian and David Grimm**	Suite: **$75**
Location: **18 mi. W of Tampa**	Open: **All year**
No. of Rooms: **4**	Breakfast: **Full**
No. of Private Baths: **2**	Pets: **Sometimes**
Max. No. Sharing Bath: **4**	Children: **Welcome**
Double/pb: **$60**	Smoking: **No**
Single/pb: **$40**	Social Drinking: **Permitted**

A premier facility in a premier location: this new Art Deco residence is 1½ miles from the Gulf of Mexico and 25 minutes from Busch Gardens, Dali Museum, and Weeki-Wachee Springs. Shopping, restaurants, churches, and public transportation are within easy walking distance. The Grimms' home has an ivory stucco exterior, with front pillars, a tile roof, and stained-glass doors. Inside, artifacts from their world travels are shown to advantage under 12-foot ceilings. Amenities include a pool and Jacuzzi, a grand piano, and bicycles for local excursions.

Gulf Beach Inn ✪
10655 GULF BEACH HIGHWAY, PENSACOLA, FLORIDA 32507

Tel: **(904) 492-4501**
Hosts: **M.J. and Lisa Krause**
Location: **50 mi. E of Mobile**
Guest Cottage: **$65**
Open: **All year**
Breakfast: **Full**

Pets: **No**
Children: **Welcome**
Smoking: **No**
Social Drinking: **Permitted**
Airport/Station Pickup: **Yes**
Foreign Languages: **German**

The Gulf Beach Inn is on the Intracoastal Waterway. Because it is located on your own private beach, it is the ideal spot for sunning, swimming, and watching sailboats, sunrises and sunsets. The Naval Aviation Museum, excellent seafood restaurants, and an outlet mall with over 100 stores are nearby. Perdido Key and the Emerald Coast of Florida are just minutes away.

Sunshine Inn ✪
508 DECATUR AVENUE, PENSACOLA, FLORIDA 32507

Tel: **(904) 455-6781**
Best Time to Call: **Early mornings**
Hosts: **The Jablonskis**
Location: **8 mi. from I-10; 4 mi. from beach**
No. of Rooms: **2**
No. of Private Baths: **1**
Max. No. Sharing Bath: **4**
Double/sb: **$35**

Suites: **$35 for 2**
Open: **All year**
Breakfast: **Full**
Pets: **No**
Children: **Welcome**
Smoking: **No**
Social Drinking: **Permitted**
Airport/Station Pickup: **Yes**
Foreign Languages: **German**

Sun and swim in the Gulf of Mexico, on the beautiful Emerald Coast of northwest Florida. Your knowledgeable host will provide you with all the touring advice you seek. Sunshine Inn is only minutes from the Naval Aviation Museum and the beach. The breakfast specialty is blueberry pancakes. There is a $5 surcharge for one-night stays.

Ruskin House Bed and Breakfast ✪
120 DICKMAN DRIVE S.W., RUSKIN, FLORIDA 33570

Tel: **(813) 645-3842**
Best Time to Call: **Anytime**
Host: **Arthur M. Miller, Ph.D.**
Location: **25 mi. S of Tampa; 30 mi. N of Sarasota**
No. of Rooms: **3**
No. of Private Baths: **1**
Max No. Sharing Bath: **4**
Double/pb: **$65**
Double/sb: **$45**
Suites: **$65**

Open: **All year**
Reduced Rates: **7th day free**
Breakfast: **Continental**
Credit Cards: **MC, VISA**
Pets: **No**
Children: **Welcome, over 6**
Smoking: **No**
Social Drinking: **Permitted**
Minimum Stay: **2 nights**
Foreign Languages: **French**

A waterfront home listed on the State Register of Historic Places, this B&B, built in 1910, is graced with verandas and furnished with period antiques. The property abounds in citrus trees, and guests can help themselves to fruit in season. Your host, a poet, editor, and literature professor at New College in Sarasota, is a third-generation inhabitant of Ruskin; his grandfather cofounded the town as a Christian Socialist venture complete with Ruskin College, tuition-free for residents and their families. (The college's only surviving building, just a block from Ruskin House, is enrolled on the National Register of Historic Places.) Ruskin is no longer a utopian community, but the beach and playground are nearby, and it's an easy drive to either Tampa or Sarasota.

Casa de la Paz
22 AVENIDA MENENDEZ, ST. AUGUSTINE, FLORIDA 32084

Tel: **(904) 829-2915**
Best Time to Call: **9 AM–9 PM**
Host: **Jan Maki**
Location: **7 mi. from I-95**
No. of Rooms: **6**
No. of Private Baths: **6**
Double/pb: **$75–$125**
Suites: **$79–$125**

Open: **All year**
Breakfast: **Full**
Credit Cards: **AMEX, MC, VISA**
Pets: **No**
Children: **No**
Smoking: **No**
Social Drinking: **Permitted**

Overlooking historic Matanzas Bay in the heart of Old St. Augustine is this three-story Mediterranean-style stucco home. The rooms are comfortably furnished in a pleasant blend of the old and new. Amenities in each room include ceiling fans, central air-conditioning and heat, high-quality linens, cable TV, and complimentary sherry or wine. The veranda rooms have private entrances. Guests are welcome to use the private, walled courtyard, well-stocked library, and delightful parlor. It is central to all attractions and convenient to fine restaurants and shops.

Castle Garden ✪
15 SHENANDOAH STREET, ST. AUGUSTINE, FLORIDA 32084

Tel: **(904) 829-3839**
Best Time to Call: **9 AM–6 PM**
Hosts: **Bruce Kloeckner and Kimmy VanKooten**
Location: **10 mi. from I-95**
No. of Rooms: **6**
No. of Private Baths: **6**
Double/pb: **$75–$150**
Open: **All year**

Reduced Rates: **20% weekly, $20 less Sun.–Thurs.; 10% seniors**
Breakfast: **Full**
Credit Cards: **AMEX, DISC, MC, VISA**
Pets: **No**
Children: **Welcome**
Smoking: **No**
Social Drinking: **Permitted**
Airport/Station Pickup: **Yes**

The only Moorish-revival dwelling in St. Augustine, Castle Garden dates to the late 1800s; the unusual coquina stone exterior has remained virtually untouched since its completion. The completely renovated interior features two magnificent bridal suites, each complete with a sunken bedroom, in-room Jacuzzi, cathedral ceiling, and other wonderful details. Park your car in the B&B's fenced lot and borrow bikes to tour the city, one of the nation's oldest. When you return, rest on the sun porch or stroll the lovely grounds. The hosts give each guest complimentary wine, and pride themselves on preparing mouthwatering country breakfasts "just like Mom used to make."

Kenwood Inn
38 MARINE STREET, ST. AUGUSTINE, FLORIDA 32084

Tel: **(904) 824-2116**
Best Time to Call: **10 AM–10 PM**
Hosts: **Mark, Kerrianne, and Caitlin Constant**
Location: **40 mi. S of Jacksonville**
No. of Rooms: **14**
No. of Private Baths: **14**
Double/pb: **$75–$105**
Single/pb: **$45–$65**

Suite: **$135**
Open: **All year**
Breakfast: **Continental**
Credit Cards: **DISC, MC, VISA**
Pets: **No**
Children: **Welcome, over 8**
Smoking: **No**
Social Drinking: **Permitted**

If you are to discover a Victorian building in Florida, how appropriate that it should be in the historic section of St. Augustine, one of the oldest cities in the U.S. This New England–style inn is a rarity in the South; this one has old-fashioned beds with color-coordinated touches right down to the sheets and linens. Breakfast may be taken in your room, in the courtyard surrounded by trees, or by the swimming pool. Tour trains, waterfront shops, restaurants, and museums are within walking distance. Flagler College is three blocks away.

St. Francis Inn ✪
279 ST. GEORGE STREET, ST. AUGUSTINE, FLORIDA 32084

Tel: **(904) 824-6068; (800) 824-6062**
Hosts: **Stan and Regina Reynolds**
Location: **2 mi. from US 1**
No. of Rooms: **14**
No. of Private Baths: **14**
Double/pb: **$55–$98**
Guest Cottage: **$140; sleeps 4–6**
Suites: **$75–$95**

Open: **All year**
Breakfast: **Continental, plus**
Credit Cards: **MC, VISA**
Pets: **No**
Children: **Welcome (crib)**
Smoking: **No**
Social Drinking: **Permitted**

Built in 1791, the Inn is a Spanish Colonial structure with a private courtyard and garden, located in the center of the restored part of town. Balconies are furnished with rocking chairs, and the swimming pool is a great cooling-off spot. The building is made of coquina, a limestone made of broken shells and coral. Due to its trapezoidal shape, there are no square or rectangular rooms. All of St. Augustine's historic and resort activities are within a three-mile radius.

Bayboro House on Old Tampa Bay
1719 BEACH DRIVE SOUTHEAST, ST. PETERSBURG, FLORIDA 33701

Tel: **(813) 823-4955**
Hosts: **Gordon and Antonia Powers**
Location: **½ mi. from I-275, Exit 9**
No. of Rooms: **4**
No. of Private Baths: **4**
Double/pb: **$95–$145**
Open: **All year**

Breakfast: **Continental**
Credit Cards: **MC, VISA**
Pets: **No**
Children: **No**
Smoking: **No**
Social Drinking: **Permitted**

Richly appointed in antiques and collectibles, the historic Bayboro House is what you would expect in a luxury waterfront bed and breakfast. All rooms have a water view, air-conditioning, TV, VCR, and a morning paper is delivered to your door. Breakfast includes fresh fruits, juice, rolls, muffins, homemade breads, cereal, coffee and tea served in the formal dining room.

Ferncourt Bed and Breakfast ✪
150 CENTRAL AVENUE, SAN MATEO, FLORIDA 32187

Tel: **(904) 329-9755**
Hosts: **Jack and Dee Morgan**
Location: **25 mi. W of St. Augustine**
No. of Rooms: **5**
No. of Private Baths: **5**
Double/pb: **$50–$70**
Suites: **$75**

Open: **All year**
Breakfast: **Full**
Pets: **No**
Children: **No**
Smoking: **No**
Social Drinking: **Permitted**

Ferncourt is a restored 1800s farm home, located in a tiny historic hamlet just a few minutes' drive from St. Augustine and Daytona Beach. Guests have use of several rooms and the wraparound veranda. Close by, restaurants serve excellent food. Cookies and tea are offered in the evening. Jack does woodworking and upholstery and many examples of his craft are on display throughout the inn. Dee dabbles in painting and loves antiques and flea markets, but her real passion is food, evidenced by the gourmet breakfast she serves. Discover North Central Florida, then retire to all the charm and hospitality of the Victorian era with your hosts.

The Dolphin Inn at Seaside ✪
P.O. Box 4732, 107 SAVANNAH STREET, SEASIDE, FLORIDA 32459

Tel: **(904) 231-5477; (800) 443-3146**
Best Time to Call: **Anytime**

Hosts: **Richard "Mac" McCullen and Nancy Judkins**

Location: **25 mi. W of Panama City**
No. of Rooms: **2**
No. of Private Baths: **2**
Double/pb: **$95**
Open: **All year**
Breakfast: **Continental**

Other Meals: **Available**
Credit Cards: **MC, VISA**
Pets: **No**
Children: **Welcome**
Smoking: **Permitted**
Social Drinking: **Permitted**

Seaside, a unique new community, recaptures the charm and tranquility of turn-of-the-century resort towns with its pastel-hued Victorian houses, white picket fences, brick streets, sugar-white beaches, and clear blue waters. The Dolphin Inn is a pink three-story Victorian cottage with stained-glass windows and dolphin-shaped gingerbread trim; inside, a 1909 piano adds to the nostalgia. Guest rooms open onto a veranda with a breathtaking view of the Gulf of Mexico. Mac is a scuba instructor and Nancy also dives, so there is a nautical air to their furnishings, including Nancy's striking shell collection. If you share Mac's passion for old cars, you'll admire his restored 1961 Impala convertible.

Knightswood ✪
P.O. BOX 151, SUMMERLAND KEY, FLORIDA 33042

Tel: **(305) 872-2246; (800) 437-5402**
Hosts: **Chris and Herb Pontin**
Location: **26 mi. E of Key West**
No. of Rooms: **2**
No. of Private Baths: **2**
Double/pb: **$85**
Single/pb: **$70**

Open: **All year**
Breakfast: **Full**
Pets: **No**
Children: **No**
Smoking: **No**
Social Drinking: **Permitted**
Minimum Stay: **2 nights**

Knightswood boasts one of the loveliest water views in the Keys. The guest apartment is self-contained and very private. Snorkeling, fishing, and boating can be enjoyed right from the Pontins' dock. You are welcome to swim in the freshwater pool, relax in the spa, or sunbathe on the white sand beach. Trips to protected Looe Key Coral Reef can be arranged. Fine dining and Key West nightlife are within easy reach.

Fiorito's Bed & Breakfast ✪
421 OLD EAST LAKE ROAD, TARPON SPRINGS, FLORIDA 34689

Tel: **(813) 937-5487**
Best Time to Call: **8 AM–9 PM**
Hosts: **Dick and Marie Fiorito**
Location: **2 mi. E of US 19**
No. of Rooms: **1**
No. of Private Baths: **1**
Double/pb: **$40**
Single/pb: **$35**

Open: **All year**
Breakfast: **Full**
Pets: **No**
Children: **No**
Smoking: **Restricted**
Social Drinking: **Permitted**
Airport/Station Pickup: **Yes**

Just off a quiet road that runs along Lake Tarpon's horse country, this meticulously maintained home on two-and-a-half acres offers respite for the visitor. The guest room and bath are decorated in tones of blue, enhanced with beautiful accessories. Fresh fruit, cheese omelette, homemade bread and jam, and a choice of beverage is the Fioritos' idea of breakfast. It is beautifully served on the tree-shaded, screened terrace. They'll be happy to direct you to the Greek Sponge Docks, deep-sea fishing opportunities, golf courses, beaches, and great restaurants.

Heartsease ✪
272 OLD EAST LAKE ROAD, TARPON SPRINGS, FLORIDA 34689

Tel: **(813) 934-0994**	Reduced Rates: **Available**
Best Time to Call: **After 7 PM**	Breakfast: **Continental**
Hosts: **Gerald and Sharon Goulish**	Pets: **No**
No. of Rooms: **1 cottage**	Children: **No**
No. of Private Baths: **1**	Smoking: **No**
Double/pb: **$60**	Social Drinking: **Permitted**
Single/pb: **$55**	Airport Pickup: **Yes**
Open: **All year**	

You'll find plenty of "heartsease," meaning peace of mind and tranquility, at Gerald and Sharon's guest cottage. Wicker and pine furniture and a green and mauve color scheme create a light, airy feeling. Amenities include a private entrance, a mini-kitchen stocked with a microwave and breakfast fixings, cable TV, private bath, tennis court, and a deck overlooking the in-ground pool. Pluck an orange or a grapefruit from one of the many fruit trees and then settle in the gazebo, an ideal place for observing the bald eagles that nest nearby. Golf courses, Tampa's Old Hyde Park, Harbour Island, and Tarpon Springs' famed sponge docks are all within a short drive.

Inn on the Bayou ✪
P.O. BOX 1545, TARPON SPRINGS, FLORIDA 34688

Tel: **(813) 942-4468**	Single/sb: **$45**
Host: **Al Stark**	Open: **All year**
Location: **15–20 mi. NW of Tampa**	Reduced Rates: **Available**
No. of Rooms: **3**	Breakfast: **Continental**
No. of Private Baths: **1**	Pets: **No**
Max. No. Sharing Bath: **2**	Children: **Welcome, over 7**
Double/pb: **$50**	Smoking: **No**
Single/pb: **$45**	Social Drinking: **Permitted**
Double/sb: **$50**	Airport Pickup: **Yes**

Come stay at this beautiful, contemporary home situated on a quiet bayou. Fish for a big red or watch the blue herons and pelicans nesting in a bird sanctuary behind the B&B. Go for a swim in your host's solar-heated pool or soak your cares away in a whirlpool spa. Then take a stroll through the famous sponge docks and do some antiquing in town. The Inn is located just minutes from a white sandy beach with breathtaking sunsets. Busch Gardens and Adventure Islands are close by. Private tours with transportation are available.

West Palm Beach Bed & Breakfast ☉
419 32ND STREET, OLD NORTHWOOD HISTORIC DISTRICT, WEST PALM BEACH, FLORIDA 33407-4809

Tel: (800) 736-4064; (407) 848-4064; fax: (407) 842-1688
Best Time to Call: 9 AM–10 PM
Host: Dennis Keimel
No. of Rooms: 4
No. of Private Baths: 4
Double/pb: $75–$115
Open: All year

Reduced Rates: May–Oct.
Breakfast: Continental, plus
Credit Cards: AMEX, DC, MC, VISA
Pets: No
Children: No
Smoking: No
Social Drinking: Permitted
Airport/Station Pickup: Yes

West Palm Beach Bed & Breakfast sits on a cozy but deceptively large property reminiscent of a Key West guest house with poolside cottages. The main house is pastel pink with aqua striped awnings and white picket fences. Inside, bright colors, whimsical decorations and white wicker furniture make for a fun, comfortable island atmosphere. All guest rooms have air-conditioning, color cable TV and paddle fans, each with its own style. The warm hospitality and ideal location near beaches, Palm Beach, and the downtown waterfront have made this B&B extremely popular with guests, including Europeans and Canadians. Enjoy a tropical breakfast buffet each morning prior to your adventures, or just relax by the pool.

GEORGIA

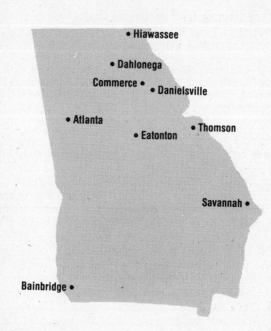

Quail Country Bed & Breakfast, Ltd.
1104 OLD MONTICELLO ROAD, THOMASVILLE, GEORGIA 31792

Tel: (912) 226-7218; 226-6882
Coordinators: **Mercer Watt and Kathy Lanigan**
States/Regions Covered: **Thomas County, Thomasville**

Rates (Single/Double):
 Average: **$30 / $40**
 Luxury: **$40 / $50**
Credit Cards: **No**

Mercer and Kathy have a wide selection of homes, several with swimming pools, in lovely residential areas. There's a lot to see and do, including touring historic restorations and plantations. Enjoy the Pebble Hill Plantation Museum, historic Glen Arven Country Club, and the April Rose Festival. There is a $5 surcharge for one-night stays.

Atlanta's Woodruff Bed & Breakfast
223 PONCE DE LEON AVENUE, ATLANTA, GEORGIA 30308

Tel: **(404) 875-9449; (800) 473-9449**
Hosts: **Joan and Douglas Jones**
No. of Rooms: **12**
No. of Private Baths: **10**
Max. No. Sharing Bath: **4**
Double/pb: **$79**
Single/pb: **$69**
Suites: **$129**
Open: **All year**

Reduced Rates: **10% seniors**
Breakfast: **Full**
Credit Cards: **AMEX, DISC, MC, VISA**
Pets: **Sometimes**
Children: **Welcome**
Smoking: **No**
Social Drinking: **Permitted**
Foreign Languages: **Spanish, French**

The moment you step into Atlanta's Woodruff Bed & Breakfast you'll experience the slower pace of times gone by. Joan and Douglas have exquisitely restored this turn-of-the-century home, keeping the old charm and character that once was. There are three Jacuzzi hot tubs, three fireplaces and several porches to insure a stay to everyone's liking. Centrally located to fine restaurants, cultural activities, and to most convention centers, yet bordering the residential area, the home was designed and built by a premier architect of the 1900s for a prominent family. In the 1950s, Bessie Woodruff purchased the home, where she and nineteen female assistants operated a licensed physiotherapy center. Many of Atlanta's finest politicians availed themselves of this needed therapy. A full Southern breakfast and true Southern hospitality will get your day started. Free pickup is provided from the MARTA, Atlanta's subway system.

Magnolia Station
1020 EDGEWOOD AVENUE NORTHEAST, ATLANTA, GEORGIA 30307

Tel: **(404) 523-2005**
Hosts: **Jim Piroli and Raymond Manci**
No. of Rooms: **3**
No. of Private Baths: **1**
Max. No. Sharing Bath: **4**
Double/pb: **$75**
Single/pb: **$65**
Double/sb: **$65**
Single/sb: **$55**

Open: **All year**
Reduced Rates: **10% after 4th night**
Breakfast: **Continental**
Credit Cards: **MC, VISA**
Pets: **No**
Children: **No**
Smoking: **No**
Social Drinking: **Permitted**

Magnolia Station is located in the Inman Park Historic District, one of the last enclaves of Atlanta's Victorian architecture. Relax by the pool or stroll the quiet streets where the city's most affluent resided, including the inventor and founders of Coca-Cola. Beautifully restored and furnished with antiques and 18th-century reproductions, Magnolia Station stands on the site of the Civil War Battle of Atlanta and is across the street from the rapid-rail station. Walk to parks, the Carter Presidential Center, and the Little Five Points and Virginia-Highlands business districts. There is easy rail access to downtown, malls, and Atlanta's airport.

The White House B&B

320 WASHINGTON STREET, BAINBRIDGE, GEORGIA 31717

Tel: **(912) 248-1703**
Hosts: **John and Mary Patterson**
Location: **45 mi. NW of Tallahassee,
  Florida**
No. of Rooms: **3**
No. of Private Baths: **1**
Max. No. Sharing Bath: **4**
Double/pb: **$45**
Single/pb: **$40**
Double/sb: **$40**

Single/sb: **$35**
Open: **All year**
Reduced Rates: **Over 3 days**
Breakfast: **Continental**
Pets: **No**
Children: **Welcome, over 10**
Smoking: **No**
Social Drinking: **No**
Airport/Station Pickup: **Yes**

This antebellum dogtrot-style home (circa 1840–50) in the historic district of Bainbridge features original hand-hewn columns and rived pine floors. The decor is a blend of family antiques, heirloom fabrics, and needlework. Guests are encouraged to enjoy the swimming pool and gazebo, gallery library, and sitting room. Nearby attractions include historic homes, antique shops, Lake Seminole for fishing and water sports, May Artsfest, and local celebrations. Convenient for business and leisure travelers, it is an easy drive from Plains, Tallahassee, Florida, the Gulf beaches, and Florida theme parks.

The Pittman House
81 HOMER ROAD, COMMERCE, GEORGIA 30529

Tel: (706) 335-3823
Best Time to Call: 7 AM–9 PM
Hosts: Tom and Dot Tomberlin
Location: 60 mi. NE of Atlanta
No. of Rooms: 4
No. of Private Baths: 3
Max. No. Sharing Bath: 4
Double/pb: $65
Double/sb: $55

Single/sb: $50
Open: All year
Breakfast: Full
Credit Cards: MC, VISA
Pets: No
Children: Welcome, over 12
Smoking: No
Social Drinking: No

This gracious white Colonial, built in 1890, is decorated throughout with period pieces. If the furniture inspires you, visit Granny's Old Things, an antique shop right next door. Other points of interest include Château Elan Winery, in neighboring Braselton, and the Crawford W. Long Museum—honoring the doctor who discovered the use of ether as an anesthetic—in the town of Jefferson. Swimmers and sailors have their choice of Lake Lanier and Lake Hartwell; Hurricane Shoals is another lovely outdoor recreational area.

The Mountain Top Lodge
ROUTE 7, BOX 150, DAHLONEGA, GEORGIA 30533

Tel: (706) 864-5257; (800) 526-9754
Best Time to Call: 10 AM–6 PM
Host: Karen A. Lewan
Location: 70 mi. N of Atlanta
No. of Rooms: 13
No. of Private Baths: 13
Double/pb: $65–$85

Suites: $115–$125
Open: All year
Breakfast: Full
Pets: No
Children: Welcome, over 12
Smoking: No
Social Drinking: Permitted

Flanked by porches and decks, this gambrel-roofed, rustic cedar lodge is a secluded rural retreat on 40 acres, with a 360-degree mountain view. Decorated with art and antiques, the pine furniture and accessories made by mountain craftsmen add to the charm. Dahlonega was the site of America's first gold rush, and nature buffs will appreciate the Chattahoochee National Forest and Amicalola Falls State Park. Rafting, hiking, and horseback riding are all nearby. Don't miss the "Alpine village" of Helen, Georgia, only 30 minutes away. It now offers deluxe rooms with in-bath Jacuzzi whirlpool tubs and gas-log fireplaces.

Royal Guard Inn
203 SOUTH PARK STREET, DAHLONEGA, GEORGIA 30533

Tel: (706) 864-1713
Best Time to Call: 10 AM–9 PM

Hosts: John and Farris Vanderhoff
Location: 50 mi. N of Atlanta

No. of Rooms: **5**
No. of Private Baths: **5**
Double/pb: **$65–$75**
Open: **All year**
Reduced Rates: **10% seniors,
  Sun.–Thurs.**

Breakfast: **Full**
Credit Cards: **MC, VISA**
Pets: **No**
Children: **By arrangement**
Smoking: **No**
Social Drinking: **Permitted**

Located in the northeast Georgia mountains, Dahlonega is where the first major U.S. gold rush occurred in 1828. Dahlonega Gold Museum, Price Memorial Hall—on the site of one of the first U.S. branch mints—and gold-panning areas are all in the heart of the historic downtown. Royal Guard Inn, a half-block from the old town square, is a restored and enlarged old home. John and Farris serve complimentary wine and cheese on the great wraparound porch. Breakfast, served on fine china and silver on crisp white linen, includes a casserole, pastries, or hotcakes from an old family recipe, and fresh fruit and whipped cream.

Honey Bear Hideaway Farm
**ROUTE 4, BOX 4106, ROGERS MILL ROAD, DANIELSVILLE,
GEORGIA 30633**

Tel: **(706) 789-2569**
Best Time to Call: **After 4 PM**
Hosts: **Ray and Natachia Dodd**
Location: **12 mi. N of Athens**
No. of Rooms: **4**
No. of Private Baths: **3**
Double/pb: **$50–$100**
Single/pb: **$45–$90**
Open: **All year**
Breakfast: **Full**

Other Meals: **Available**
Credit Cards: **MC, VISA**
Pets: **Horses**
Children: **Welcome, over 12**
Smoking: **No**
Social Drinking: **Permitted**
Airport/Station Pickup: **Yes**

This 125-year-old farmhouse is nestled among pecan and walnut trees, with a lake nearby. Ray and Natachia are artists who converted the property's two barns into studios. The house is a virtual gallery of antiques and curios; one bedroom is decorated with old-fashioned purses. Visitors will wake up to a Southern, country-style breakfast, with farm-fresh eggs, ham or sausage, and homemade breads and jellies.

The Crockett House
671 MADISON ROAD, EATONTON, GEORGIA 31024

Tel: **(706) 485-2248**
Hosts: **Christa and Peter Crockett**
Location: **73 mi. E of Atlanta**
No. of Rooms: **6**
No. of Private Baths: **6**
Double/pb: **$65–$75**
Single/pb: **$55–$65**
Open: **All year**

Reduced Rates: **10% Nov.–Feb.;**
   extended stays; seniors; families
Breakfast: **Full**
Pets: **No**
Children: **Welcome**
Smoking: **No**
Social Drinking: **Permitted**
Airport Pickup: **Yes**

This stately and gracious turn-of-the-century home captures the history and charm of a bygone era. Guests receive a warm welcome and comfortable accommodations year-round. The home features seven bedrooms and eleven fireplaces. The large cozy bedrooms are thoughtfully decorated, some with private baths and fireplaces. Separate innkeepers' quarters insure the privacy of guests. Wander throughout the home and enjoy the principal rooms (equipped with telephones and TVs), balcony, wraparound porch, and tranquil setting of the three-acre yard.

Henson Cove Place ○

3840 CAR MILES ROAD, HIAWASSEE, GEORGIA 30546-9585

Tel: (800) 714-5542	Open: All year
Best Time to Call: After 10 AM	Breakfast: Full
Hosts: Bill and Nancy Leffingwell	Credit Cards: MC, VISA
Location: 2 hrs. N of Atlanta	Pets: No
No. of Rooms: 2	Children: Welcome, over 10
No. of Private Baths: 2	Smoking: No
Double/pb: $55	Social Drinking: Permitted
Suites: $55	Minimum Stay: 2 nights weekends

Henson Cove Place has a warm homey atmosphere that will envelop you as you head for your room. The furniture and decorations are from Bill and Nancy's families and have stories behind them. You can browse through the magazine collection, read any of 2000 books, watch TV in the sitting room, and relax on the front porch. Or attend a festival, country music show, hike or stop in the many small shops in the area. In the morning you'll be greeted with hot coffee and breakfast. A typical menu might be fruit cup, juice, muffins, rolled stuffed omelette, apple French toast with baby sausages, or sausage strata. Bill is a furniture maker specializing in reproductions. Nancy operates a business service above his workshop. Both like talking to guests and making their stay an enjoyable one.

R.S.V.P. Savannah—B&B Reservation Service

9489 WHITFIELD AVENUE, BOX 49, SAVANNAH, GEORGIA 31406

Tel: (912) 232-7787; (800) 729-7787	Savannah, St. Simons Island, Tybee
Best Time to Call: 9:30 AM–5:30 PM	Island; South Carolina—Beaufort,
Mon.–Fri.	Charleston
Coordinator: Sonja Lazzaro	Rates (Single/Double): $60–$225
States/Regions Covered: Brunswick,	Credit Cards: AMEX, DISC, MC, VISA

Accommodations include elegantly restored inns, guest houses, private homes, and even a villa on the water. They're located in the best historic districts as well as along the coast, from South Carolina's Low Country to Georgia's Sea Islands. A special blend of cordial hospitality, comfort, and services is provided. All are air-conditioned in the summer. Facilities for children and the disabled are often available. Please note that while some hosts accept credit cards, some do not.

Joan's on Jones

17 WEST JONES STREET, SAVANNAH, GEORGIA 31401

Tel: (912) 234-3863	Location: 140 mi. N of Jacksonville, FL
Hosts: Joan and Gary Levy	Suites: $95–$110; sleeps 2–4

Open: **All year**
Reduced Rates: **Weekly**
Breakfast: **Continental**
Pets: **Sometimes**
Children: **Welcome**

Smoking: **No**
Social Drinking: **Permitted**
Minimum Stay: **3 days for St. Patrick's Day week only**

Clip-clopping along the brick streets of the city's historic district, horse-drawn carriages take you back to a more serene and elegant era. This bed and breakfast maintains the old-fashioned mood, with its original heart-pine floors, antique furnishings, and Savannah gray brick walls. (Note the late nineteenth-century documents that slipped behind one of the fireplace mantels.) All the historic places of interest, including the famous squares, are a short walk away. Joan and Gary, former restaurateurs, live upstairs and invite you to tour their home if you're staying at least two nights.

Lion's Head Inn
120 EAST GASTON STREET, SAVANNAH, GEORGIA 31401

Tel: **(912) 232-4580**
Host: **Christy Dell'orco**
Location: **Downtown Savannah**
No. of Rooms: **6**
No. of Private Baths: **6**
Double/pb: **$85–$95**
Single/pb: **$85–$95**
Suites: **$110–$135**
Open: **All year**

Reduced Rates: **Available**
Breakfast: **Continental**
Credit Cards: **AMEX, MC, VISA**
Pets: **No**
Children: **Welcome**
Smoking: **No**
Social Drinking: **Permitted**
Airport/Station Pickup: **Yes**

This elegant nineteenth-century mansion is tastefully adorned with pristine Empire furniture and accessories. A collection of European and American art, Italian marble, and French bronze sculptures and 19th-century lighting beautify each room. The Inn is located on Gaston Street, the prime residential street in the historic district. Stroll across the street to picturesque Forsyth Park and enjoy all the historic attractions and amenities within walking distance. The innkeeper, Christy, a retired sales manager, now is a registered Savannah tour guide and antiquarian. She'll help you enjoy gracious living at its best and experience true nineteenth-century grandeur at the Lion's Head Inn.

Four Chimneys B&B
2316 WIRE ROAD SOUTHEAST, THOMSON, GEORGIA 30824

Tel: **(706) 597-0220**
Best Time to Call: **9 AM–10 PM**
Hosts: **Maggie and Ralph Zieger**
Location: **35 mi. W of Augusta**
No. of Rooms: **4**

No. of Private Baths: **3**
Double/pb: **$50**
Single/pb: **$45**
Open: **All year**
Breakfast: **Continental**

Credit Cards: **MC, VISA**
Pets: **No**
Children: **Welcome, over 12**

Smoking: **Permitted**
Social Drinking: **Permitted**
Foreign Languages: **German**

Escape from the modern world at this early 1800s country house with a rocking-chair porch. The old-fashioned landscape features a large herb garden and heirloom flowers. Antique and reproduction furniture complement the original heart-pine interior. A small library and a cozy parlor invite you to relax at your leisure. Guest rooms have four-poster beds and working fireplaces. Restaurants, golf courses, and antique shops are nearby. Fox hunts and other equestrian events take place throughout the year.

For key to listings, see inside front or back cover.

✪ This star means that rates are guaranteed through December 31, 1996, to any guest making a reservation as a result of reading about the B&B in *Bed & Breakfast U.S.A.*—1996 edition.

Important! To avoid misunderstandings, always ask about cancellation policies when booking.

Please enclose a self-addressed, stamped, business-size envelope when contacting reservation services.

For more details on what you can expect in a B&B, see Chapter 1.

Always mention *Bed & Breakfast U.S.A.* when making reservations!

If no B&B is listed in the area you'll be visiting, use the form on page 249 to order a copy of our "List of New B&Bs."

We want to hear from you! Use the form on page 251.

KENTUCKY

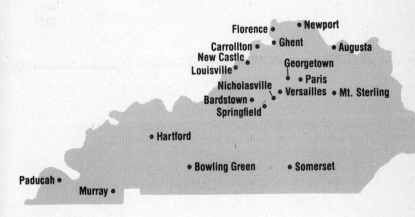

Bluegrass Bed & Breakfast Reservation Service ✪
ROUTE 1 BOX 263, VERSAILLES, KENTUCKY 40383

Tel: **(606) 873-3208**
Best Time to Call: **9 AM–4 PM**
Coordinator: **Betsy Pratt**
States/Regions Covered: **Berea,
Danville, Frankfort, Georgetown,
Lexington, Louisville, Maysville,
Midway, Paris, Versailles, Winchester**

Rates (Single/Double):
Modest: **$60**
Average: **$75**
Luxury: **$100**

Betsy's B&B's are beautiful old houses that grace the country roads of
the area. You may choose among a stone house built in 1796, a
separate private cottage on a farm, or a country home where your
bedroom windows look out on thoroughbred horses. Visit Shaker-
town, where weavers, smiths, and woodworkers display their skills in
a restored 1839 village. Take a ride on the winding Kentucky River in
a paddlewheel boat. Tour exquisite historic mansions or see the

picturesque homes of such Derby winners as Secretariat and Seattle Slew. And don't miss the 1000-acre Kentucky Horse Park that includes a theater, museum, track, barns, and hundreds of horses. You may even take a horseback ride, because this place will inspire you.

Augusta White House Inn B&B ✪

307 MAIN STREET, AUGUSTA, KENTUCKY 41002

Tel: **(606) 756-2004**	Open: **All year**
Best Time to Call: **9–11 AM**	Reduced Rates: **Available**
Host: **Rebecca Spencer**	Breakfast: **Full**
Location: **50 mi. SE of Cincinnati, Ohio**	Credit Cards: **MC, VISA**
No. of Rooms: **5**	Pets: **No**
Max. No. Sharing Bath: **4**	Children: **No**
Double/sb: **$79**	Smoking: **No**
Single/sb: **$59**	Social Drinking: **No**
Guest Cottage: **$75**	Airport/Station Pickup: **Yes**

AWHIBB is located in the downtown section of historic Augusta, in a beautifully restored, two-story brick structure (the Buger Tin Shop, circa 1840) that combines Victorian elegance and Southern hospitality. Comfortably sized rooms with flowered wallpaper and high, crown-molded ceilings may well remind you of your grandparents' home, albeit with all modern conveniences. In addition to their own room, guests have use of the parlor, formal dining and living rooms, and outside garden deck. Breakfast includes fresh-baked bread with an array of gourmet entrees and side dishes to please even the most discriminating palates. Antique shops and excellent restaurants are a short stroll away.

Jailer's Inn ✪

111 WEST STEPHEN FOSTER AVENUE, BARDSTOWN, KENTUCKY 40004

Tel: **(502) 348-5551; (800) 948-5551**	Reduced Rates: **Available**
Best Time to Call: **10 AM–5 PM**	Breakfast: **Continental, plus**
Hosts: **Challen and Fran McCoy**	Credit Cards: **AMEX, DISC, MC, VISA**
Location: **35 mi. S of Louisville**	Pets: **No**
No. of Rooms: **6**	Children: **Welcome**
No. of Private Baths: **6**	Smoking: **No**
Double/pb: **$65–$95**	Social Drinking: **Permitted**
Open: **Mar.–Dec.**	Station pickup: **Yes**

For the ultimate in unusual experiences, spend the night in "jail" without having committed a crime. Built in 1819, this former jailer's residence originally housed prisoners upstairs, and has been completely remodeled and furnished with fine antiques and oriental rugs. An adjacent building, once used as the women's cell, has been transformed into a charming suite, where bunk beds are suspended from a brick wall and the decor is black-and-white checks instead of stripes. The town is famous for *The Stephen Foster Story*, an outdoor musical production. Take time to visit the Getz Museum of Whiskey History and a Civil War museum, and take a tour of My Old Kentucky Home conducted by guides in antebellum costumes.

Alpine Lodge ○
5310 MORGANTOWN ROAD, BOWLING GREEN, KENTUCKY 42101

Tel: **(502) 843-4846**	Suites: **$75**
Best Time to Call: **9 AM–9 PM**	Open: **All year**
Hosts: **Dr. and Mrs. David Livingston**	Reduced Rates: **Weekly**
Location: **60 mi. N of Nashville, Tenn.**	Breakfast: **Full**
No. of Rooms: **5**	Other Meals: **Available**
No. of Private Baths: **3**	Pets: **Dogs welcome**
Max. No. Sharing Bath: **4**	Children: **Welcome**
Double/pb: **$50**	Smoking: **Permitted**
Single/pb: **$40**	Social Drinking: **Permitted**
Double/sb: **$45**	Airport/Station Pickup: **Yes**
Single/sb: **$35**	Foreign Languages: **Spanish**
Guest Cottage: **$150, sleeps 6**	

The lush Bluegrass Region of Kentucky is the setting for this spacious Swiss chalet–style home that's situated on four lovely acres and furnished with many antiques. A typical Southern breakfast of eggs, sausage, biscuits and gravy, fried apples, grits, coffee cake, and beverage starts your day. If you can manage to get up from the table, stroll the grounds complete with nature trails and gardens or take a swim in the pool. Afterwards, take in the sights and sounds of Opryland, Mammoth Cave, or the battlefields of historic Bowling Green. In the evening, relax in the living room, where Dr. Livingston, a music professor, may entertain you with selections played on the grand piano.

Bowling Green Bed & Breakfast ○
3313 SAVANNAH DRIVE, BOWLING GREEN, KENTUCKY 42104

Tel: **(502) 781-3861**	Double/sb: **$55**
Best Time to Call: **Before 10 PM**	Single/sb: **$45**
Hosts: **Dr. Norman and Ronna Lee Hunter**	Open: **All year**
	Reduced Rates: **20% families**
Location: **3.5 mi. from I-65, exit 22**	Breakfast: **Full**
No. of Rooms: **3**	Pets: **No**
No. of Private Baths: **1**	Children: **Welcome, over 14**
Max. No. Sharing Bath: **4**	Smoking: **No**
Double/pb: **$55–$65**	Social Drinking: **Permitted**
Single/pb: **$45**	Station Pickup: **Yes**

Upon entering this lovely home in an attractive, quiet neighborhood, guests receive a warm welcome. Whether you choose the antique walnut twin room or either of the double-bedded rooms, you will find a comfortable, relaxed atmosphere. Enjoy the library and TV in the den, read or chat in the lounge, or take an evening walk to the duck pond and the woods. Breakfast is set out in the dining room, with special dietary needs considered. Afternoon tea is also served. This B&B is located between Mammoth Cave National Park and Nashville, Tennessee. Restaurants, shopping, Western Kentucky University and the historic downtown square are all close by. Your hosts, a retired chemistry professor and a nurse, are involved with foreign exchange and love to travel and meet people.

Baker House Bed & Breakfast ✪
406 HIGHLAND AVENUE, CARROLLTON, KENTUCKY 41008

Tel: (502) 732-4210; (800) 74 BAKER [742-1537], outside Kentucky	Open: All year
Host: Maggie Klein	Guest Cottage: $125, sleeps 6
Location: 5 mi. N of I-71 exit 44	Breakfast: Full
No. of Rooms: 3	Credit Cards: MC, VISA
No. of Private Baths: 3	Pets: No
Double/pb: $75	Children: Welcome, over 10
Single/pb: $65	Smoking: Restricted
	Social Drinking: Permitted

Upon entering this large Victorian home, listed on the National Register of Historic Places, one gets the feeling of having stepped back to the 1800s. The high ceilings, heavy walnut doors, hand-carved cherry staircase, oil lamp chandeliers, and elegant antiques embellish the careful restoration of this ornate house. Upon arrival, you are graciously welcomed with a snack and beverage. A bowl of fresh fruit in your room, a potpourri gift, and breakfast served on antique china and crystal are just some of the special touches. Recreational diversions abound in this area located midway between Cincinnati and Louisville.

Twin Pines ✪
28 LACRESTA DRIVE, FLORENCE, KENTUCKY 41042

Tel: (606) 282-0456	Single/sb: $40
Best Time to Call: 8 AM–10 PM	Open: All year
Hosts: Coleen and Mike Detzel	Reduced Rates: 10% seniors
Location: 10 mi. S of Cincinnati, Ohio	Breakfast: Full
No. of Rooms: 3	Credit Cards: MC, VISA
No. of Private Baths: 1	Pets: Sometimes
Max. No. Sharing Bath: 4	Children: Welcome, over 10
Double/pb: $60	Smoking: No
Single/pb: $50	Social Drinking: Permitted
Double/sb: $50	Airport/Station Pickup: Yes

Twin Pines is a classic brick ranch, beautifully decorated and filled with lots of interesting collectibles and antiques. Enjoy reading or relaxing in the living room, or try the 1950s style lower level featuring TV, games, and a pinball machine. Its home-cooked Kentucky breakfast includes pancakes, homemade syrup, biscuits and gravy, fresh eggs, fried apples, and several cold cereals for those wanting lighter fare. Your hosts Coleen and Mike will tell you about the great shopping, restaurants, and excellent attractions close by.

Jordan Farm Bed & Breakfast ✪
4091 NEWTOWN PIKE, GEORGETOWN, KENTUCKY 40324

Tel: (502) 863-1944, 868-9002	Pets: No
Best Time to Call: Anytime	Children: Welcome
Hosts: Harold and Becky Jordan	Smoking: No
Location: 8 mi. N of Lexington	Social Drinking: Permitted
Suites: $75, sleeps 4	Minimum Stay: 2 nights weekends Apr.
Open: All year	and Oct.
Breakfast: Continental	Airport/Station Pickup: Yes

Derby fans will want to stay on this 100-acre thoroughbred farm in the middle of Kentucky's legendary horse country. Indeed, the Kentucky Horse Park is only five minutes away. From the guest room's private deck, you can watch the Jordans' horses cavort in the fields. Or drop a line into the fishing pond and try your luck. Separate guest house with two large Jacuzzi suites and mini-kitchens.

Log Cabin Bed and Breakfast ✪
350 NORTH BROADWAY, GEORGETOWN, KENTUCKY 40324

Tel: (502) 863-3514	Breakfast: Continental
Hosts: Clay and Janis McKnight	Pets: Welcome
Location: 10 mi. N of Lexington	Children: Welcome
Guest Cottage: $75 for 2	Smoking: Permitted
Open: All year	Social Drinking: Permitted

This rustic log cabin was built, circa 1809, with a shake shingle roof and chinked logs. Inside, the living room is dominated by a huge fieldstone fireplace. The master bedroom and bath are on the ground floor and a loft bedroom will sleep additional people with ease. The house has been fully restored and air-conditioned by the McKnights, and is filled with period furnishings. The dining-kitchen wing is equipped with all new appliances and modern amenities. The Log Cabin is located in a quiet neighborhood close to Kentucky Horse Park, Keeneland, and many other historic places. This is the perfect spot to bring the kids and give them a taste of authentic American tradition.

Ghent House B&B ✪

411 MAIN STREET, U.S. 42, GHENT, KENTUCKY 41045

Tel: **(502) 347-5807** weekends; **(606) 291-0168** weekdays	Suites: **$100**
Best Time to Call: **After 7 PM; weekends**	Open: **All year**
	Reduced Rates: **Available**
Hosts: **Wayne and Diane Young**	Breakfast: **Full**
Location: **12 mi. N and E of I-71 exit 44**	Pets: **No**
No. of Rooms: **3**	Children: **Welcome (crib)**
No. of Private Baths: **3**	Smoking: **No**
Double/pb: **$60**	Social Drinking: **Permitted**
Single/pb: **$50**	Airport/Station Pickup: **Yes**

Ghent House is a gracious antebellum residence, built in the usual style of the day—a central hall with rooms on either side and the kitchen and dining room in the rear. A beautiful fantail window and two English coach lights enhance the front entrance. Guests can look out over the Ohio River and imagine the time when steamboats regularly traveled the waterways. The view includes the lovely homes of the Vevay, Indiana, side of the river.

Ranney Porch Bed & Breakfast ✪

3810 HIGHWAY 231 NORTH, HARTFORD, KENTUCKY 42347

Tel: **(502) 298-7972**	Single/pb: **$40**
Best time to Call: **After 4 PM**	Open: **All year**
Hosts: **Peggy Jo and Rance Ranney**	Breakfast: **Full**
Location: **17.7 mi. S of Owensboro**	Pets: **No**
No. of Rooms: **1**	Children: **Welcome**
No. of Private Baths: **1**	Smoking: **No**
Double/pb: **$50**	Social Drinking: **No**

One of the unique features of this country B&B is the fifty-seven-foot porch spanning the length of the building, which is modeled after a Georgia tenant house. The exterior has blue trim, black shutters, and a candy apple red door. Inside, a Story and Clark piano sits on the foyer's red brick floor tiles, which came from the roof of a train depot. In the living room, cherry furniture complements the cherry wood floor. The bedroom's antique quilts and firm mattress assure you a good night's sleep. Numerous special events throughout the year, such as the Bar-be-que Festival, Yellow Banks Dulcimer Festival, and Bluegrass Music Festival, make this a place to visit often.

The Victorian Secret Bed & Breakfast ✪

1132 SOUTH FIRST STREET, LOUISVILLE, KENTUCKY 40203

Tel: **(502) 581-1914**	Location: **1 mi. S of downtown Louisville**
Hosts: **Nan and Steve Roosa**	

No. of Rooms: **3**
No. of Private Baths: **1**
Max. No. Sharing Bath: **3**
Double/pb: **$68–$89**
Double/sb: **$58–$68**
Open: **All year**

Reduced Rates: **Weekly**
Breakfast: **Continental**
Pets: **No**
Children: **Welcome**
Smoking: **Permitted**
Social Drinking: **Permitted**

An elegant brick Victorian with lavish woodwork, this B&B has modern amenities like an exercise room with a bench press and a rowing machine, and color TVs in guest rooms. The Louisville area is rich in historic homes. Railbirds and would-be jockeys will want to make pilgrimages to the famous tracks at Churchill Downs (site of the Kentucky Derby) and Louisville Downs (home of harness races).

The Trimble House ○
321 NORTH MAYSVILLE STREET, MT. STERLING, KENTUCKY 40353

Tel: **(606) 498-6561, 498-7078**
Best Time to Call: **9 AM–10 PM**
Hosts: **Jim and June Hyska**
Location: **29 mi. E of Lexington**
No. of Rooms: **4**
No. of Private Baths: **3**
Max. No. Sharing Bath: **4**
Double/pb: **$60**
Single/pb: **$45**

Double/sb: **$55**
Open: **All year**
Reduced Rates: **10% seniors**
Breakfast: **Full**
Credit Cards: **AMEX, MC, VISA**
Pets: **No**
Children: **Welcome, over 12**
Smoking: **Permitted**
Social Drinking: **Permitted**

An "Old South" plantation-style home located in Mt. Sterling's historic district, the Trimble House (1872) is listed on the Kentucky

Historic Register. Visitors can enjoy air-conditioning, comfortable beds, Granny's handmade quilts, and antiques. Pool, exercise room, Jacuzzi, bicycles, and limo available for horse racing events and bluegrass horse farm tours.

Diuguid House Bed & Breakfast ✪
603 MAIN STREET, MURRAY, KENTUCKY 42071

Tel: **(502) 753-5470**	Reduced Rates: **Seventh night free**
Best Time to Call: **4–10 PM**	Breakfast: **Full**
Hosts: **Karen and George Chapman**	Credit Cards: **MC, VISA**
Location: **45 mi. S of Paducah**	Pets: **No**
No. of Rooms: **3**	Children: **Welcome**
Max. No. Sharing Bath: **5**	Smoking: **No**
Double/sb: **$40**	Social Drinking: **Permitted**
Open: **All year**	Airport/Station Pickup: **Yes**

Upon walking into this 1890s Queen Anne, listed on the National Register of Historic Places, guests see an impressive sweeping oak staircase and unusual hallway fretwork. In addition to their rooms, visitors have use of the parlor, TV lounge, and dining room. Murray State University houses a local history museum, an art gallery, and the National Boy Scout Museum. The town, a top-rated retirement community, offers lots of theatrical and musical events. For outdoor activities, take the twenty-minute drive to Land Between the Lakes, where you can hike, hunt, fish, admire the resident buffalo herd, or see a working historical farm.

The Oldham House B&B and Antiques ✪
P.O. BOX 628, NEW CASTLE, KENTUCKY 40050

Tel: **(502) 845-0103**	Breakfast: **Full**
Hosts: **Emmy and Alan Blincoe**	Credit Cards: **MC, VISA**
Location: **35 mi. NE of Louisville**	Pets: **No**
No. of Rooms: **2**	Children: **Welcome, over 12**
No. of Private Baths: **2**	Smoking: **No**
Double/pb: **$70**	Social Drinking: **Permitted**
Single/pb: **$65**	Airport Pickup: **Yes**
Suite: **$75**	Foreign Languages: **Dutch, French,**
Open: **All year**	**German**
Reduced Rates: **Available**	

A Federal period structure built in 1820, Oldham House is located a short distance north of the Bluegrass Region and convenient to Louisville, Lexington, and Cincinnati. The B&B is decorated in primitive antiques and accessories, most of which are for sale at Emmy's antique shop located on the property. The kitchen had once been the slave kitchen with separate quarters above. The original smokehouse still remains on the property. Things to do include horse racing twice a year in Louisville and Lexington horse farms, visiting scenic Ohio River towns and state parks, golfing, and of course, antiquing galore.

Gateway Bed and Breakfast ○
326 EAST 6TH STREET, NEWPORT, KENTUCKY 41071

Tel: **(606) 581-6447**
Best Time to Call: **After 4:30 PM**
Hosts: **Ken and Sandy Clift**
Location: **1 mi. South of Cincinnati, Ohio**
No. of Rooms: **3**
No. of Private Baths: **1**
Max. No. Sharing Bath: **4**
Double/pb: **$70**
Single/pb: **$70**

Double/sb: **$60**
Single/sb: **$60**
Open: **All year**
Breakfast: **Full**
Credit Cards: **AMEX, MC, VISA**
Pets: **No**
Children: **Welcome**
Smoking: **No**
Social Drinking: **Permitted**
Airport/Station Pickup: **Yes**

This 1878 town house in East Newport's National Historic District won 1992's Great American Homes Award for Bed and Breakfast Restoration from the National Trust for Historic Preservation. Gateway is elegantly decorated in the Victorian period, complete with antique musical devices: a 1910 pump organ, a 1904 Edison Fireside Phonograph, and a 1928 player piano. A full breakfast will be served especially for you in the formal dining room. The inn is conveniently located five minutes from downtown Cincinnati, next door to Palm Beach Mill Outlet. Fine dining can be found along River Row on the scenic Ohio River.

Sandusky House Bed & Breakfast ○
1626 DELANEY FERRY ROAD, NICHOLASVILLE, KENTUCKY 40356

Tel: **(606) 223-4730**
Best Time to Call: **8 AM–10 PM**
Hosts: **Jim and Linda Humphrey**
Location: **6 mi. SW of Lexington**
No. of Rooms: **3**
No. of Private Baths: **3**
Double/pb: **$69**
Open: **All year**

Reduced Rates: **Available**
Breakfast: **Full**
Credit Cards: **MC, VISA**
Pets: **No**
Children: **Welcome, over 12**
Smoking: **No**
Social Drinking: **Permitted**
Airport/Station Pickup: **Yes**

The tree-lined drive to the Sandusky House is just a prelude to the handsome Greek Revival residence built about 1850 from bricks fired on the premises. Once the property was a one thousand-acre farm owned by Revolutionary War veteran Jacob Sandusky—he acquired the site in a 1780 land grant from Patrick Henry, then the governor of Virginia. Today the B&B sits on a ten-acre estate amid horse farms, yet close to downtown Lexington, Keeneland Race Track, Kentucky Horse Park, and many other attractions.

Ehrhardt's B&B ✪

285 SPRINGWELL LANE, PADUCAH, KENTUCKY 42001

Tel: **(502) 554-0644**
Best Time to Call: **7–9 AM; 4–6 PM**
Hosts: **Eileen and Phil Ehrhardt**
Location: **1 mi. from I-24**
No. of Rooms: **2**
Max. No. Sharing Bath: **4**
Double/sb: **$35**
Single/sb: **$30**
Open: **All year**

Reduced Rates: **10% seniors**
Breakfast: **Full**
Other Meals: **Available**
Pets: **No**
Children: **Welcome, over 12**
Smoking: **Permitted**
Social Drinking: **Permitted**
Airport/Station Pickup: **Yes**

This brick Colonial ranch home is just a mile off I-24, which is famous for its beautiful scenery. Your hosts hope to make you feel at home in antique-filled bedrooms and a den with a fireplace. Homemade biscuits and jellies, and country ham and gravy are breakfast specialties. Enjoy swimming in the Ehrhardts' pool and boating at nearby Lake Barkley, Ky Lake, and Land Between the Lakes. Paducah features quarterhorse racing from June through November, and the National Quilt Show in April.

Rosedale ✪
1917 CYPRESS STREET, PARIS, KENTUCKY 40361 ✪

Tel: **(606) 987-1845**
Best Time to Call: **9 AM–9 PM**
Hosts: **Jim and Katie Haag**
Location: **18 mi. NE of Lexington**
No. of Rooms: **6**
No. of Private Baths: **2**
Max. No. Sharing Bath: **4**
Double/pb: **$90**
Double/sb: **$65**
Suites: **$100**

Open: **All year**
Breakfast: **Full**
Credit Cards: **MC, VISA**
Pets: **No**
Children: **Welcome, over 12**
Smoking: **No**
Social Drinking: **Permitted**
Minimum Stay: **2 nights weekends Apr. and Oct.**
Airport Pickup: **Yes**

Tucked into three secluded acres, Rosedale invites you to take time for yourself and leave the cares of the world at the end of the driveway. This 14-room Italianate house—built in 1862 for Civil War General John T. Croxton—is decorated in warm colors and filled with antiques and oriental rugs. Guests are welcome to curl up in front of a fire in the mahogany paneled library, formal living room, or the casual den. The property offers hidden retreats with garden benches, a hammock for quiet solitude, as well as croquet, horseshoes, and bocce ball for recreational activities.

Shadwick House ✪
411 SOUTH MAIN STREET, SOMERSET, KENTUCKY 42501

Tel: **(606) 678-4675**
Best Time to Call: **Anytime**
Host: **Ann Epperson**
Location: **84 mi. S of Lexington**
No. of Rooms: **4**
Max. No. Sharing Bath: **4**
Double/sb: **$40**
Single/sb: **$40**

Open: **All year**
Breakfast: **Full**
Credit Cards: **MC, VISA**
Pets: **No**
Children: **Welcome**
Smoking: **No**
Social Drinking: **Permitted**

Shadwick House has been known for its Southern hospitality for more than seventy years—the home was built in 1920 by Nellie Stringer Shadwick, great-grandmother of the present owner. The first floor has been converted into an antique and crafts shop. Kentucky ham and biscuits are served for breakfast in the original dining room. This B&B is tucked into the Cumberland Mountain foothills, near Lake Cumberland. Other local attractions are Renfro Valley, Cumberland Falls State Park, Tombstone Junction, and Big South Fork National Park.

Maple Hill Manor B&B ✪
2941 PERRYVILLE ROAD, SPRINGFIELD, KENTUCKY 40069

Tel: **(606) 336-3075**
Hosts: **Bob and Kay Carroll**

No. of Rooms: **7**
No. of Private Baths: **7**

Double/pb: **$60–$85**
Single/pb: **$50**
Open: **All year**
Reduced Rates: **Available**
Breakfast: **Full**

Credit Cards: **MC, VISA**
Pets: **No**
Children: **Welcome (crib)**
Smoking: **No**
Social Drinking: **Permitted**

This hilltop manor house built in 1851 is situated on 14 tranquil acres in the scenic Bluegrass Region of Kentucky. Listed on the National Register of Historic Places, its Italianate design features 13-foot ceilings, 9-foot windows and doors, a profusion of fireplaces, and a solid cherry spiral staircase. The bedrooms are large, airy, and beautifully decorated with carefully chosen antique furnishings. The romantic honeymoon bed chamber has a canopy bed and Jacuzzi bath. In the evening, Bob and Kay graciously offer complimentary beverages and homemade dessert. Within an hour of Lexington and Louisville, you can visit Perryville Battlefield and Shaker Village and take a tour of distilleries. Murder mystery packages and gift certificates available.

Shepherd Place ✪
31 HERITAGE ROAD (U.S. 60), VERSAILLES, KENTUCKY 40383

Tel: **(606) 873-7843**
Hosts: **Marlin and Sylvia Yawn**
Location: **10 mi. W of Lexington**
No. of Rooms: **2**
No. of Private Baths: **2**
Double/pb: **$65–$70**
Single/pb: **$60**
Open: **All year**

Breakfast: **Full**
Credit Cards: **MC, VISA**
Pets: **No**
Children: **Welcome, over 12**
Smoking: **No**
Social Drinking: **Permitted**
Airport/Station Pickup: **Yes**

Marlin and Sylvia encourage you to make yourself comfortable in their pre–Civil War home, built around 1815. Rest in a spacious, beautifully decorated bedroom or relax in the parlor. Enjoy the lovely scenery while sitting on the patio or the porch swing. You might even want to pet the resident ewes, Abigail and Victoria. Brochures, menus, and plenty of ideas will be available to help you plan the rest of your stay.

For key to listings, see inside front or back cover.

✪ This star means that rates are guaranteed through December 31, 1996, to any guest making a reservation as a result of reading about the B&B in *Bed & Breakfast U.S.A.*—1996 edition.

Important! To avoid misunderstandings, always ask about cancellation policies when booking.

Please enclose a self-addressed, stamped, business-size envelope when contacting reservation services.

For more details on what you can expect in a B&B, see Chapter 1.

Always mention *Bed & Breakfast U.S.A.* when making reservations!

If no B&B is listed in the area you'll be visiting, use the form on page 249 to order a copy of our "List of New B&Bs."

We want to hear from you! Use the form on page 251.

LOUISIANA

Shreveport •

St. Francisville •

• Slidell
• New Orleans

• Plaquemine

Lafitte •

Victoria Inn
HIGHWAY 45, BOX 545B, LAFITTE, LOUISIANA 70067

Tel: **(800) 689-4797**
Best Time to Call: **8 AM–8 PM**
Hosts: **Roy and Dale Ross**
Location: **30 mi. S of New Orleans**
No. of Rooms: **5**
No. of Private Baths: **3**
Max. No. Sharing Bath: **4**
Double/pb: **$85**
Double/sb: **$75**
Single/sb: **$65**
Suites: **$90–$125**

Open: **All year**
Reduced Rates: **Available**
Breakfast: **Full**
Credit Cards: **AMEX, DISC, MC, VISA**
Pets: **Sometimes**
Children: **Welcome**
Smoking: **No**
Social Drinking: **Permitted**
Minimum Stay: **2 nights weekends, 3
nights special events, Mardi Gras,
Jazz Fest**

Roy and Dale are the hosts of two homes on a six-acre property. There
are five guest rooms, a dining room, kitchen, and sitting room in one
home, and two guest rooms, a sitting room, hosts' quarters, and office
in the other. The rooms are individually decorated with antiques,

wicker and rattan. A subtropical feeling is offered here with ceiling fans, large windows, and French doors that open onto galleried porches. Things to do include visiting Jean Lafitte National Historic Park, power boating, dock fishing, canoeing, hiking, swamp tours, scuba diving, and a Cajun Fais Do Do dance every Sunday afternoon. Special events include the Seafood Festival, Louisiana Oyster Festival, and Mardi Gras. Guests will enjoy a unique variety of breakfast specialties: eggs Victoria, which features sauteed crab claws, pecan waffles, Andouille sausage, or ethnic Huevos Rancheros. Guests can stay here for over ten days and never (unless requested) have a breakfast repeated.

Bed & Breakfast, Inc.—New Orleans ✪
1021 MOSS STREET, BOX 52257, NEW ORLEANS, LOUISIANA 70152-2257

Tel: **(504) 488-4640; (800) 729-4640;**
  fax: (504) 488-4639
Coordinator: **Hazell Boyce**
States/Regions Covered: **New Orleans**
Descriptive Directory: **Free**

Rates (Single/Double):
  Modest: **$30–$40 / $40–$50**
  Average: **$40–$75 / $40–$75**
  Luxury: **$70–$85 / $70–$85**
Credit Cards: **No**

New Orleans is called The City That Care Forgot. You are certain to be carefree, visiting the French Quarter, taking Mississippi riverboat rides, taking plantation tours, as well as dining in fine restaurants and attending jazz concerts. Hazell's hosts, many with historic properties along the streetcar line and in the French Quarter, will help you get the most out of your stay.

New Orleans Bed & Breakfast and Accommodations ✪
P.O. BOX 8163, NEW ORLEANS, LOUISIANA 70182-8163

Tel: **(504) 838-0071, 838-0072; fax:**
  (504) 838-0140
Best Time to Call: **8:30 AM–4:30 PM**
Coordinator: **Sarah-Margaret Brown**
States/Regions Covered:
  Louisiana—Covington, Jeanerette,
  Lafayette, Mandeville, Natchitoches,
  New Iberia, New Orleans,
  Shreveport, St. Francisville

Rates (Single/Double):
  Modest: **$30–$45 / $40–$45**
  Average: **$45–$50 / $50–$55**
  Luxury: **$65–$200**
Credit Cards: **AMEX, DISC, MC, VISA**
  (for deposit only)
Minimum Stay: **5 nights Mardi Gras,**
  Jazz Festival; 3 nights Sugar Bowl

Since 1979 Sarah-Margaret has arranged accommodations for visitors in private homes, apartments, and condos. Tell her what you want and she will do her best to please you. Care is given to guests' safety, comfort, and special interests. Discount tickets are available for many attractions.

Beau Séjour ✪
1930 NAPOLEON AVENUE, NEW ORLEANS, LOUISIANA 70115

Tel: (504) 897-3746	Open: All year
Best Time to Call: 10 AM–8 PM	Breakfast: Continental
Hosts: Gilles and Kim Gagnon	Pets: No
No. of Rooms: 5	Children: Welcome
No. of Private Baths: 5	Smoking: Permitted
Double/pb: $85	Social Drinking: Permitted
Single/pb: $75	Minimum Stay: 2 nights
Suites: $125	Foreign Languages: French

Kim and Gilles recently restored their 1906 Beau Séjour house to its original character, with beautiful detailing and wood floors. It is decorated in the best New Orleans style, blending country and European antiques with Louisiana and New Orleans touches. Located in one of the most picturesque neighborhoods of New Orleans, surrounded by lush tropical plantings, and on the Mardi Gras parade route, the mansion is convenient to convention and tourist attractions. Kim and Gilles are dedicated to New Orleans preservation and enjoy sharing their knowledge of local restaurants, excursions, and the culture of the "Big Easy."

The Chimes Bed & Breakfast
CONSTANTINOPLE AT COLISEUM, BOX 52257, NEW ORLEANS, LOUISIANA 70152-2257

Tel: (504) 488-4640; (800) 729-4640	Suites: $86–$126
Best Time to Call: 10 AM–5 PM Mon.–Fri.	Open: All year
	Reduced Rates: Available
Hosts: Jill and Charles Abbyad and Susan Smith	Breakfast: Continental, plus
	Pets: Sometimes
Location: In New Orleans	Children: Welcome
No. of Rooms: 4	Social Drinking: Permitted
No. of Private Baths: 4	Minimum Stay: Special events
Double/pb: $66–$73	Foreign Languages: French

These quaint guest quarters sit behind a Victorian uptown home. Stained and leaded glass windows, French doors, cypress staircases, and a brick courtyard enhance the friendly, relaxed atmosphere here. Caring for a property of this magnitude is an ongoing commitment and truly a labor of love. Your hosts, who are coming to the end of a two-year renovation, typify Southern hospitality. Three blocks from St. Charles Avenue, the Chimes cottages are minutes away from major New Orleans attractions including the French Quarter, convention centers, Audubon Zoological Gardens with the walk-through Louisiana Swamp Exhibit, the Mississippi River, and universities. The historic St. Charles Avenue streetcar makes the famous restaurants, jazz clubs, art galleries, and antique shops accessible without an auto.

Your hosts live on the second floor of the main house—their door is always open! They willingly share their vast knowledge of New Orleans, offering suggestions for tours and restaurants. For your convenience, each suite has a telephone, tea/coffeepot, television set, and stereo. Laundry facilities and use of a refrigerator are available.

The Glimmer Inn ✪
1631 SEVENTH STREET, NEW ORLEANS, LOUISIANA 70115

Tel: **(504) 897-1895**	Double/sb: **$65**
Best Time to Call: **9 AM–9 PM**	Single/sb: **$55**
Hosts: **Sharon Agiewich and Cathy Andros**	Open: **All year**
	Breakfast: **Continental, plus**
No. of Rooms: **6**	Pets: **No**
No. of Private Baths: **1**	Children: **Welcome, by arrangement**
Max. No. Sharing Bath: **4**	Smoking: **Permitted**
Double/pb: **$85**	Social Drinking: **Permitted**

This restored 1891 Victorian home has wonderful period elements: twelve-foot cove ceilings, cypress woodwork, side and front galleries, a wraparound front porch, and an enclosed brick patio. Public rooms are comfortably furnished for reading, TV viewing and musical enjoyment. The main house's guest rooms are beautifully appointed, with antiques, ceiling fans, and individually controlled air-conditioning and heat. Also offered is a private carriage house with bath, refrigerator, and central air-conditioning and heating. Glimmer Inn is across the street from the historic Garden District, a block from the trolley line and Mardi Gras parade route, and fifteen minutes from the French Quarter. Let Cathy and Sharon know your interests; they pride themselves on meeting guests' travel needs in a relaxed but attentive atmosphere.

Sully Mansion
2631 PRYTANIA STREET, NEW ORLEANS, LOUISIANA 70130

Tel: **(504) 891-0457**	Breakfast: **Continental**
Best Time to Call: **7 AM–10 PM**	Credit Cards: **MC, VISA**
Host: **Maralee Prigmore**	Pets: **Sometimes**
No. of Rooms: **5**	Children: **No**
No. of Private Baths: **5**	Smoking: **No**
Double/pb: **$85–$150**	Social Drinking: **Permitted**
Suites: **$175**	Minimum Stay: **2 nights weekends, 5**
Open: **All year**	**nights special events**
Reduced Rates: **June 15–Sept. 1**	

A Queen Anne named to honor its architect, Sully Mansion shows his discerning eye in its 12-foot ceilings, 10-foot doors, grand staircase, and stained glass. The house is furnished with a blend of yesterday's antiques and today's comfortable pieces, and most of the bedrooms have fireplaces. Other architectural jewels fill the surrounding historic Garden District; board the St. Charles streetcar for a 15-minute ride to New Orleans's main attractions.

Old Turnerville B&B ✪
23230 NADLER STREET, PLAQUEMINE, LOUISIANA 70764

Tel: **(504) 687-5337**	Cottage: **$75**
Best Time to Call: **10 AM–4 PM**	Open: **All year**
Host: **Brenda Bourgoyne Blanchard**	Reduced Rates: **10% seniors**
Location: **20 mi. S of Baton Rouge**	Breakfast: **Continental**
No. of Rooms: **1**	Pets: **No**
No. of Private Baths: **1**	Children: **Welcome**
Double/pb: **$65**	Smoking: **Permitted**
Single/pb: **$60**	Social Drinking: **Permitted**

Old Turnerville is an 1800s village on the Mississippi in the heart of plantation country. Bed and breakfast accommodations are available at Miss Louise's House, built more than a century ago. The antique-furnished home includes a guest bedroom with private bath, TV, air-conditioning, and ceiling fan. Guests can enjoy the swing and rockers on the wide front gallery and stroll along the top of the Mississippi River levee. A separate guest cottage sleeps up to four. Restaurants and historic attractions are close by. Tariff includes guided tour of Miss Louise's House and Marietta's House, an 1800s cottage across the street.

Barrow House B&B ✪
P.O. BOX 700, 9779 ROYAL STREET, ST. FRANCISVILLE, LOUISIANA 70775-0700

Tel: **(504) 635-4791**	Suites: **$115–$135**
Host: **Shirley Dittloff**	Open: **All year, except Dec. 21–25**
Location: **25 mi. N of Baton Rouge**	Breakfast: **Continental**
No. of Rooms: **8**	Pets: **No**
No. of Private Baths: **8**	Children: **Welcome**
Double/pb: **$85–$95**	Smoking: **Permitted**
Single/pb: **$75**	Social Drinking: **Permitted**

A saltbox erected in 1809, with a Greek Revival wing that was added some four decades later, Barrow House is listed on the National Register of Historic Places. Appropriately enough, Shirley furnished her B&B with 19th-century pieces from the American South. Other notable homes are in the area; Shirley likes to send guests on a cassette walking tour of the neighborhood. Afterward, sit on the screened front porch and sip a glass of wine or iced tea. Breakfast options range from a simple Continental meal to a full-course New

Orleans spread. Shirley is a fabulous cook, and private candlelight dinners, featuring Cajun and Creole specialties, can also be arranged.

Butler Greenwood ✪

8345 U.S. HIGHWAY 61, ST. FRANCISVILLE, LOUISIANA 70775

Tel: **(504) 635-6312**	Breakfast: **Continental, plus**
Best Time to Call: **Anytime**	Credit Cards: **MC, VISA**
Host: **Anne Butler**	Pets: **Sometimes**
Location: **25 mi. N of Baton Rouge**	Children: **Welcome**
Guest Cottages: **$80–$90, sleeps 2–6**	Smoking: **Permitted**
Open: **All year**	Social Drinking: **Permitted**
Reduced Rates: **Families**	

Butler Greenwood offers five cottages on picturesque plantation grounds. Choose from the 1796 kitchen with exposed beams and skylights, the nineteenth-century cook's cottage with a fireplace and porch swing, the romantic gazebo with antique stained glass windows, the treehouse at the edge of a steep wooded ravine with a wonderful 3-level deck and fireplace, or the pond house on its own pond. All sites have private baths, partial kitchens, and cable TV. Rates include a tour of the main house—listed on the National Register of Historic Places—and the extensive grounds. A tour book is available, describing the area's history and attractions. Continental-plus breakfast is served; other amenities include a pool, nature walks, and ballooning.

2439 Fairfield "A Bed and Breakfast Inn" ◐
2439 FAIRFIELD AVENUE, SHREVEPORT, LOUISIANA 71104

Tel: **(318) 424-2424**	Open: **All year**
Best Time to Call: **8 AM–10 PM**	Reduced Rates: **Available**
Hosts: **Jimmy and Vicki Harris**	Breakfast: **Full**
Location: **½ mi from I-20**	Credit Cards: **AMEX, DC, MC, VISA**
No. of Rooms: **4**	Pets: **No**
No. of Private Baths: **4**	Children: **No**
Double/pb: **$95–$150**	Smoking: **No**
Single/pb: **$95–$150**	Social Drinking: **Permitted**

2439 Fairfield is a meticulously restored three-story Victorian mansion located in the Highland historic district and was featured on the front cover of the 1992 edition of *Bed & Breakfast U.S.A.* This home is surrounded by century-old oaks, rose gardens, and azaleas—you can enjoy the scenic view from your own private balcony complete with porch swings and rocking chairs. The gracious guest rooms are furnished with antiques, Amish quilts, quality linens, feather beds, and down pillows and comforters. Each guest bath has a whirlpool tub. Hearty English breakfasts are served in the morning room. Then it's off to the races at nearby Louisiana Downs. The Strand Theatre, art galleries, and fine restaurants are all within reasonable driving distances.

Salmen-Fritchie House Circa 1895 ✪
127 CLEVELAND AVENUE, SLIDELL, LOUISIANA 70458

Tel: **(504) 643-1405; (800) 235-4168,** **for reservations**	Best Time to Call: **8 AM–9 PM** Hosts: **Homer and Sharon Fritchie**

Location: **30 mi. N of New Orleans**
No. of Rooms: **5**
No. of Private Baths: **5**
Double/pb: **$75–$85**
Single/pb: **$75–$85**
Suites: **$115–$150**
Open: **All year**
Reduced Rates: **Available**

Breakfast: **Full**
Credit Cards: **AMEX, MC, VISA**
Pets: **No**
Children: **Welcome, over 12**
Smoking: **No**
Social Drinking: **Permitted**
Station Pickup: **Yes**

You'll feel the sense of history as you step inside this magnificent sixteen-room house listed on the National Register of Historic Places. From the front door to the back, the great hall measures twenty feet wide and eighty-five feet long! All the rooms are filled with beautiful antiques, reminiscent of days gone by. Hospitality is a way of life here. Arrive by 4 PM and you can join your hosts for tea in the parlor and afterward, a tour of the house and grounds. In the morning, you'll receive fresh hot coffee in your room. Then you'll enjoy a full Southern breakfast in the bright, cheery breakfast room.

MARYLAND

Smithsburg •
Hagerstown •
Sharpsburg •
• Taneytown
• Westminster
• Frederick
• Elkton
• North East
Ellicott City • • Baltimore
Poolesville •
Burtonsville •
• Bryantown
• Annapolis
Bethesda •
Chevy Chase •
• St. Michaels
• Vienna
Scotland •

Bed & Breakfast of Maryland/The Traveller in Maryland, Inc. ✪
P.O. BOX 2277, ANNAPOLIS, MARYLAND 21404-2277

Tel: **(410) 269-6232; (800) 736-4667;**
  fax: **(410) 263-4841**
Best Time to Call: **9 AM–5 PM**
Coordinator: **Greg Page**
States/Regions Covered: **Annapolis, Baltimore, Central Maryland, Eastern and Southern shore, Western Maryland; London, England, United Kingdom**

Descriptive Directory: $5
Rates (Single/Double):
  Modest: **$55 / $60**
  Average: **$60 / $70**
  Luxury: **$80 / $100**
Credit Cards: **AMEX, MC, VISA**

Maryland is the home of Annapolis, site of the United States Naval Academy; Baltimore, home to the restored Inner Harbor and locale of historic Fort McHenry of "Star-Spangled Banner" fame; and Chesapeake Bay, known for its excellent harbors and fabulous fishing.

Greg's carefully selected hosts are anxious to show off their expertise in helping you discover all of those special places that will make your visit memorable.

Chesapeake Bay Lighthouse B&B ✪
1423 SHARPS POINT ROAD, ANNAPOLIS, MARYLAND 21401

Tel: **(410) 757-0248**	Breakfast: **Continental, plus**
Hosts: **Bill and Janice Costello**	Credit Cards: **AMEX, MC, VISA**
Location: **6 mi. from historic Annapolis**	Pets: **No**
No. of Rooms: **3**	Children: **No**
No. of Private Baths: **3**	Smoking: **No**
Double/pb: **$85**	Social Drinking: **Permitted**
Open: **All year**	Minimum Stay: **2 nights**
Reduced Rates: **10% seniors**	

For the vacation of a lifetime, come to Annapolis, a picturesque Colonial town with cobblestone streets, the Naval Academy, the Chesapeake, and blue crab and sailboats galore. Join your hosts on the breezy bay shore in a full-size replica of a typical cottage-style lighthouse. On this three-acre setting you'll enjoy panoramic views from every room: you'll see osprey and blue heron feeding, plus spectacular vistas of the Bay Bridge, Thomas Point Lighthouse, and the entrance to the Annapolis harbor. For closer views, you can borrow binoculars from Bill and Janice. Other amenities include individually controlled air-conditioning units in all guest rooms, and an upstairs common room with a well-stocked refrigerator.

College House Suites ✪
ONE COLLEGE AVENUE, ANNAPOLIS, MARYLAND 21401

Tel: **(410) 263-6124**	Credit Cards: **MC, VISA**
Best Time to Call: **10 AM–4 PM**	Pets: **No**
Hosts: **Jo Anne and Don Wolfrey**	Children: **No**
Suites: **$160**	Smoking: **No**
Open: **All year**	Social Drinking: **Permitted**
Breakfast: **Continental**	Minimum Stay: **2 nights**

This brick town house is nestled between the U.S. Naval Academy and St. John's College. The Annapolitan suite has a fireplace, Laura Ashley decor, and a private entrance through the ivy-covered courtyard. The Colonial suite has superb oriental rugs, antiques, and views of the Academy. The hosts pay close attention to details such as fresh flowers, fruit baskets, and chocolates. College House Suites is a short walk to the city dock, Paca House and Gardens, fine restaurants, fascinating shops and boutiques, art and antique galleries, museums, historic buildings, churches, and theater. A "breakfast-out" option is available.

Amanda's B&B Reservation Service ✪
1428 PARK AVENUE, BALTIMORE, MARYLAND 21217

Tel: (410) 225-0001; fax (410) 728-8957
Best Time to Call: 8:30 AM–5:30 PM Mon.–Fri.; 8:30 AM–noon Sat.
Coordinator: Betsy Grater
States/Regions Covered: Delaware, District of Columbia, Maryland, New Jersey, Pennsylvania, Virginia, West Virginia
Descriptive Directory of B&Bs: $3
Rates (Single/Double):
 Modest: $60
 Luxury: $75–$125
Credit Cards: AMEX, DISC, MC, VISA

Amanda's is a regional reservation service for private homes, small inns and yachts. This service represents almost 200 properties throughout Maryland and the six surrounding states. Accommodations include everything from economical to luxury rooms with Jacuzzis and private baths.

Betsy's Bed and Breakfast ✪
1428 PARK AVENUE, BALTIMORE, MARYLAND 21217

Tel: (410) 383-1274
Best Time to Call: 9:30 AM–10 PM
Host: Betsy Grater
No. of Rooms: 3
No. of Private Baths: 3
Double/pb: $85
Single/pb: $65
Open: All year
Breakfast: Full
Credit Cards: AMEX, MC, VISA
Pets: No
Children: Welcome
Smoking: No
Social Drinking: Permitted

A petite estate, this four-story row house is in Bolton Hill, a historic Baltimore neighborhood listed on the National Registry. The interior features 12-foot ceilings with center medallions, a hall floor inlaid with oak and walnut, crown moldings, and carved marble fireplaces. This charming old house is uniquely decorated with a large collection of original brass rubbings, heirloom quilts, and interesting wall groupings. Modern amenities include a hot tub. Betsy's B&B is just a few blocks from a new light-rail stop at "Cultural Station," and steps away from Meyerhoff Symphony Hall, the Lyric Opera House, Antique Row, and the Maryland Institute of Art. The Inner Harbor is seven minutes away by car.

The Winslow Home ✪
8217 CARAWAY STREET, CABIN JOHN, BETHESDA, MARYLAND 20818

Tel: (301) 229-4654
Best Time to Call: After 5 PM
Host: Jane Winslow
Location: 7 mi. W of Washington, D.C.
No. of rooms: 2
Max. No. Sharing Bath: 4

Double/sb: **$45**
Single/sb: **$35**
Open: **All year**
Breakfast: **Full**

Pets: **No**
Children: **Welcome**
Smoking: **No**
Social Drinking: **No**

You may enjoy the best of two worlds while staying at Jane's. This comfortable home is located in a lovely residential section of Bethesda, just 20 minutes from downtown Washington, D.C. Imagine touring the capital with some extra pocket money saved on high hotel costs. You are welcome to use the kitchen, laundry facilities, and piano. Georgetown, George Washington, and American universities are close by. There's a $5 surcharge for one-night stays.

Shady Oaks of Serenity ✪
P.O. BOX 842, BRYANTOWN, MARYLAND 20617-0842

Tel: **(800) 597-0924**
Best Time to Call: **4–11 PM**
Hosts: **Kathy and Gene Kazimer**
Location: **35 mi. from Washington, D.C.**
Suites: **$65**

Open: **All year**
Breakfast: **Continental**
Pets: **No**
Children: **Welcome, over 14**
Smoking: **No**
Social Drinking: **Permitted**

Shady Oaks of Serenity is a new Georgia Victorian situated on three acres and surrounded by trees. This secluded home is off the beaten path, yet within a 45-minute drive of the nation's capital and Annapolis, home of the U.S. Naval Academy. Just down the road is Amish country with antiques and unique shops, historic churches, the renowned Dr. Mudd Home, and Gilbert Run Park, a favorite county stop. Also, this retreat may be of interest to those visiting patients at the Charlotte Hall Veterans Home, only minutes away. Decorated with the Amish theme, the suite has a private bath. Visitors are welcome to gather in the sitting room, the front porch or enjoy an evening on the deck. This room has a king-size bed for a peaceful night's rest. Kathy and Gene cordially invite you to be a guest in their home and visit historic Charles County. The morning brings fresh coffee, homemade muffins or breads and a variety of fresh fruits.

The Taylors' B&B ✪
P.O. BOX 238, BURTONSVILLE, MARYLAND 20866-0238

Tel: **(301) 236-4318**
Best Time to Call: **9–11 AM; 7–9 PM**
Hosts: **Ruth and Fred Taylor**
Location: **30 min. from Washington, D.C., and the Inner Harbor**
No. of Rooms: **1**
No. of Private Baths: **1**
Double/pb: **$60**

Open: **All year**
Breakfast: **Continental**
Pets: **No**
Children: **No**
Smoking: **No**
Social Drinking: **Permitted**
Foreign Languages: **French**

This gracious two-story Colonial home offers a breath of fresh country air just 30 minutes from Washington, D.C., and Baltimore's Inner Harbor district. Guests can enjoy the grand piano, the extensive collection of books in the library, and Ruth's paintings. In warm weather, cool drinks are served in the gazebo; in winter, guests gather by the fireplace in the family room. Both of your hosts are retired. Ruth likes to read, sew, paint, and cook; Fred enjoys reading, writing, history, and music. They've traveled extensively and know how to make guests feel welcome. Tennis courts, horseback riding, and nature trails are nearby.

Chevy Chase Bed & Breakfast
6815 CONNECTICUT AVENUE, CHEVY CHASE, MARYLAND 20815

Tel: (301) 656-5867; fax (301) 656-5867
Best Time to Call: Anytime
Host: S. C. Gotbaum
Location: 1 mi. N of Washington
No. of rooms: 2
No. of Private Baths: 2
Double/pb: $65

Single/pb: $55
Open: All year
Reduced Rates: Families
Breakfast: Continental, plus
Pets: No
Children: Welcome
Smoking: No
Social Drinking: Permitted

Enjoy the convenience of being close to the transportation and sights of Washington, D.C., and Maryland's Montgomery County while staying at a relaxing, turn-of-the century, country-style house. Rooms have beamed ceilings and are filled with rare tapestries, oriental rugs, baskets, copperware, and native crafts from Mexico to the Mideast. The garden room has a cathedral ceiling and private deck. The gabled skylight room has a king-size bed. Your host is a sociologist with a private consulting business. Breakfast items include homemade breads, jams, pancakes, French toast, and a special blend of Louisiana coffee. When you want to take a break from touring, the lovely garden is there for you. There is a $5 surcharge for one-night stays.

The Garden Cottage at Sinking Springs Herb Farm ❂
234 BLAIR SHORE ROAD, ELKTON, MARYLAND 21921

Tel: (410) 398-5566
Best Time to Call: 9 AM–9 PM
Hosts: Ann and Bill Stubbs
Location: 4½ mi. from Rte. 40
No. of Rooms: 1
No. of Private Baths: 1
Guest Cottage: $85 for 2; sleeps 3
Open: All year
Reduced Rates: 5% seniors

Breakfast: Full
Credit Cards: MC, VISA
Other Meals: Available
Pets: No
Children: Welcome
Smoking: No
Social Drinking: Permitted
Airport/Station Pickup: Yes

Guests frequently comment on the peaceful beauty of this 128-acre historic farm. The garden cottage has a sitting room and fireplace adjoining the bedroom. Breakfast features coffee ground from organically grown beans, herbal teas, homemade buns, fruit, and juice. A full country breakfast prepared with unprocessed food fresh from the farm is available at no extra charge. Lectures on herbs and craft classes are available, and a gift shop is on the premises. Longwood Gardens and the famed Winterthur Museum are close by. Historic Chesapeake City is five minutes away.

Hayland Farm
5000 SHEPPARD LANE, ELLICOTT CITY, MARYLAND 21042

Tel: **(410) 531-5593**	Double/sb: **$40**
Host: **Dorothy Mobley**	Single/sb: **$25**
Location: **Bet. Baltimore and D.C.**	Open: **All year**
No. of Rooms: **3**	Breakfast: **Full**
No. of Private Baths: **1**	Pets: **No**
Max. No. Sharing Bath: **4**	Children: **No**
Double/pb: **$60**	Smoking: **No**
Single/pb: **$40**	Social Drinking: **Permitted**

When you breathe the country-fresh air, it may surprise you that Baltimore and Washington, D.C., are only a short drive away. At Hayland Farm you will find gracious living in a large manor house furnished in a handsome, yet comfortable, style. Dorothy is retired and has traveled extensively. She enjoys sharing conversation with her guests. In warm weather, the 20- by 50-foot swimming pool is a joy.

Middle Plantation Inn ✪
9549 LIBERTY ROAD, FREDERICK, MARYLAND 21701

Tel: **(301) 898-7128**	Open: **All year**
Best Time to Call: **6–10 PM**	Breakfast: **Continental**
Hosts: **Shirley and Dwight Mullican**	Credit Cards: **MC, VISA**
Location: **5 mi. E of Frederick**	Pets: **No**
No. of Rooms: **4**	Children: **Welcome, over 15**
No. of Private Baths: **4**	Smoking: **No**
Double/pb: **$85–$95**	Social Drinking: **Permitted**

Dwight and Shirley have furnished their handsome stone and log home with antiques collected on their travels. Their rustic B&B will appeal to Civil War buffs, since Gettysburg, Pennsylvania, Sharpsburg, Maryland, and Harpers Ferry, West Virginia, are all 40 minutes away by car. Closer to home, Frederick's 33-block historic district boasts a fascinating mix of museums, galleries, antique shops, and eateries. And for more antiquing, guests should head to nearby New Market.

Beaver Creek House Bed and Breakfast ✪
20432 BEAVER CREEK ROAD, HAGERSTOWN, MARYLAND 21740

Tel: **(301) 797-4764**
Best Time to Call: **Anytime**
Hosts: **Don and Shirley Day**
Location: **4 mi. E of Hagerstown**
No. of Rooms: **5**
No. of Private Baths: **5**
Double/pb: **$90**
Single/pb: **$80**
Open: **All year**

Reduced Rates: **$10 less Mon.–Thurs.**
Breakfast: **Full**
Credit Cards: **AMEX, DISC, MC, VISA**
Pets: **No**
Children: **Welcome, over 10**
Smoking: **No**
Social Drinking: **Permitted**
Airport/Station Pickup: **Yes**

This turn-of-the-century country home enjoys a wonderful view of South Mountain. Start your day with a bountiful country breakfast served on the wraparound screened porch. Then it's off to South Mountain for a hike along the Appalachian Trail. Or perhaps you'd rather bicycle along the scenic country roads. Civil War buffs will want to visit nearby historic parks like Antietam Battlefield and Harpers Ferry, while duffers can choose between two professional courses. Whatever your pleasure, save time to explore the beautifully maintained B&B grounds, with their gardens, fish pond, and patio.

Lewrene Farm B&B ✪
9738 DOWNSVILLE PIKE, HAGERSTOWN, MARYLAND 21740

Tel: **(301) 582-1735**
Hosts: **Lewis and Irene Lehman**
Location: **3½ mi. from I-70 and I-81**
No. of Rooms: **5**
No. of Private Baths: **3**
Max. No. Sharing Bath: **4**
Double/pb: **$75–$90**
Double/sb: **$50–$65**

Suites: **$90**
Open: **All year**
Breakfast: **Full**
Children: **Welcome**
Smoking: **No**
Social Drinking: **No**
Foreign Languages: **Spanish**

Lewis and Irene will help you discover the peaceful beauty of their 125-acre farm located in a historic area near the Antietam Battlefield. Guests are treated like old friends and are welcome to lounge in front of the fireplace or to play the piano in the Colonial-style living room. You're invited to enjoy snacks and a video in the evening. Harpers Ferry, Fort Frederick, the C&O Canal, and Gettysburg are nearby. Irene sells antiques and collectibles on the premises.

Sunday's Bed & Breakfast ✪
39 BROADWAY, HAGERSTOWN, MARYLAND 21740

Tel: **(800) 221-4828**
Best Time to Call: **Anytime**
Host: **Bob Ferrino**

Location: **70 mi. NW of Washington, D.C.**
No. of Rooms: **3**

No. of Private Baths: **3**
Double/pb: **$95**
Single/pb: **$75**
Open: **All year**
Reduced Rates: **Available**
Breakfast: **Full**

Other Meals: **Available**
Pets: **Sometimes**
Children: **Welcome**
Smoking: **No**
Social Drinking: **Permitted**
Airport Pickup: **Yes**

Built in 1890, this elegant Queen Anne Victorian is located in Hagerstown's historic north end, on a street lined with other grand old homes. Relax in your room or in the many public areas and porches. You may want to visit the area's numerous attractions, such as the National Historical Parks of Antietam, Harpers Ferry, Whitetails Ski Resort, and the C&O Canal. Or choose among the myriad other historic sites, antique shops, fishing areas, golf courses, museums, shopping outlets, and theaters.

The Wingrove Manor Inn ✪
635 OAK HILL AVENUE, HAGERSTOWN, MARYLAND 21740

Tel: **(301) 797-7769; fax (301) 797-8659**
Host: **Winnie Price**
Location: **70 mi. NW of Washington, D.C.**
Suites: **$85–$125**
Open: **All year**
Reduced Rates: **Available**

Breakfast: **Continental**
Credit Cards: **MC, VISA**
Pets: **Sometimes**
Children: **Welcome, off-season**
Smoking: **No**
Social Drinking: **Permitted**
Minimum Stay: **2 nights peak season**
Airport Pickup: **Yes**

The Wingrove Manor is a beautifully restored bed and breakfast on a street lined with Victorian mansions. Relax in the wicker rockers stretched across a large Southern porch surrounded by 23 white columns, ceramic tiled floors, and breathtaking beauty. Inside you will find magnificent turn-of-the-century craftsmanship, marble fireplaces, a winding staircase, oriental rugs, crystal chandeliers, and towering white columns—all reflecting the home's lineage. The common rooms are elegant. Featured on the first floor is the Canopy Suite with a queen-size bed, marble fireplace, private entrance, TV, VCR, and a full bath with a Jacuzzi, ideally suited for honeymooners. On the second floor are three spacious rooms all with TV, VCR, telephone, double-thick towels, fragrant sprays, sweet soaps, and queen beds that bid travelers welcome and promise a good night's sleep.

The Mill House B&B ✪
102 MILL LANE, NORTH EAST, MARYLAND 21901

Tel: **(410) 287-3532**	Single/sb: **$60–$70**
Best Time to Call: **Before 9 AM; after 4 PM**	Open: **March 1–Dec. 1**
	Breakfast: **Full**
Hosts: **Lucia and Nick Demond**	Credit Cards: **MC, VISA**
Location: **40 mi. NE of Baltimore**	Pets: **No**
No. of Rooms: **2**	Children: **Welcome, over 12**
Max. No. Sharing Bath: **4**	Smoking: **No**
Double/sb: **$65–$75**	Social Drinking: **Permitted**

A genuine mill house that dates to the early 18th century, this B&B is furnished entirely in antiques. You'll see picturesque mill ruins and wildflowers on the grounds, but you won't see the parlor's original Queen Anne paneling; that was purchased by Henry Francis Du Pont and installed in his Winterthur estate bedroom. The Winterthur Museum and the Brandywine River Museum are less than an hour's drive away, as is Baltimore's Inner Harbor. Sightseers will be sustained with a full breakfast, including homemade breads fresh from the oven.

Rocker Inn ✪
17924 ELGIN ROAD, POOLESVILLE, MARYLAND 20837

Tel: **(301) 972-8543**	Single/pb: **$40**
Best Time to Call: **After 5:30 PM**	Open: **All year**
Host: **Nancy Hopkinson**	Breakfast: **Continental**
Location: **25 mi. NW of Washington, D.C.**	Pets: **Sometimes**
	Children: **Welcome**
No. of Rooms: **2**	Smoking: **No**
No. of Private Baths: **1**	Social Drinking: **Permitted**
Double/pb: **$45**	

Built in 1915 as a local telephone house, Rocker Inn takes its name from the rocking chairs and two swings that fill its 48-foot front porch.

Inside, the home is decorated in an informal country mode. Walking tours of Poolesville and Frederick, along with a hike on the C&O Canal, are minutes away. For more ambitious excursions, Harpers Ferry, Gettysburg Battlefield, and historic Leesburg are within an hour's drive.

Parsonage Inn ✪
210 NORTH TALBOT STREET, ST. MICHAELS, MARYLAND 21663

Tel: **(800) 394-5519**
Hosts: **Anthony and Jodie Deyesu**
Location: **11 mi. off Rte. 50**
No. of Rooms: **8**
No. of Private Baths: **8**
Double/pb: **$100–$130**
Open: **All year**
Reduced Rates: **10% seniors; $20 less midweek**

Breakfast: **Full**
Credit Cards: **MC, VISA**
Pets: **No**
Children: **Welcome**
Smoking: **No**
Social Drinking: **Permitted**

Built in the 1880s with bricks fired in the St. Michaels brickyard, the Parsonage Inn was completely restored in 1985. This striking Victorian B&B is part of the town's historic district, and it's an easy stroll to shops, restaurants, and the Chesapeake Bay Maritime Museum. More ambitious guests may borrow the Inn's 12-speed bicycles and venture farther afield.

St. Michael's Manor B&B
ST. MICHAEL'S MANOR, SCOTLAND, MARYLAND 20687

Tel: **(301) 872-4025**	Open: **All year**
Hosts: **Joe and Nancy Dick**	Breakfast: **Full**
Location: **9 mi. S of St. Marys City**	Pets: **No**
No. of Rooms: **4**	Children: **By arrangement**
Max. No. Sharing Bath: **4**	Smoking: **Downstairs**
Double/sb: **$70**	Social Drinking: **Permitted**
Single/sb: **$50**	

St. Michael's Manor was built in 1805 on land patented to Leonard Calvert during the seventeenth century. Today, the white stucco manor home on picturesqure Long Neck Creek is included in the state's Pilgrimage Tour. The beautiful handcrafted woodwork has been preserved and is complemented by antiques and handcrafts. Your hosts offer you the use of a canoe, paddleboat, bikes, spa, and swimming pool. Estate wine tasting is also available. The manor house is near Point Lookout State Park, the Chesapeake Bay, and historic St. Marys City.

Jacob Rohrbach Inn
P.O. BOX 607, SHARPSBURG, MARYLAND 21782

Tel: **(301) 432-5079**	Single/pb: **$70**
Best Time to Call: **After 11 AM**	Open: **All year**
Hosts: **Chris and Denise Yeager**	Reduced Rates: **10% seniors**
Location: **70 mi. NW of Washington,**	Breakfast: **Full**
D.C.	Pets: **No**
No. of Rooms: **2**	Children: **Welcome, over 6**
No. of Private Baths: **2**	Smoking: **No**
Double/pb: **$80**	Social Drinking: **Permitted**

This great brick and stone house survived the Battle of Antietam with relatively minor damage only to have its owner murdered by Confederate raiders in 1864. Today, the Jacob Rohrbach Inn looks much as it did during the Civil War, permitting patrons a unique view into the past. Antietam Battlefield surrounds the Inn and Harpers Ferry Historical Park is just twenty minutes away. Tour the battlefield, bicycle the C&O Canal, visit quaint country shops, or just curl up with a book in front of a warm fire. White-water rafting, horseback riding, and skiing are nearby; if you'd rather travel by car, a leisurely one-hour trip leads through the Shenandoah Valley to the Skyline Drive.

Blue Bear Bed & Breakfast ✪
13810 FRANK'S RUN ROAD, SMITHSBURG, MARYLAND 21783

Tel: **(800) 381-2292**
Best Time to Call: **After 4 PM**
Hosts: **Ellen Panchula and Marilyn Motter**
Location: **6 mi. from I-70, exit 35**
No. of Rooms: **2**
No. of Private Baths: **2**
Double/pb: **$60–$65**

Single/pb: **$50–$55**
Open: **All year**
Breakfast: **Continental**
Pets: **No**
Children: **Welcome, over 12**
Smoking: **No**
Social Drinking: **Permitted**

Ellen, a full-time schoolteacher, and her sister Marilyn, a professional dog groomer, have joined together at the Blue Bear B&B to offer guests year-round hospitality. Their home is decorated in an informal country mode, with several antiques and a charming collection of friendly-faced teddy bears throughout the house. Guests can relax and enjoy beautiful views from the front porch or tour nearby battlefields. Breakfast consists of fresh fruits, homemade breads, pastries and coffee cake. Snacks are offered in the evening.

Null's Bed & Breakfast ✪
4910 BAPTIST ROAD, TANEYTOWN, MARYLAND 21787

Tel: **(410) 756-6112**
Host: **Betty Null**
Location: **8 mi. S of Gettysburg, Penn.**
No. of Rooms: **2**
No. of Private Baths: **1**
Max. No. Sharing Bath: **4**
Double/pb: **$55**
Single/pb: **$50**

Double/sb: **$50**
Single/sb: **$45**
Open: **All year**
Breakfast: **Full**
Pets: **No**
Children: **Welcome**
Smoking: **No**
Social Drinking: **Permitted**

While it is no longer a working farm, the property's 22 acres invite exploration. Ask your host about the furniture; some pieces are genuine antiques, others are artful reproductions. Taneytown is about nine miles from Gettysburg, and Baltimore, Washington, D.C., and Amish country are all accessible by car. Homemade bread and jam accompany Betty's full breakfasts.

The Tavern House ✪
111 WATER STREET, P.O. BOX 98, VIENNA, MARYLAND 21869

Tel: **(410) 376-3347**
Hosts: **Harvey and Elise Altergott**
Location: **15 mi. NW of Salisbury**
No. of Rooms: **4**
Max. No. Sharing Bath: **4**
Double/sb: **$65–$75**
Single/sb: **$60–$70**

Open: **All year**
Breakfast: **Full**
Credit Cards: **MC, VISA**
Pets: **No**
Children: **Welcome, over 12**
Smoking: **Permitted**
Social Drinking: **Permitted**

Vienna is a quiet little town on the Nanticoke River, where one can escape the stress of the 20th century. Careful restoration has brought back the simple purity of this Colonial tavern. The stark white "lime, sand, and hair" plaster accents the authentic furnishings. This is a place for those who enjoy looking at the river and marshes, watching an osprey, or taking a leisurely walk. Days begin with a special full breakfast and end with complimentary cheese and a beverage. For the sports minded, there's tennis, boating, and flat roads for bicycling, all within easy reach. This is an excellent base for exploring the Eastern Shore, interesting small towns, and Blackwater National Wildlife Refuge.

Winchester Country Inn ○

111 STONER AVENUE, WESTMINSTER, MARYLAND 21157

Tel: **(410) 876-7373; (800) 887-3950**
Best Time to Call: **9 AM–7 PM**
Hosts: **Estella Williams and Cynthia Rosembloom**
Location: **35 mi. NW of Baltimore**
No. of Rooms: **5**
No. of Private Baths: **3**
Max. No. Sharing Bath: **4**
Double/pb: **$39.95–$65**

Open: **All year**
Reduced Rates: **Sun.–Thurs.**
Breakfast: **Full**
Credit Cards: **MC, VISA**
Pets: **No**
Children: **Welcome, over 6**
Smoking: **No**
Social Drinking: **Permitted**

Built in the 1760s, this inn is one of the oldest inns in Carroll County. It is furnished with period antiques that enhance the interior. It is only a quarter of a mile to the historic Carroll County Farm Museum, which is the site of special events such as the Maryland Wine Festival. It is within walking distance of the Farmers Market, where produce, flowers, and crafts may be bought. Breakfast includes farm-fresh eggs and country sausage or ham.

MISSISSIPPI

Iuka •

• West

Port Gibson •

Lincoln, Ltd. Bed & Breakfast—Mississippi Reservation Service

P.O. BOX 3479, 2303 23RD AVENUE, MERIDIAN, MISSISSIPPI 39303

Tel: (601) 482-5483; resv. only: (800)
633-MISS [6477]; fax: (601) 693-
7447
Best Time to Call: 9 AM–5 PM
Coordinator: **Barbara Lincoln Hall**
States/Regions Covered:
**Mississippi—Natchez to Memphis,
Alabama**

Descriptive Directory: $3.50
Rates (Single/Double):
Average: **$55–$65 / $65–$75**
Luxury: **$85–$125 / $95–$165**
Credit Cards: **AMEX, MC, VISA**

For the traveling businessperson or for the vacationer, a stay with one
of Barbara's hosts offers a personal taste of the finest Southern
hospitality. All rooms have private baths. Mississippi abounds with
historic-house tours, called "pilgrimages," in March and April, and
Natchez and Vicksburg have similar pilgrimages in autumn. In May,

Meridian is host to the Jimmie Rodgers Festival. Accommodations range from a cozy, historic log cabin to an elegant antebellum mansion.

Natchez Trace B&B Reservation Service—Mississippi ✪
PO BOX 193, HAMPSHIRE, TENNESSEE 38461

Tel: **(800) 377-2770**
Best Time to Call: **Evenings; weekends**
Coordinator: **Kay Jones**
States/Regions Covered: **Mississippi: Church Hill, Corinth French Camp, Jackson, Kosciusko, Lorman, Natchez, Port Gibson, Vicksburg**

Descriptive Directory of B&Bs: **Free**
Rates (Single/Double):
  Modest: **$55 / $65**
  Average: **$70 / $80**
  Luxury: **$90 / $115**
Credit Cards: **MC, VISA**

Kay can help you plan your trip and give you access to homes ranging from rustic, woodsy sites to fine antebellum mansions. Call her for a free list of homes.

Eastport Inn Bed & Breakfast ✪
100 SOUTH PEARL STREET, IUKA, MISSISSIPPI 38852

Tel: **(601) 423-2511**
Best Time to Call: **8 AM–5 PM**
Host: **Betty Watson**
No. of Rooms: 7
No. of Private Baths: 7
Double/pb: **$50**
Single/pb: **$40**
Suites: **$50**
Open: **All year**

Reduced Rates: **Available**
Breakfast: **Continental**
Other Meals: **Available**
Credit Cards: **AMEX, DC, DISC, MC, VISA**
Pets: **No**
Children: **Welcome**
Smoking: **No**
Social Drinking: **Permitted**

This gracious home was built in 1864 and is decorated in period style, with four-poster beds and floral bedspreads. For swimming and boating, Pickwick Lake is six miles away; Shiloh National Park, Tishomingo State Park, Coleman State Park, and the Natchez Trace Drive are also nearby.

Oak Square Plantation ✪
1207 CHURCH STREET, PORT GIBSON, MISSISSIPPI 39150

Tel: **(601) 437-4350; (800) 729-0240**
Best Time to Call: **Anytime**
Hosts: **Mr. and Mrs. William D. Lum**
Location: **On Hwy. 61 between Natchez and Vicksburg**
No. of Rooms: **12**
No. of Private Baths: **12**
Double/pb: **$85–$95**

Single/pb: **$70–$75**
Open: **All year**
Breakfast: **Full**
Credit Cards: **AMEX, DISC, MC, VISA**
Pets: **No**
Children: **Welcome**
Smoking: **No**
Social Drinking: **Permitted**

Port Gibson is the town that Union General Ulysses S. Grant said was "too beautiful to burn." Oak Square is the largest and most palatial antebellum mansion, circa 1850, in Port Gibson, and is listed on the National Register of Historic Places. The guest rooms are all furnished with family heirlooms, and all have canopied beds. Guests will enjoy the courtyard, gazebo, and beautiful grounds. A chairlift for upstairs rooms is available. You will enjoy the delightful Southern breakfast and tour of the mansion. Your hosts offer complimentary wine, tea, or coffee, and will enlighten you on the many historic attractions in the area.

The Alexander House ✪
210 GREEN STREET, P.O. BOX 187, WEST, MISSISSIPPI 39192

Tel: **(601) 967-2266**
Hosts: **Ruth Ray and Woody Dinstel**
Location: **70 mi. N of Jackson**
No. of Rooms: **5**
No. of Private Baths: **3**
Max. No. Sharing Bath: **4**
Double/pb: **$65**
Double/sb: **$65**
Suites: **$110**

Open: **All year**
Breakfast: **Full**
Other Meals: **Available**
Pets: **Sometimes**
Children: **Welcome, over 10**
Smoking: **No**
Social Drinking: **Permitted**
Station pickup: **Yes**

The Alexander House, which has been dated to the 1880s, opened as a bed and breakfast in March 1994. Located in the town historic district, the house has been carefully restored with authentic decor, but with added conveniences. A full breakfast is served each morning and may include hot biscuits, fruit compote, grits, eggs, or casseroles. The two-story home has three bedrooms and a suite.

NORTH CAROLINA

Winston-Salem Germanton
Sparta •   • Madison •   • Weldon
Boone •   Manson •   • Tarboro
Spruce Pine • • Banner Elk   • Durham   Kill Devil Hills
          • Burnsville   Siler City • Wilson
Marshall • • Asheville
Lake Junaluska • • Clyde   • Taylorsville   • Washington
Waynesville •   • Hendersonville
Franklin •,   • Pisgah Forest Statesville   New Bern •   • Morehead City
Murphy • Highlands   • Tryon   • Charlotte   Cape Carteret • • Beaufort
                                                    • Swansboro
                                               • Wilmington
            Tabor City • • Shallotte

Abbington Green Bed and Breakfast Inn
46 CUMBERLAND CIRCLE, ASHEVILLE, NORTH CAROLINA 28801

Tel: **(704) 251-2454**
Best Time to Call: **10 AM–9 PM**
Hosts: **Valerie, Gabrielle and Julie Larrea**
Location: **¾ mi from I-240 Exit 4C**
No. of Rooms: **6**
No. of Private Baths: **6**
Double/pb: **$85–$120**
Suites: **$150**

Open: **All year**
Breakfast: **Full**
Credit Cards: **AMEX, MC, VISA**
Pets: **No**
Children: **Welcome, over 10**
Smoking: **No**
Social Drinking: **Permitted**
Minimum Stay: **2 nights weekends**

Enjoy elegance with a romantic English flavor. This sunlit 1908 Colonial Revival home in the Montford Historic District is a delight to behold inside and out. Stylishly appointed guest rooms are named after parks and gardens around London; each has a canopy-draped queen-size bed, antiques, fine rugs, and air-conditioning. Three guest rooms have fireplaces. Play piano or chess, daydream, or relax with a good book beside the parlor or living room fireplaces. Start each morning with a homemade breakfast featuring crepes or quiche. Abbington Green is located minutes from Biltmore House, Blue Ridge Parkway, University of North Carolina, and fine restaurants and shops.

A Bed of Roses ✪
135 CUMBERLAND AVENUE, ASHEVILLE, NORTH CAROLINA 28801

Tel: **(704) 258-8700**	Breakfast: **Full**
Best Time to Call: **10 AM–9 PM**	Credit Cards: **AMEX**
Host: **Caroline Logie**	Pets: **No**
Location: **½ mi. N of Asheville**	Children: **Welcome, over 12, in main**
No. of Rooms: **4**	**house, under 12 in cottage**
No. of Private Baths: **4**	Smoking: **No**
Double/pb: **$80–$95**	Social Drinking: **Permitted**
Suites: **$110 for 2**	Minimum Stay: **2 nights holidays, in**
Open: **All year**	**season weekends**
Reduced Rates: **10% seniors,**	
Jan.–Mar.	

Styled after an English country cottage, this inn is a cheery Queen Anne Victorian, circa 1897, listed on the Register of Historic Homes. Each guest room is uniquely decorated, some with antique bath fixtures and claw-footed tubs. Guests are invited to relax in the backyard hot tub, or enjoy a cool glass of lemonade or iced tea and cookies on the front porch rockers. Breakfast consists of homemade granola, muffins, seasonal fruit, waffles and crepes. Gourmet coffees and English teas are always available. Biltmore House and Gardens, the Thomas Wolfe Memorial, botanical gardens, and the Blue Ridge Parkway are just minutes from the inn.

Acorn Cottage
25 SAINT DUNSTANS CIRCLE, ASHEVILLE, NORTH CAROLINA 28803

Tel: **(704) 253-0609; (800) 699-0609**	Open: **All year**
Best Time to Call: **10 AM–9 PM**	Breakfast: **Full**
Host: **Connie Stahl**	Credit Cards: **MC, VISA**
Location: **1¼ mi. from Route I40, exit**	Pets: **No**
50/50B	Children: **Welcome (crib)**
No. of Rooms: **4**	Smoking: **No**
No. of Private Baths: **4**	Social Drinking: **Permitted**
Double/pb: **$75–$85**	Minimum Stay: **2 nights weekends,**
Single/pb: **$70–$80**	**March 15–Dec. 31**

An English country cottage in the woodsy heart of Asheville, Acorn is built of local granite; the interior boasts maple floors and a granite fireplace. The guest rooms feature queen-size beds, fine linens, air-conditioning, TV, and baths stocked with special soaps. A delicious full breakfast is served each morning with fresh fruit, varied entrees, juice, coffee, tea, and an assortment of breads, muffins, and coffee cakes. Then you're ready for the quarter-mile trip to the Biltmore Estate.

Applewood Manor
62 CUMBERLAND CIRCLE, ASHEVILLE, NORTH CAROLINA 28801

Tel: **(704) 254-2244**
Best Time to Call: **11 AM–9 PM**
Hosts: **Susan Poole and Maryanne Young**
Location: **¾ mi. from Rte. 240, Exit 4C**
No. of Rooms: **4**
No. of Private Baths: **4**
Double/pb: **$85–$95**
Single/pb: **$80–$90**
Guest Cottage: **$115**
Suite: **$105**
Open: **All year**
Reduced Rates: **10% Jan.–Feb.; 10% seniors (Sept. only)**
Breakfast: **Full**
Credit Cards: **DISC, MC, VISA**
Pets: **No**
Children: **Welcome, over 12**
Smoking: **No**
Social Drinking: **Permitted**
Minimum Stay: **2 nights weekends**

Built in 1908, this Colonial Revival home boasts wide porches with rockers and a swing, and two manicured acres perfect for a game of badminton or croquet. Fine lace curtains, antique furnishings, heart-pine floors covered with oriental rugs, and bright and airy rooms, most with fireplaces and balconies, are found throughout. Breakfast always includes something special, such as orange-pecan waffles or apple and brie omelets. It's only a mile away from fine restaurants, antique and crafts shops, an art museum, theater, and the Thomas Wolfe Memorial.

Cairn Brae
217 PATTON MOUNTAIN ROAD, ASHEVILLE, NORTH CAROLINA 28804

Tel: **(704) 252-9219**
Hosts: **Milli and Ed Adams**
No. of Rooms: **3**
No. of Private Baths: **3**
Double/pb: **$90**
Suites: **$105–$140**
Open: **Apr. 1–Nov. 30**
Breakfast: **Full**
Credit Cards: **DISC, MC, VISA**
Pets: **No**
Children: **Welcome, over 10**
Smoking: **No**
Social Drinking: **Permitted**
Airport/Station Pickup: **Yes**

Cairn Brae is a secluded mountain retreat on wooded acreage, just minutes from downtown Asheville. Enjoy the beautiful mountain views and walking trails, or relax by the fireplace in the cozy guest living room. Afternoon refreshments are served on the terrace, and a full homemade breakfast is offered in the morning.

Carolina Bed & Breakfast ✪

177 CUMBERLAND AVENUE, ASHEVILLE, NORTH CAROLINA 28801

Tel: (704) 254-3608
Best Time to Call: 10 AM–9 PM
Hosts: Sam and Karin Fain
Location: ½ mi. from route 240, Exit 4C
No. of Rooms: 5
No. of Private Baths: 5
Double/pb: $80–$90
Open: All year

Breakfast: Full
Credit Cards: MC, VISA
Pets: No
Children: Welcome, over 12
Smoking: No
Social Drinking: Permitted
Minimum Stay: 2 nights holidays, in season weekends

This turn-of-the-century Colonial Revival home has been painstakingly restored; feel free to relax on the front and back porches, or just take in the view from the second-floor guest rooms, with their distinctive, twelve-over-one panes. In springtime, the grounds bloom with dogwoods and rhododendrons. On cooler days, you can curl up in front of one of the house's seven fireplaces. Your hosts serve a different full breakfast each day; the usual fare includes eggs or quiche and fresh bread and muffins.

The Colby House

230 PEARSON DRIVE, ASHEVILLE, NORTH CAROLINA 28801

Tel: (704) 253-5644; (800) 982-2118
Hosts: Everett and Ann Colby
No. of Rooms: 4
No. of Private Baths: 4
Double/pb: $80–$110
Open: All year

Breakfast: Full
Credit Cards: MC, VISA
Pets: No
Children: Welcome, over 12
Smoking: Restricted
Social Drinking: Permitted

This elegant Dutch-Tudor house in the Montford Historic District is a special place, thanks to its porch, beautiful gardens, and inviting fireplaces. Each guest room has its own individual decor and queen-size beds. Refreshments are available at all times, and wine and cheese are served in the evening. Breakfasts vary daily, but are always served on fine china, with heirloom crystal and silver. Southern hospitality abounds in your hosts' personal attention to every guest's needs.

Corner Oak Manor ✪

53 ST. DUNSTANS ROAD, ASHEVILLE, NORTH CAROLINA 28803

Tel: (704) 253-3525
Best Time to Call: 9 AM–9 PM
Hosts: Karen and Andy Spradley
Location: 1¼ mi. from Rte. 40, Exit 50
No. of Rooms: 4
No. of Private Baths: 4

Double/pb: $85–$100
Single/pb: $70–$85
Cottage: $130
Open: All year
Breakfast: Full
Credit Cards: AMEX, DISC, MC, VISA

Pets: **No**
Children: **Welcome, over 12**

Smoking: **No**
Social Drinking: **Permitted**

Surrounded by maple, oak, and evergreen trees, this lovely English Tudor home is located minutes away from the famed Biltmore Estate and Gardens. The rooms have queen-size beds beautifully covered in fine linen. The window treatments and coordinated wall coverings could easily grace the pages of a decorating magazine. Handmade wreaths, weavings, and stitchery complement the furnishings. Breakfast specialties include orange French toast, blueberry-ricotta pancakes, or four-cheese-herb quiche. A living room fireplace, baby grand piano, outdoor deck, and Jacuzzi are among the gracious amenities.

Flint Street Inns
100 & 116 FLINT STREET, ASHEVILLE, NORTH CAROLINA 28801

Tel: **(704) 253-6723**
Hosts: **Rick, Lynne, and Marion Vogel**
Location: **¼ mi. from Rte. 240**
No. of Rooms: **8**
No. of Private Baths: **8**
Double/pb: **$85**
Single/pb: **$70**

Open: **All year**
Breakfast: **Full**
Credit Cards: **AMEX, DISC, MC, VISA**
Pets: **No**
Children: **No**
Smoking: **Permitted**
Social Drinking: **Permitted**

These turn-of-the-century homes on an acre with century-old trees are listed on the National Register of Historic Places. Stained glass, pine floors, and a claw-footed bathtub are part of the Victorian decor. The Inns are air-conditioned for summer comfort; some have fireplaces for winter coziness. Guests are served coffee and soft drinks. The Blue Ridge Parkway is close by.

The Banner Elk Inn Bed & Breakfast ✪
ROUTE 3, BOX 1134, HIGHWAY 194 NORTH, BANNER ELK, NORTH CAROLINA 28604

Tel: **(704) 898-6223**
Best Time to Call: **9 AM–10 PM**
Host: **Beverly Lait**
Location: **17 mi. W of Boone**
No. of Rooms: **5**
No. of Private Baths: **4**
Double/pb: **$75–$100**
Single/pb: **$65–$90**
Suites: **$100–$150; sleeps 4**
Open: **All year**
Reduced Rates: **Available**

Breakfast: **Full**
Credit Cards: **MC, VISA**
Pets: **Yes**
Children: **Welcome, Sun.–Thurs.**
Smoking: **No**
Social Drinking: **Permitted**
Minimum Stay: **Mid-July; first 2 weeks of Oct.; ski season Dec. 25–Mar. 30; 2 nights weekends**
Foreign Languages: **Spanish, German**

Your host, Beverly, spent years with the Foreign Service, and original tapestries, artwork, and antiques from around the world fill her stunningly renovated historic home. The Inn is located halfway between the Sugar Resort and Beech Mountain ski slopes, near such major tourist attractions as Grandfather Mountain and Natural Habitat, Linville Falls, Valle Crucis, and the Blue Ridge Parkway. You'll have energy to visit all these places after Beverly's full breakfasts of homemade breads, eggs, fruit, juice, and coffee or tea.

Delamar Inn ✪
217 TURNER STREET, BEAUFORT, NORTH CAROLINA 28516

Tel: **(919) 728-4300**	Open: **All year**
Best Time to Call: **Anytime**	Breakfast: **Continental, plus**
Hosts: **Tom and Mabel Steepy**	Credit Cards: **MC, VISA**
Location: **140 mi. SE of Raleigh**	Pets: **No**
No. of Rooms: **3**	Children: **Welcome, over 10**
No. of Private Baths: **3**	Smoking: **Restricted**
Double/pb: **$85**	Social Drinking: **Permitted**
Single/pb: **$85**	Airport/Station Pickup: **Yes**

The Delamar Inn, built in 1866, is located in historic Beaufort, North Carolina's third oldest town. The Inn offers three guest rooms furnished with antiques, each room with a private bath. After a delightful breakfast, stroll down to the historic restoration grounds, maritime museum, or the open-air bus, or browse in the waterfront specialty shops. Tom and Mabel, your hosts, can offer directions to local beaches for shell collecting, sunbathing, or fishing. Try a short ride to Fort Macon, Tryon Palace, or the ferry to the Outer Banks. A selection of the '91 and '92 historic homes tour, the Delamar Inn welcomes you.

Estes Mountain Retreat ✪
ROUTE 1, BOX 1316A (OFF BAKER'S CREEK ROAD), BURNSVILLE, NORTH CAROLINA 28714

Tel: **(704) 682-7264**	Open: **All year**
Best Time to Call: **After 7 PM**	Reduced Rates: **15% weekly; 10% seniors**
Hosts: **Bruce and Maryallen Estes**	
Location: **37 mi. NE of Asheville**	Breakfast: **Full**
No. of Rooms: **2**	Pets: **No**
No. of Private Baths: **1**	Children: **Welcome, over 3**
Max. No. Sharing Bath: **4**	Smoking: **No**
Double/pb: **$60**	Social Drinking: **Permitted**
Double/sb: **$55**	Foreign Languages: **French**

Breathtaking mountain views await you at this three-level cedar log home with a rock chimney, fireplace, and porches. Because Burnsville is in Pisgah National Forest, you won't have to travel far to go rafting, fishing, hiking, and rock and gem hunting, and there's golfing next door at Mountain Air Country Club. Mt. Mitchell, Linville Caverns, outdoor theater, the Biltmore Mansion, and the Carl Sandburg Home are all within an hour's drive.

Hamrick Inn ✪
7787 HIGHWAY 80 SOUTH, BURNSVILLE, NORTH CAROLINA 28714

Tel: **(704) 675-5251**	Single/pb: **$55–$65**
Best Time to Call: **Mornings**	Open: **Apr. 2–Oct. 31**
Hosts: **Neal and June Jerome**	Reduced Rates: **Weekly**
Location: **55 mi. NE of Asheville; 16 mi. from I-40, Exit 72**	Breakfast: **Full**
No. of Rooms: **4**	Pets: **No**
No. of Private Baths: **4**	Children: **Welcome**
Double/pb: **$60–$70**	Smoking: **Permitted**
	Social Drinking: **Permitted**

This charming three-story Colonial-style stone inn is nestled at the foot of Mt. Mitchell, the highest mountain east of the Mississippi River. Much of the lovely furniture was built by Neal and June. The den has a fine selection of books as well as a TV set for your enjoyment. There is a private porch off each bedroom, where you may take in the view and the cool mountain breezes. Golfing, hiking, fishing, rock hounding, crafts shopping, and fall foliage wandering are local activities. Pisgah National Park, Linville Caverns, Crabtree Meadows, and the Parkway Playhouse are area diversions.

Harborlight Guest House ✪
332 LIVE OAK DRIVE, CAPE CARTERET, NORTH CAROLINA 28584

Tel: **(800) 624-VIEW [8439]; (919) 393-6868**	Best Time to Call: **Noon–9:30 PM**
	Hosts: **Bobby and Anita Gill**

Location: **15 mi. from 70E, exit 24W**
No. of Rooms: 7
No. of Private Baths: 7
Double/pb: **$75–$110**
Single/pb: **$60**
Suites: **$125–$155**
Open: **All year**
Reduced Rates: **Waterview rooms $15 per night winter**

Breakfast: **Full**
Credit Cards: **AMEX, MC, VISA**
Pets: **No**
Children: **Welcome, over 16**
Smoking: **No**
Social Drinking: **Permitted**
Minimum Stay: **2 nights weekends**
Airport Pickup: **Yes**

Located on a secluded waterfront on the central North Carolina coast, Harborlight Guest House offers seven luxury suites and rooms—all having private entrances, private baths, and spectacular water view. The luxury suites have two-person Jacuzzis, fireplaces, and in-suite breakfasts. Activities include golf, antique shopping, and Barrier Island excursions by boat. The waterfront villages of Beaufort and Swansboro offer unique gift shops and intimate restaurants. Water sports include deep-sea fishing, swimming and boating, and ocean-front horseback rides. In the morning guests enjoy a gourmet breakfast consisting of egg and cheese dishes, fresh fruits, and fresh breads. Visit the coast and experience the waterfront sunset amidst graceful palms and the tranquility of Harborlight Guest House.

The Elizabeth Bed & Breakfast ✪
2145 EAST 5TH STREET, CHARLOTTE, NORTH CAROLINA 28204

Tel: **(704) 358-1368**
Best Time to Call: **Evening**
Host: **Joan Mastny**
Location: **3 mi. from Rte I-77, Exit 10B**
No. of Rooms: 3
No. of Private Baths: 3
Double/pb: **$58–$78**
Single/pb: **$55–$70**

Guest cottage: **$80–$88**
Open: **All year**
Breakfast: **Full, Continental**
Credit Cards: **MC, VISA**
Pets: **No**
Children: **Welcome, over 12**
Smoking: **No**
Social Drinking: **Permitted**

This 1927 lavender "lady" is in historic Elizabeth, Charlotte's second oldest neighborhood. Rooms are decorated in European country style and are beautifully appointed with antiques, ceiling fans, decorator linens, and unique collections. For privacy a guest cottage is available, furnished in an elegant Southwestern style. All rooms have central air-conditioning; some have TV and phone. Enjoy a full breakfast on weekends and Continental on weekdays. Guests may relax in the garden courtyard complete with a charming gazebo or stroll beneath giant oak trees to convenient restaurants and shopping.

The Homeplace
5901 SARDIS ROAD, CHARLOTTE, NORTH CAROLINA 28270

Tel: **(704) 365-1936**
Hosts: **Peggy and Frank Dearien**

Location: **10 mi. from I-77; I-85**
No. of Rooms: 2

No. of Private Baths: **2**
Double/pb: **$88**
Single/pb: **$78**
Suite: **$115**
Open: **All year**
Breakfast: **Full**

Credit Cards: **AMEX, MC, VISA**
Pets: **No**
Children: **Welcome, over 10**
Smoking: **No**
Social Drinking: **No**

The warm and friendly atmosphere hasn't changed since 1902. The minute you arrive at this country Victorian and walk up to the wraparound porch with its rockers, you'll feel you've "come home." The handcrafted staircase, 10-foot beaded ceilings, and heart-pine floors add to the interior's beauty. It's convenient to malls, furniture and textile outlets, and treasure-filled antique shops.

Still Waters ○
6221 AMOS SMITH ROAD, CHARLOTTE, NORTH CAROLINA 28214

Tel: **(704) 399-6299**
Best Time to Call: **Evenings**
Hosts: **Janet and Rob Dyer**
Location: **3 mi. W of Charlotte**
No. of Rooms: **3**
No. of Private Baths: **3**
Double/pb: **$65–$85**
Open: **All year**

Reduced Rates: **Available**
Breakfast: **Full**
Credit Cards: **MC, VISA**
Pets: **No**
Children: **Welcome**
Smoking: **No**
Social Drinking: **Permitted**

Relax on the river just outside Charlotte city limits—only minutes away from downtown, the airport, or the interstates, but a world away from the bustle of everyday life. Visit this lakefront log home on two wooded acres. Enjoy the deck, garden, dock, and boat ramp, or play on the sport court. Guests stay in either of two large rooms or in a suite. Full breakfasts always feature homemade sourdough rolls and fresh-ground coffee.

Windsong: A Mountain Inn ✪
120 FERGUSON RIDGE, CLYDE, NORTH CAROLINA 28721

Tel: **(704) 627-6111**
Best Time to Call: **8 AM–9 PM**
Hosts: **Donna and Gale Livengood**
Location: **36 mi. W of Asheville**
No. of Rooms: **5**
No. of Private Baths: **5**
Double/pb: **$90–$150**
Single/pb: **$81–$89.10**
Open: **All year**

Reduced Rates: **10%, singles and weekly bookings**
Breakfast: **Full**
Credit Cards: **DISC, MC, VISA**
Pets: **No**
Children: **Welcome, over 8**
Smoking: **No**
Social Drinking: **Permitted**

From its mountainside perch near Waynesville, this immense contemporary log home affords spectacular views of the surrounding countryside. Inside, the house is bright and airy, thanks to the large windows and skylights and the high exposed-beam ceilings. Each oversized room boasts its own patio, fireplace, and deep tubs for two. There is a tennis court and in-ground pool, plus a billiard table and an extensive video library with in-room VCRs. You'll love their llama herd with group pack trips going into the national forests. Nearby attractions include horseback riding, white-water rafting, Cherokee Indian Reservation, Great Smoky Mountain National Park, Biltmore House, and the Appalachian Trail. You'll relish home-baked breakfast goods. Typical entrees are buckwheat banana pancakes and egg-sausage strata with mushrooms.

The Blooming Garden Inn ✪
513 HOLLOWAY STREET, DURHAM, NORTH CAROLINA 27701

Tel: **(919) 687-0801**
Best Time to Call: **Evenings**
Hosts: **Frank and Dolly Pokrass**
Location: **Downtown Durham**
No. of Rooms: **5**
No. of Private Baths: **5**
Double/pb: **$85–$105**
Suites: **$145–$160**
Open: **All year**

Reduced Rates: **Available**
Breakfast: **Full**
Credit Cards: **AMEX, DC, DISC, MC, VISA**
Pets: **No**
Children: **Welcome**
Smoking: **No**
Social Drinking: **Permitted**

If you appreciate flowers—and who doesn't?—you'll love staying at this restored 1892 Victorian with glorious gardens at every turn. The house is handsome, too, with its gabled roof, beveled and stained-glass windows, and wraparound porch supported by Tuscan columns. What's more, you're right in the center of Durham's historic Holloway District, just moments from shops, galleries, theaters, Duke University, and the University of North Carolina. For the ultimate in pampering, luxury suites with Jacuzzis are available. A big feature at Blooming Garden Inn is the gourmet breakfast.

Buttonwood Inn ○

190 GEORGIA ROAD, FRANKLIN, NORTH CAROLINA 28734

Tel: **(704) 369-8985**	Double/sb: **$55**
Best Time to Call: **After 5 PM**	Single/sb: **$45**
Host: **Liz Oehser**	Suites: **$95**
Location: **75 mi. SW of Asheville**	Open: **Apr. 15–Nov. 15**
No. of Rooms: **4**	Breakfast: **Full**
No. of Private Baths: **2**	Pets: **No**
Max. No. Sharing Bath: **4**	Children: **Welcome, over 10**
Double/pb: **$60–$75**	Smoking: **Permitted**
Single/pb: **$50**	Social Drinking: **Permitted**

The Buttonwood is a small country inn surrounded by towering pines, a spacious lawn, and mountain views. The original residence was a small cottage built in the late 1920s adjacent to the greens of the Franklin golf course. Years later, a new wing was added with rustic, charming rooms. Guests may choose from comfortable bedrooms decorated with antiques, cozy quilts, and handcrafts, many of which are offered for sale. Breakfast selections include sausage-apple ring, eggs Benedict, or cheese frittata, with coffee cake and plenty of hot coffee or tea. Golfers will be glad to be so close to the beautiful fairways and Bermuda grass greens right next door. Nearby there are also crafts shops, hiking trails, the Blue Ridge Parkway, gem mines, and plenty of places to swim and ride.

Heritage Inn ○

101 HERITAGE HOLLOW, FRANKLIN, NORTH CAROLINA 28734

Tel: **(704) 524-4150**	Reduced Rates: **10% less Nov.–Mar.**
Best Time to Call: **9 AM-9 PM**	Breakfast: **Full**
Host: **Sally Wade**	Pets: **No**
Location: **135 mi. NE Atlanta, Georgia**	Children: **Welcome, over 12**
No. of Rooms: **4**	Smoking: **No**
No. of Private Baths: **4**	Social Drinking: **Permitted**
Double/pb: **$55–$65**	Minimum Stay: **2 nights, holiday and**
Single/pb: **$48**	**October weekends**
Cottage: **$75–$110, sleeps 6**	Airport Pickup: **Yes**
Open: **All year**	

Rocking on the veranda over a cascading waterfall is one of the favorite pastimes at this tin-roofed, in-town country inn. Nestled in the Smoky Mountains tall pines, it is close to gem mining, white-water rafting, hiking trails, and country auctions, within walking distance of museums, mountain crafts and antique shops. On the premises is a gallery of tribal art and artifacts that Sally collected in her world travels. Each immaculate, tastefully furnished room has its own entrance and porch for added privacy. Kitchenettes are available. A full breakfast and evening dessert are served. Complimentary beverages are offered throughout the day and evening at the lovely, creekside gazebo.

MeadowHaven Bed & Breakfast ✪
NC HIGHWAY 8, P.O. BOX 222, GERMANTON,
NORTH CAROLINA 27019

Tel: **(910) 593-3996**
Best Time to Call: **9 AM–9 PM**
Hosts: **Samuel and Darlene Fain**
Location: **16 mi. N of Winston-Salem**
No. of Rooms: **3**
No. of Private Baths: **3**
Double/pb: **$65–$90**
Cabins: **$125–$175**
Open: **All year**

Breakfast: **Full, Continental, plus**
Pets: **No**
Children: **No**
Smoking: **No**
Social Drinking: **Permitted, in guest rooms**
Minimum Stay: **2 nights weekends, holidays and special event weeks**

MeadowHaven is a chalet-style retreat on 25 acres, with stunning mountain views from the B&B's large deck. Immerse yourself in the hot tub or the heated indoor pool, grab some snacks from the pantry, and test your skills in the game room, at the fishing pond, or on the archery ranges. For honeymooners, the Lovebirds' Retreat, with its whirlpool tub and steam shower, is ideal. You won't have to travel far for horseback riding, canoeing, and golf; other local attractions include a winery, an art gallery, and Sauratown Mountain. Darlene, a former controller for the Marriott Corporation, runs her family's construction business, and Sam is a retail manager interested in greenhouse gardening, magic, and birds.

The Waverly Inn ✪
783 NORTH MAIN STREET, HENDERSONVILLE,
NORTH CAROLINA 28792

Tel: **(800) 537-8195; (704) 693-9193**
Best Time to Call: **9:30 AM–10 PM**
Hosts: **John and Diane Sheiry**
Location: **20 mi. S of Asheville**
No. of Rooms: **14**
No. of Private Baths: **14**
Double/pb: **$79–$149**
Single/pb: **$79**

Open: **All year**
Reduced Rates: **Off-season**
Breakfast: **Full**
Credit Cards: **AMEX, DISC, MC, VISA**
Pets: **No**
Children: **Welcome**
Smoking: **Restricted**
Social Drinking: **Permitted**

Built as a boardinghouse in 1898, the Waverly is distinguished by its handsome Eastlake staircase—a factor that earned the Inn a listing on the National Register of Historic Places. Furnishings like four-poster canopy beds and claw-footed tubs combine Victorian stateliness and Colonial Revival charm. You'll walk away sated from all-you-can-eat breakfasts of pancakes and French toast. Noteworthy local sites include the Biltmore Estate, the Carl Sandburg house, the Blue Ridge Parkway, and the Flat Rock Playhouse.

Colonial Pines Inn ○

ROUTE 1, BOX 22B, HICKORY STREET, HIGHLANDS, NORTH CAROLINA 28741

Tel: **(704) 526-2060**	Guest Cottages: **$85–$200; sleep 4–6**
Best Time to Call: **Afternoons**	Open: **All year**
Hosts: **Chris and Donna Alley**	Reduced Rates: **Winter**
Location: **80 mi. SW of Asheville**	Breakfast: **Full**
No. of Rooms: 7	Credit Cards: **MC, VISA**
No. of Private Baths: 7	Pets: **No**
Double/pb: **$90**	Children: **Welcome, in cottage only**
Single/pb: **$80**	Smoking: **No**
Suites: **$100**	Social Drinking: **Permitted**

Located in a charming, uncommercial mountain resort town, this white Colonial is flanked by tall columns and is surrounded by two acres. The scenic view may be enjoyed from comfortable rocking chairs on the wide veranda. Donna, a former interior decorator, has furnished the Inn with antiques, art, and interesting accessories. Chris is a classical guitarist, woodworker, and great cook. The hearty breakfast includes a variety of homemade breads.

The Guest House ○

RT. 2, BOX 64914 (HWY E 64), HIGHLANDS, NORTH CAROLINA 28741

Tel: **(704) 526-4536**	Breakfast: **Full**
Best Time to Call: **9 AM–9 PM**	Credit Cards: **MC, VISA**
Host: **Juanita Hernandez**	Pets: **No**
Location: **100 mi. NE of Atlanta**	Children: **Welcome**
No. of Rooms: 4	Smoking: **No**
No. of Private Baths: 4	Social Drinking: **Permitted**
Double/pb: **$68–$85**	Minimum Stay: **Weekends July–Sept.,**
Single/pb: **$60–$70**	**holidays, and October**
Open: **All year**	Foreign Languages: **Spanish, German**
Reduced Rates: **Available**	

A charming Alpine-style mountain chalet nestled among stately trees, this B&B is more ample than its compact looks suggest. Inside you'll admire the plush, cream-colored carpeting, chestnut paneling, light wallcoverings, teakwood furniture, and native stone fireplace. Deep contemporary seats invite guests to slip off their shoes and relax. Partake of the spectacular view from the open deck, with its sun umbrella and rocking chairs. After a restful night in your tastefully decorated room—accented with Juanita's artistic touches—you'll wake up to one of her superb breakfasts.

Lakeside Inn ✪
ROUTE 1, BOX 189A, HIGHLANDS, NORTH CAROLINA 28741

Tel: **(704) 526-4498**
Best Time to Call: **10 AM–9 PM**
Hosts: **Cathy and Hank Ross**
Location: **120 mi. NE of Atlanta**
No. of Rooms: **4**
No. of Private Baths: **4**
Double/pb: **$75**
Single/pb: **$70**
Open: **All year**

Breakfast: **Full**
Credit Cards: **MC, VISA**
Pets: **No**
Children: **Welcome**
Smoking: **No**
Social Drinking: **Permitted**
Minimum Stay: **June–Oct. 2 nights weekends**

Nestled among the oaks and hemlocks, Lakeside Inn has a lovely view of Lake Sequoyah and borders the Nantahala National Forest. You can enjoy the scenery from the patio of this restored 1930s lodge or use the canoe that is provided by your hosts for a leisurely ride. Lakeside Inn offers cozy rooms and has a common area with a fireplace, cable TV, books and games. Breakfast entrees include French toast, burritos, fresh fruits, and freshly baked muffins. Area activities range from hiking, horseback riding, mountain biking, fishing, rappelling, and white-water rafting to enjoying the quaint town of Highlands.

Ye Olde Stone House
ROUTE 2, BOX 7, HIGHLANDS, NORTH CAROLINA 28741

Tel: **(704) 526-5911**
Best Time to Call: **Afternoons;
   evenings**
Hosts: **Jim and Rene Ramsdell**
Location: **80 mi. SW of Asheville**
No. of Rooms: **4**
No. of Private Baths: **4**
Double/pb: **$65–$75**
Single/pb: **$60–$65**
Chalet: **$95–$115, sleeps 4**
Open: **All year**

Reduced Rates: **10% Sun.–Thurs.;
   weekly**
Breakfast: **Full**
Credit Cards: **MC, VISA**
Pets: **No**
Children: **Welcome**
Smoking: **No**
Social Drinking: **Permitted**
Minimum Stay: **2 nights holiday
   weekends**

Built of stones taken from a local river by mule and wagon, the house is less than a mile from the center of town, where you will find a nature center, museum, galleries, tennis courts, swimming pool, and shops offering antiques or mountain crafts. The rooms are bright, cheerful, and comfortably furnished. The sun room and porch are perfect spots to catch up on that book you've wanted to read. On cool evenings, the Ramsdells invite you to gather round the fireplace for snacks and conversation.

Cherokee Inn Bed & Breakfast ☉
**500 NORTH VIRGINIA DARE TRAIL, KILL DEVIL HILLS,
NORTH CAROLINA 27948**

Tel: **(919) 441-6127; (800) 554-2764**
Best Time to Call: **Evenings**
Hosts: **Bob and Kaye Combs**
Location: **75 mi. S of Norfolk**
No. of Rooms: **6**
No. of Private Baths: **6**
Double/pb: **$55–$85**
Open: **Apr. 1–Oct. 30**
Reduced Rates: **$5 less per night,
   seniors**

Breakfast: **Continental**
Credit Cards: **AMEX, MC, VISA**
Pets: **No**
Children: **No**
Smoking: **No**
Social Drinking: **Permitted**
Minimum Stay: **2 nights July–Aug.; 3
   nights holidays**

Only 500 feet from the Atlantic Ocean you'll find this beach house with wraparound porches, soft cypress interiors, and white ruffled curtains. Cherokee Inn is near the historic Roanoke Island settlement, Cape Hatteras, and the Wright Brothers Memorial at Kitty Hawk. Of course, you may just want to spend the day at the beach. In the evening, curl up with a book or watch TV. You'll start the next day with coffee and pastries.

The Laurels ✪
P.O. BOX 1354, LAKE JUNALUSKA, NORTH CAROLINA 28745

Tel: (704) 456-7186	Single/sb: $55
Hosts: Mary and Roger Kayler	Open: All year
Location: 20 mi. W of Asheville	Breakfast: Full
No. of Rooms: 3	Credit Cards: MC, VISA
No. of Private Baths: 1	Pets: No
Max. No. Sharing Bath: 4	Children: Welcome, over 12
Double/pb: $75	Smoking: No
Single/pb: $65	Social Drinking: Permitted
Double/sb: $65	Airport/Station Pickup: Yes

This two-story, four-square house sits on 1.5 acres, shaded by lovely old hemlocks, stately white oaks, and surrounded by rhododendrons and laurels. Recently restored, The Laurels is furnished with treasured family antiques, many crafted with wood from local forests. It maintains the warmth and charm of a stately mountain home. Rock on the expansive side porch or relax in the parlor with a glass of sherry. Fine linens, down comforters and pillows, terry robes, flowers, and gourmet chocolates pamper guests. A full breakfast, casual in atmosphere, is served on fine china, crystal, and old family silver. The Laurels lies in the heart of the Blue Ridge Mountains near Waynesville, Maggie Valley and adjacent to the Methodist Assembly at Lake Junaluska. This area offers many outdoor activities and shopping opportunities.

The Boxley Bed & Breakfast ✪
117 EAST HUNTER STREET, MADISON, NORTH CAROLINA 27025

Tel: (800) 429-3516	Open: All year
Best Time to Call: 8 AM–8 PM	Reduced Rates: 10% seniors, weekly
Hosts: JoAnn and Monte McIntosh	Breakfast: Full
Location: 22 mi. N of Greensboro	Credit Cards: AMEX, MC, VISA
No. of Rooms: 4	Pets: No
No. of Private Baths: 4	Children: Welcome
Double/pb: $65	Smoking: No
Single/pb: $55	Social Drinking: Permitted

This Greek Federal-style home, was built in 1825 on over an acre, located in the historic district of Madison. Furnished with oriental rugs, antiques, fine linens and china, the house possesses an aura of simple elegance, charm and grace. Guests will enjoy the peacefulness and serenity of this 19th-century setting. A gourmet breakfast is served in the country kitchen, dining room or on the porch. JoAnn and Monte are full-time hosts; their interests are in gardening and refinishing furniture. The Boxley is your home away from home.

Kimball Oaks
ROUTE 1, BOX 158, MANSON, NORTH CAROLINA 27553

Tel: **(919) 456-2153**	Open: **All year**
Best Time to Call: **8 AM–6 PM**	Reduced Rates: **10% after 1st night**
Hosts: **Allen and Jeanette Kimball**	Breakfast: **Full**
Location: **50 mi. N of Raleigh, Durham**	Other Meals: **Available**
No. of Rooms: **3**	Pets: **No**
No. of Private Baths: **2**	Children: **Welcome, over 12**
Max. No. Sharing Bath: **4**	Smoking: **No**
Double/pb: **$70–$80**	Social Drinking: **Permitted**
Double/sb: **$60**	Foreign Languages: **Italian**

Allen and Jeanette invite you to their two-story home in a grove of 200-year-old oaks surrounded by lawns, flower/herb beds and a vegetable garden, set in the middle of a farm community. Portions of their Colonial home date back to the 1840s. Rooms are decorated in light airy colors and tastefully furnished in traditional style with many antiques. Guests are greeted with iced tea and lemonade, with fresh fruit and flowers in the rooms. Participate in a lawn game—horseshoes, badminton, croquet, bocce or volleyball/basketball for the young at heart—or take a good book down to the shade-covered beaver pond for relaxed reading. Your hosts are a retired Army officer and his wife whose entertaining skills have been honed by years of military and diplomatic living in Brussels, Geneva, Verona, Rome, and Washington. Come for a real treat!

The Gingerbread House ✪
300 HIGHWAY 213, P.O. BOX 907, MARSHALL, NORTH CAROLINA 28753

Tel: **(704) 649-3922**	Open: **All year**
Best Time to Call: **8–9:30 AM**	Reduced Rates: **10% seniors, mid-week, off-season**
Host: **Jim Goshorn**	
Location: **15 mi. N of Asheville**	Breakfast: **Continental**
No. of Rooms: **3**	Credit Cards: **AMEX, MC, VISA**
No. of Private Baths: **1**	Pets: **No**
Max. No. Sharing Bath: **4**	Children: **Welcome**
Double/pb: **$65**	Smoking: **No**
Double/sb: **$55**	Social Drinking: **Permitted**
Single/sb: **$45**	Foreign Languages: **German**

The Gingerbread House is a lavishly decorated two-story Victorian farmhouse with three beautifully furnished bedrooms, a parlor and a breakfast room with five-sided bay windows. The unusual scrollwork on the balconies and porches has made The Gingerbread House a landmark and has earned it enrollment on the National Historic Register. The Peach Room has a queen-size brass bed, private bath, and a wood-burning fireplace. The Green Room has a four-poster queen bed and the Blue Room has two extra-long twin beds. The cheerful rooms and hearty breakfast will earn this bed and breakfast a place in your heart.

Morehead Manor Bed & Breakfast ✪
107 NORTH TENTH STREET, MOREHEAD CITY, NORTH CAROLINA 28557

Tel: (919) 726-9233	Reduced Rates: $10 less Sun.–Thurs.
Hosts: Bob and Brenda Thorne	Breakfast: Full
Location: 160 mi. SE of Raleigh	Credit Cards: MC, VISA
No. of Rooms: 8	Pets: No
No. of Private Baths: 3	Children: Welcome, over 5
Max. No. Sharing Bath: 4	Smoking: No
Double/pb: $75	Social Drinking: Permitted
Single/pb: $65	Minimum Stay: Holidays, 2 nights
Double/sb: $59	Airport Pickup: Yes
Single/sb: $55	
Open: Memorial weekend thru Labor Day	

Venture out and explore the treasures of this pleasant coastal community. Cape Lookout National Seashore, wild ponies, historic Beaufort, and miles of sandy beach await you. Within walking distance are the restaurants, shops, and charter boats of the waterfront district. The inn offers a casual, laid-back atmosphere reminiscent of grandma's house. Old and new blend gracefully together in this refreshing summer place. With three porches and a courtyard laced with shrubs and flowers, there's room to socialize or just sit and rock your cares away. Bob and Brenda invite you to join them on the crystal coast.

Huntington Hall Bed and Breakfast ✪
500 VALLEY RIVER AVENUE, MURPHY, NORTH CAROLINA 28906

Tel: (704) 837-9567; (800) 824-6189; fax: (704) 837-2527	Reduced Rates: 15% Dec.–Feb., based on availability
Best Time to Call: 8 AM–9 PM	Breakfast: Full
Hosts: Bob and Kate DeLong	Credit Cards: AMEX, DC, DISC, MC, VISA
Location: 100 mi. N. of Atlanta, Georgia	Pets: No
No. of Rooms: 5	Children: Welcome
No. of Private Baths: 5	Smoking: No
Double/pb: $65–$85	Social Drinking: Permitted
Single/pb: $49–$65	Airport/Station Pickup: Yes
Open: All year	

Two huge maple trees shade this pleasant clapboard home, circa 1881; tall columns accent the front porch, and English ivy and Virginia creeper climb the low stone wall surrounding the property. Each spacious bedroom blends the old-world charm of tall windows, wooden floors, and Victorian decor with such modern amenities as cable TV and private baths. Wonderful breakfasts served on the sunporch precede the day's explorations of the historical district in nearby Brasstown, or of the Valley River Valley—original home of the Cherokee Indians and site of their "Trail of Tears." Both Bob and Kate are outdoor enthusiasts, eager to help guests plan white-water rafting trips on the Nanathala and Ocoee Rivers and hikes in Great Smoky Mountain National Park.

The Aerie ☉
509 POLLOCK STREET, NEW BERN, NORTH CAROLINA 28560

Tel: **(919) 636-5553; (800) 849-5553**
Hosts: **Howard and Dee Smith**
Location: **120 mi. E of Raleigh**
No. of Rooms: **7**
No. of Private Baths: **7**
Double/pb: **$79–$89**
Single/pb: **$54–$64**
Open: **All year**

Breakfast: **Full**
Credit Cards: **AMEX, DISC, MC, VISA**
Pets: **No**
Children: **Welcome**
Smoking: **No**
Social Drinking: **Permitted**
Airport/Station Pickup: **Yes**

Just one block from Tryon Palace, The Aerie has the closest accommodations to all of New Bern's historic attractions. This Victorian inn was a private residence for almost a century. Today it is furnished with fine antiques and reproductions. Each of the seven individually decorated rooms has a modern bath, telephone, and cable TV. Complimentary wine, beer, soft drinks, and light refreshments are offered throughout your stay, and a generous country breakfast awaits you each morning in the dining room.

New Berne House Bed and Breakfast Inn ☉
709 BROAD STREET, NEW BERN, NORTH CAROLINA 28560

Tel: **(919) 636-2250; (800) 842-7688**
Hosts: **Marcia Drum and Howard Bronson**
Location: **1 mi. from Hwy. 70**
No. of Rooms: **7**
No. of Private Baths: **7**
Double/pb: **$80**
Single/pb: **$60**
Open: **All year**

Reduced Rates: **AAA, AARP**
Breakfast: **Full**
Credit Cards: **AMEX, MC, VISA**
Pets: **No**
Children: **Welcome, over 12**
Smoking: **No**
Social Drinking: **Permitted**
Airport/Station Pickup: **Yes**

Located in the heart of New Bern's historic district, this brick Colonial is furnished in the style of an English country manor with a mixture of antiques, traditional pieces, and attic treasures. Guests are pampered with afternoon tea or coffee served in the parlor. A sweeping stairway leads upstairs to romantic bedchambers, one with a brass bed reportedly rescued in 1897 from a burning brothel. Breakfast specialties such as praline and cream waffles, honey-glazed ham, and homemade breads and muffins are served in the dining room. New Berne House is within walking distance of Tryon Palace, North Carolina's Colonial capitol, and the governor's mansion. Ask about the exciting Mystery Weekends.

Key Falls Inn ○
151 EVERETT ROAD, PISGAH FOREST, NORTH CAROLINA 28768

Tel: **(704) 884-7559**
Best Time to Call: **9 AM–9 PM**
Hosts: **Clark and Patricia Grosvenor, and Janet Fogleman**
No. of Rooms: **4**
No. of Private Baths: **4**
Double/pb: **$60–$75**
Single/pb: **$50–$65**

Suites: **$90**
Open: **All year**
Breakfast: **Full**
Credit Cards: **AMEX, DC, MC, VISA**
Pets: **No**
Children: **Welcome, over 6**
Smoking: **No**
Social Drinking: **Permitted**

Visitors to this B&B will be able to make the most of western North Carolina's natural and cultural attractions. Key Falls Inn is situated on a 28-acre estate with its own tennis court, pond, and outdoor barbecue. For quieter moments, sit on one of the porches and enjoy the mountain views. Music lovers will want to get tickets to the acclaimed Brevard Festival, an annual summer event.

Breakfast Creek ○
4361 OCEAN BREEZE AVENUE SW, SHALLOTTE, NORTH CAROLINA 28470

Tel: **(910) 754-3614**
Best Time to Call: **Mornings**
Hosts: **Tim Tryon and Diane Turtle**
Location: **35 mi. S of Wilmington**
No. of Rooms: **3**
No. of Private Baths: **2**
Max. No. Sharing Bath: **4**
Double/pb: **$60**

Suite: **$75**
Open: **All year**
Breakfast: **Full**
Pets: **No**
Children: **Welcome**
Smoking: **No**
Social Drinking: **Permitted**

Breakfast Creek is a modest white brick house filled with sunlight and antiques. It overlooks the Atlantic Ocean, Shallotte Inlet, Intracoastal Waterway, and acres of living wetlands. Diane is a devoted gardener, Tim is a musician and woodworker; both love sailing and the beach. The B&B is located fifteen minutes from Ocean Isle, and twenty minutes from Holden Beach, Calabash, Southport, Fort Fisher, Wilmington, and the Grand Strand. None of these are reachable without passing at least one golf course. During his first visit, a guest said, "It's like staying with friends at the beach without the sand."

Bed and Breakfast at Laurel Ridge ✪

**3188 SILER CITY–SNOW CAMP ROAD, SILER CITY,
NORTH CAROLINA 27344**

Tel: (800) 742-6049; (919) 742-6049
Best Time to Call: **9 AM–9 PM**
Hosts: **David Simmons and Lisa
 Reynolds**
Location: **35 mi. SE of Greensboro**
No. of Rooms: **3**
No. of Private Baths: **1**
Max. No. Sharing Bath: **4**
Double/pb: **$95**
Single/pb: **$85**
Double/sb: **$50–$65**

Single/sb: **$40–$55**
Suites: **$95**
Open: **All year**
Reduced Rates: **6th night free**
Breakfast: **Full**
Credit Cards: **AMEX, MC, VISA**
Pets: **No**
Children: **Welcome, over 10**
Smoking: **No**
Social Drinking: **Permitted**

Bed and Breakfast at Laurel Ridge is a contemporary rustic post and beam home situated on 26 forested acres that border the Rocky River. Centrally located in the heart of North Carolina, between the Triad furniture markets, Research Triangle Park, North Carolina Zoo, and Seagrove Pottery, this guest house provides visitors with many choices of things to do. David, a professional chef for over 25 years, prepares the best breakfast in North Carolina using locally grown, organic products. The menu may include soufflés, specialty pancakes, and stuffed French toast.

Turby Villa B&B ✪

STAR ROUTE 1, BOX 48, SPARTA, NORTH CAROLINA 28675

Tel: (910) 372-8490
Host: **Mrs. Maybelline Turbiville**
No. of Rooms: **3**
No. of Private Baths: **3**
Double/pb: **$50**
Single/pb: **$35**

Open: **All year**
Breakfast: **Full**
Pets: **No**
Children: **Welcome**
Smoking: **Permitted**
Social Drinking: **Permitted**

At an altitude of 3000 feet, this contemporary two-story brick home is the centerpiece of a 20-acre farm. The house is surrounded by an acre of trees and manicured lawns, and the lovely views are of the scenic Blue Ridge Mountains. Breakfast is served either on the enclosed porch with its white wicker furnishings or in the more formal dining room with its Early American–style furnishings. Mrs. Turbiville takes justifiable pride in her attractive, well-maintained B&B.

The Richmond Inn ✪

101 PINE AVENUE, SPRUCE PINE, NORTH CAROLINA 28777

Tel: (704) 765-6993
Best Time to Call: **Anytime**
Hosts: **Lenore Boucher and Bill Ansley**

Location: **4 mi. from Blue Ridge Pkwy.,
 Exit 331**
No. of Rooms: **7**

No. of Private Baths: **7**
Double/pb: **$55–$75**
Single/pb: **$45–$65**
Open: **All year**
Breakfast: **Full**

Credit Cards: **MC, VISA**
Pets: **No**
Children: **Welcome**
Smoking: **No**
Social Drinking: **Permitted**

Surrounded by towering pines, this white wooden house trimmed with black window shutters has a stone terrace and rock walls. It is furnished in a comfortable blend of antiques and family treasures. Most mornings, Lenore fixes a Southern repast with bacon, eggs, and grits. Spruce Pine is the mineral capital of the world, and panning for gemstones such as garnets and amethysts is a popular pastime. Hiking the Appalachian Trail, playing golf, or working out at your hosts' community spa will keep you in shape. Internationally known artists schedule shows throughout the year.

Cedar Hill Farm B&B ✪
778 ELMWOOD ROAD, STATESVILLE, NORTH CAROLINA 28677

Tel: **(704) 873-4332; (800) 948-4423**
  Ext. 1254
Best Time to Call: **Before 2 PM; after 5 PM**
Hosts: **Brenda and Jim Vernon**
Location: **45 mi. N of Charlotte**
No. of Rooms: **2**
No. of Private Baths: **2**
Double/pb: **$60**

Guest Cottage: **$75**
Open: **All year**
Breakfast: **Full**
Credit Cards: **MC, VISA**
Pets: **Sometimes**
Children: **Welcome**
Smoking: **No**
Social Drinking: **Permitted**

A three-story Federal farmhouse furnished with antique and country pieces, Cedar Hill is surrounded by 32 acres of rolling green, the better to feed the Vernons' sheep. Brenda and Jim sell fleece coverlets and crafts from their own hand-spun wool; they also make furniture and cure turkey and ham in a smokehouse on site. Stay in the farmhouse or in a private cottage. Either way you'll have an air-conditioned room with a telephone and cable TV. The country breakfasts will leave you full, thanks to servings of ham, sausage, fruit, potatoes, and buttermilk biscuits with homemade preserves. You can work off calories swimming in your hosts' pool or playing badminton, but you might want to relax in a porch rocker or hammock first. The cottage now has a working fireplace.

Madelyn's Bed & Breakfast
514 CARROLL STREET, STATESVILLE, NORTH CAROLINA 28677

Tel: **(704) 872-3973; (800) 948-4473;**
  (704) 881-0713
Best Time to Call: **9 AM–9 PM**
Hosts: **John and Madelyn Hill**

Location: **45 mi. N of Charlotte**
No. of Rooms: **3**
No. of Private Baths: **3**
Double/pb: **$55–$65**

Open: **All year**
Reduced Rates: **10% seniors**
Breakfast: **Full**
Credit Cards: **MC, VISA**
Pets: **No**

Children: **Welcome, over 10**
Smoking: **No**
Social Drinking: **Permitted**
Airport/Station Pickup: **Yes**

Madelyn's B&B is nestled in a quiet neighborhood near downtown, historic districts, and a two-mile par course; outlet shopping is nearby. For more fun, Statesville hosts two annual events—the Carolina Dogwood Festival in the spring and the National Balloon Rally in the fall. Madelyn and John try to make each guest feel special. When you arrive, you'll find fresh fruit, candies, and homemade cookies in your room. A sumptuous breakfast is served where you want it: in the formal dining room, before a cozy fire in the breakfast room, on the sunporch, or even in bed. Your hosts are glad to cater to visitors' special dietary needs.

Scott's Keep ✪
308 WALNUT STREET, SWANSBORO, NORTH CAROLINA 28584

Tel: **(910) 326-1257; (800) 348-1257**
Best Time to Call: **Anytime**
Hosts: **Frank and Norma Scott**
Location: **150 mi. SE of Raleigh**
No. of Rooms: **3**
Max. No. Sharing Bath: **4**
Double/pb: **$55**
Double/sb: **$45**
Open: **All year**

Reduced Rates: **15% weekly**
Breakfast: **Full**
Credit Cards: **AMEX, DISC, MC, VISA**
Pets: **No**
Children: **Welcome, over 6**
Smoking: **No**
Social Drinking: **Permitted**
Minimum Stay: **2 nights, May 15–Sept. 15**

This simple contemporary is located on a quiet street two blocks from the waterfront. Your hosts want you to feel right at home in the bright, spacious living room and comfortable guest rooms. The larger bedroom is decorated with wicker and features an antique trunk, queen-size bed, and colorful quilts. The smaller bedroom is furnished in classic maple with twin beds and grandmother's quilts. For breakfast, Norma serves blueberry or apple spice muffins with fruit and homemade jellies. This historic seaside village is filled with inviting shops and waterside seafood restaurants. Your hosts will point the way to beautiful beaches, waterskiing, sailing, and windsurfing.

Four Rooster Inn ✪
205 PIREWAY ROAD, ROUTE 904, TABOR CITY, NORTH CAROLINA 28463

Tel: **(910) 653-3878**
Hosts: **Gloria and Bob Rogers**
Location: **24 mi. NW of Myrtle Beach, South Carolina**

No. of Rooms: **4**
No. of Private Baths: **2**
Max. No. Sharing Bath: **4**
Double/pb: **$65**

Single/pb: **$55**
Double/sb: **50–$60**
Single/sb: **$40–$50**
Open: **All year**
Reduced Rates: **Fifth night free**
Breakfast: **Full**

Credit Cards: **MC, VISA**
Pets: **No**
Children: **Welcome, by arrangement**
Smoking: **No**
Social Drinking: **Permitted**
Airport/Station Pickup: **Yes**

Experience the warm, gracious hospitality of the old South in the charm of a country setting. The Inn has been restored to a comfortable elegance with china, crystal, antiques, beautiful fabrics and fine linens. Amenities include afternoon tea, evening turn-down service accented with chocolates, and coffee or tea at your door when you awake. A full breakfast is served in the dining room and may include yam bread, French toast, or eggs Benedict. The Four Rooster Inn is located forty-five minutes from Interstate 95 and a short drive from Myrtle Beach golf courses, Waccamaw Pottery shopping, Brookgreen Gardens, and historic Wilmington. The Inn provides a comfortable haven whether traveling for business or pleasure. Gloria and Bob are dedicated to the art of service for their guests.

Little Warren ✪
304 EAST PARK AVENUE, TARBORO, NORTH CAROLINA 27886

Tel: **(919) 823-1314; (800) 309-1314**
Hosts: **Patsy and Tom Miller**
Location: **Easy access from I-95**
No. of Rooms: **3**
No. of Private Baths: **3**
Double/pb: **$65**
Single/pb: **$58**
Open: **All year**
Reduced Rates: **Corporate, upon
  request**

Breakfast: **Full**
Credit Cards: **AMEX, DISC, MC, VISA**
Pets: **No**
Children: **Welcome, over 6**
Smoking: **Permitted**
Social Drinking: **Permitted**
Airport/Station Pickup: **Yes**
Foreign Languages: **Spanish**

Little Warren is actually a large and gracious family home built in 1913. It is located along the Albemarle Trail in Tarboro's historic district. The deeply-set, wraparound porch overlooks one of the last originally chartered town commons still in existence. Inside, you'll find rooms of beautiful antiques from England and America. In the morning, choose from a full English, Southern, or expanded Continental breakfast.

Barkley House Bed & Breakfast ✪
ROUTE 6, BOX 12, TAYLORSVILLE, NORTH CAROLINA 28681

Tel: **(704) 632-9060**	Open: **All year**
Best Time to Call: **Mornings**	Breakfast: **Full**
Host: **Phyllis Barkley**	Credit Cards: **AMEX, DISC, MC, VISA**
Location: **60 mi. NW of Charlotte**	Pets: **Sometimes**
No. of Rooms: **3**	Children: **Welcome**
No. of Private Baths: **3**	Smoking: **Permitted**
Double/pb: **$49**	Social Drinking: **Permitted**
Single/pb: **$38**	Airport/Station Pickup: **Yes**

After staying in European B&Bs, Phyllis opened the first one in Taylorsville, a small town surrounded by mountains. Barkley House is a white Colonial with yellow shutters and a gracious front porch with four columns. The furnishings are homey, combining antiques and pieces from the '50s. Haystack eggs and fruity banana splits are two of Phyllis's breakfast specialties; she'll be happy to cater to guests on restricted diets.

Mill Farm Inn ✪
P.O. BOX 1251, TRYON, NORTH CAROLINA 28782

Tel: **(704) 859-6992; (800) 545-6992**	Open: **All year**
Best Time to Call: **Mornings**	Reduced Rates: **10% seniors**
Hosts: **Chip and Penny Kessler**	Breakfast: **Continental**
Location: **45 mi. SE of Asheville**	Pets: **No**
No. of Rooms: **9**	Children: **Welcome**
No. of Private Baths: **9**	Smoking: **No**
Double/pb: **$65**	Social Drinking: **Permitted**
Single/pb: **$49**	Foreign Languages: **French**
Suites: **$65–$100**	

The Pacolet River flows past the edge of this three-and-one-half-acre property in the foothills of the Blue Ridge Mountains. Sitting porches and the living room with fireplace are fine spots to relax. A hearty breakfast of fresh fruit, cereal, English muffins, preserves, and coffee is served. Crafts shops, galleries, and antiquing will keep you busy.

Acadian House Bed & Breakfast ☉

**129 VAN NORDEN STREET, WASHINGTON,
NORTH CAROLINA 27889**

Tel: **(919) 975-3967**	Suites: **$85**
Best Time to Call: **Mornings and evenings**	Open: **Feb. 1–Dec. 14**
	Breakfast: **Full**
Hosts: **Johanna and Leonard Huber**	Credit Cards: **AMEX, DISC, MC, VISA**
Location: **105 mi. E of Raleigh**	Pets: **No**
No. of Rooms: **3**	Children: **Welcome, over 12**
No. of Private Baths: **3**	Smoking: **No**
Double/pb: **$55–$60**	Social Drinking: **Permitted**
Single/pb: **$50**	

Acadian House Bed & Breakfast, a 1900 home located in Colonial Washington, features a unique herringbone-patterned brick porch. It is decorated throughout with antiques and local crafts. A Victorian staircase leads to guest rooms and the library, where books and games are provided. Johanna and Leonard, transplanted New Orleanians, serve a full breakfast featuring southern Louisiana Acadian specialties such as beignets and café au lait along with traditional breakfast foods. Acadian House is one block from the scenic Pamlico River; museums and antique shops are nearby. The business traveler will find a writing table and telephone available. Fax and copying facilities are also nearby.

Pamlico House ☉

400 EAST MAIN STREET, WASHINGTON, NORTH CAROLINA 27889

Tel: **(919) 946-7184; (800) 948-8507**	Open: **All year**
Best Time to Call: **9 AM–8 PM**	Breakfast: **Full**
Hosts: **Lawrence and Jeanne Hervey**	Credit Cards: **AMEX, DISC, MC, VISA**
Location: **20 mi. E of Greenville**	Pets: **No**
No. of Rooms: **4**	Children: **Welcome, over 6**
No. of Private Baths: **4**	Smoking: **No**
Double/pb: **$65–$75**	Social Drinking: **Permitted**
Single/pb: **$55–$65**	Airport/Station Pickup: **Yes**

Located in the center of a small, historic town, this stately Colonial Revival home's large rooms are a perfect foil for the carefully chosen antique furnishings. Guests are drawn to the classic Victorian parlor or to the spacious wraparound porch for relaxing conversation. Take a self-guided walking tour of the historic district or a stroll along the quaint waterfront. Recreational pleasures abound. Nature enthusiasts enjoy the wildlife and exotic plants in nearby Goose Creek State Park.

Should you get homesick for your favorite pet, Lawrence and Jeanne will share theirs.

Belle Meade Inn ✪

804 BALSAM ROAD, WAYNESVILLE, NORTH CAROLINA 28738 (MAILING ADDRESS: P.O. BOX 1319, WAYNESVILLE, NORTH CAROLINA 28786)

Tel: **(704) 456-3234**	Reduced Rates: **10% AARP; weekly**
Hosts: **Gloria and Al DiNofa**	Breakfast: **Full**
Location: **27 mi. W of Asheville**	Credit Cards: **DISC, MC, VISA**
No. of Rooms: **4**	Pets: **No**
No. of Private Baths: **4**	Children: **Welcome, over 6**
Double/pb: **$55–$60**	Smoking: **No**
Single/pb: **$50–$55**	Social Drinking: **Permitted**
Open: **All year**	

Nestled in the mountains, and within easy reach of the Great Smoky National Park, this elegant home is a frame dwelling built in the craftsman style popular in the early 1900s. The warm richness of the chestnut woodwork in the formal rooms and the large stone fireplace in the living room complement the appealing blend of antique and traditional furnishings. The friendly attention to guests' needs is exemplified in such thoughtful touches as "early bird" coffee brought to your door, complimentary refreshments on the veranda, and fresh flowers and mints in your room. Nearby attractions include Biltmore House, Catalooche Ski Slope, mountain art and crafts festivals, and white-water rafting and tubing.

Weldon Place Inn ✪
500 WASHINGON AVENUE, WELDON, NORTH CAROLINA 27890

Tel: **(919) 536-4582; (800) 831-4470**
Best Time to Call: **Anytime**
Hosts: **Angel and Andy Whitby**
Location: **2 mi. E of I-95, exit 173**
No. of Rooms: **4**
No. of Private Baths: **3**
Max. No. Sharing Bath: **3**
Double/pb: **$60–$65**
Single/pb: **$55–$60**
Double/sb: **$55**

Single/sb: **$50**
Open: **All year**
Reduced Rates: **Available**
Breakfast: **Full**
Credit Cards: **AMEX, MC, VISA**
Pets: **No**
Children: **No**
Smoking: **Restricted**
Social Drinking: **No**

If you love antiques and country elegance, step back in time as you cross the threshold of Weldon Place Inn. Sleep in a canopy bed, wake to singing sparrows, and savor a gourmet breakfast. Then explore this historic neighborhood: the Inn, built in 1913, stands amid homes that date to the mid 1800s, and nearby, there is a canal system aqueduct that is two decades older. Breakfast specialties like sausage-and-cheese-stuffed French toast and strawberry bread will help to fuel your excursions.

Anderson Guest House ✪
520 ORANGE STREET, WILMINGTON, NORTH CAROLINA 28401

Tel: **(910) 343-8128**
Best Time to Call: **8 AM–5 PM**
Hosts: **Landon and Connie Anderson**
No. of Rooms: **2**
No. of Private Baths: **2**
Double/pb: **$75**
Single/pb: **$60**

Open: **All year**
Breakfast: **Full**
Pets: **Sometimes**
Children: **Welcome**
Smoking: **No**
Social Drinking: **Permitted**
Airport/Station Pickup: **Yes**

This 19th-century town house has a private guest house overlooking a garden. The bedrooms have ceiling fans, fireplaces, and air-conditioning. Enjoy cool drinks upon arrival and a liqueur before bed. Breakfast specialties are eggs Mornay, blueberry cobbler, and crepes. Your host can point out the sights of this historic town and direct you to the beaches.

Catherine's Inn ✪
**410 SOUTH FRONT STREET, WILMINGTON,
NORTH CAROLINA 28401**

Tel: **(910) 251-0863; (800) 476-0723**
Best Time to Call: **8 AM–10 PM**
Hosts: **Walter and Catherine Ackiss**

Location: **Wilmington's historical
district**
No. of Rooms: **3**

No. of Private Baths: **3**
Double/pb: **$75–$80**
Single/pb: **$60–$65**
Open: **All year**
Reduced Rates: **Available**
Breakfast: **Full**

Credit Cards: **AMEX, MC, VISA**
Pets: **No**
Children: **Welcome, by arrangement**
Smoking: **No**
Social Drinking: **Permitted**
Airport Pickup: **Yes**

Located in Wilmington's historic district, this Italianate home features wrought-iron fences, a gate, a Colonial Revival wraparound front porch and a two-story screened rear porch. The 300-foot lawn overlooks a sunken garden and the picturesque Cape Fear River. Inside, furnishing includes antiques and tasteful reproductions, high ceilings and an heirloom baby grand piano. Start your day with coffee delivered to your door, followed by an appetizing homemade breakfast served in the dining room on silver, china, and crystal. An evening turn-down service is provided, and a nightcap, too.

Taylor House Inn ○

14 NORTH SEVENTH STREET, WILMINGTON, NORTH CAROLINA 28401

Tel: **(910) 763-7581**
Best Time to Call: **After 11 AM**
Host: **Glenda Moreadith**
Location: **120 mi. SE of Raleigh**
No. of Rooms: **4**
No. of Private Baths: **4**
Double/pb: **$85**
Single/pb: **$65**
Suites: **$80–$140**
Open: **All year**

Breakfast: **Full**
Credit Cards: **AMEX, MC, VISA**
Pets: **No**
Children: **Welcome, over 12**
Smoking: **No**
Social Drinking: **Permitted**
Minimum Stay: **2 nights weekends May–Aug.**
Airport/Station Pickup: **Yes**

Upon entering the foyer of the Taylor House Inn, one is in awe of its stately elegance and warmth. The golden oak staircase with two stained glass windows, high ceilings, and parquet floors provide a dramatic expression of a long-lost art. Guest rooms include a bridal suite with an off-white color scheme and a king-size bed with a huge canopy, and a Garden Room with a gas fireplace, brass bed and a melon color scheme. A gourmet breakfast is served in the formal dining room, with bone china, crystal and white linen. Taylor House is located in the historic district, within walking distance to the riverfront, antique shops, and museums. Walking tours and horse-drawn tours are also available. Wonderful beaches are a 15-minute drive.

Miss Betty's Bed & Breakfast Inn

600 WEST NASH STREET, WILSON, NORTH CAROLINA 27893-3045

Tel: **(919) 243-4447; (800) 258-2058**
  (for reservations only)

Best Time to Call: **9 AM–9 PM**
Hosts: **Betty and Fred Spitz**

Location: **50 mi. E of Raleigh**
No. of Rooms: **10**
No. of Private Baths: **10**
Double/pb: **$60–$70**
Single/pb: **$50–$60**
Suites: **$75**
Open: **All year**

Breakfast: **Full**
Credit Cards: **AMEX, CB, DC, DISC, MC, VISA**
Pets: **No**
Children: **No**
Smoking: **No**
Social Drinking: **Permitted**

One of the best places to stay in the South, Miss Betty's is located in the downtown historic section of Wilson. The B&B comprises three beautifully restored homes—the Davis-Whitehead-Harris House (circa 1858), the adjacent Riley House, and Rosebud (circa 1943)—that recapture bygone elegance and style. Guests can browse for antiques in any of the numerous shops that have given Wilson the title of "Antique Capital of North Carolina." The town is also renowned for its tasty barbecue, gorgeous golf courses, and numerous tennis courts.

Mickle House ✪
927 WEST FIFTH STREET, WINSTON-SALEM, NORTH CAROLINA 27101

Tel: **(910) 722-9045**
Best Time to Call: **9 AM–10 PM**
Host: **Barbara Garrison**
Location: **1 mi. from Rte. 40, Broad St. exit**
No. of Rooms: **2**
No. of Private Baths: **2**
Double/pb: **$65–$75**

Single/pb: **$60–$65**
Open: **All year**
Breakfast: **Full**
Credit Cards: **MC, VISA**
Pets: **No**
Children: **No**
Smoking: **No**
Social Drinking: **Permitted**

Step back in time to visit a quaint Victorian cottage painted a soft yellow, with dark green shutters and gingerbread trim. The fully restored home, located in the National Historic District of West End, is furnished with lovely antiques, such as the canopy and poster beds in the guest rooms. Dessert is served in the afternoon or evening, and a full breakfast, with fresh fruit and freshly-baked breads and muffins, awaits you in the morning. Old Salem, the Medical Center, and the Convention Center are five minutes away; fine restaurants, parks, shops, and the library are within walking distance.

Wachovia B&B, Inc. ✪
513 WACHOVIA STREET, WINSTON-SALEM, NORTH CAROLINA 27101

Tel: **(910) 777-0332**
Best Time to Call: **9 AM–5 PM**
Host: **Susan Bunting**
Location: **½ mi. S of Winston-Salem**
No. of Rooms: **5**
No. of Private Baths: **2**

Max. No. Sharing Bath: **4**
Double/pb: **$65**
Single/pb: **$55**
Double/sb: **$55**
Single/sb: **$45**
Open: **All year**

Breakfast: **Full**
Pets: **No**
Children: **Welcome (crib)**

Smoking: **No**
Social Drinking: **Permitted**

This white and rose Victorian cottage, with its appealing wraparound porch, is just outside the Old Salem historic district, and antique shops, excellent restaurants, and a scenic strollway are within a one-block radius. Noted institutions like North Carolina School of the Arts and Wake Forest University are only a few miles away. This is a good area for cycling. Susan's experience as a pastry chef for a local restaurant is apparent in her full breakfasts.

For key to listings, see inside front or back cover.

✪ This star means that rates are guaranteed through December 31, 1996, to any guest making a reservation as a result of reading about the B&B in *Bed & Breakfast U.S.A.*—1996 edition.

Important! To avoid misunderstandings, always ask about cancellation policies when booking.

Please enclose a self-addressed, stamped, business-size envelope when contacting reservation services.

For more details on what you can expect in a B&B, see Chapter 1.

Always mention *Bed & Breakfast U.S.A.* when making reservations!

If no B&B is listed in the area you'll be visiting, use the form on page 249 to order a copy of our "List of New B&Bs."

We want to hear from you! Use the form on page 251.

OKLAHOMA

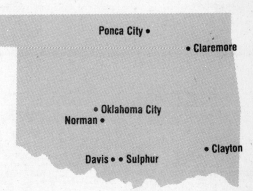

Ponca City •

• Claremore

• Oklahoma City
Norman •

Davis • • Sulphur

• Clayton

Country Inn
ROUTE 3, BOX 1925, CLAREMORE, OKLAHOMA 74017

Tel: **(918) 342-1894**
Best Time to Call: **8 AM–8 PM**
Hosts: **Leland and Kay Jenkins**
Location: **25 mi. NE of Tulsa**
No. of Rooms: **3**
No. of Private Baths: **3**
Double/pb: **$52**
Single/pb: **$35**

Suite: **$65**
Open: **All year**
Reduced Rates: **10% seniors**
Breakfast: **Full**
Children: **No**
Smoking: **No**
Social Drinking: **Permitted**

Leland and Kay look forward to making you feel right at home in the charming barn-style guest quarters, separate from the main house. They invite you to enjoy the swimming pool, improve your suntan, or just sit back in the shade and enjoy a cool drink. The Will Rogers Memorial, the J. M. Davis Gun Museum, the 29,500-acre Oologah Lake, and Oral Roberts University are close by.

Clayton Country Inn ✪
ROUTE 1, BOX 8, HIGHWAY 271, CLAYTON, OKLAHOMA 74536

Tel: **(918) 569-4165, 627-1956**
Best Time to Call: **8 AM–9 PM**
Hosts: **Betty Lundgren, Eula and Al Taylor**
Location: **140 mi. SE of Tulsa**
No. of Rooms: **11**
No. of Private Baths: **11**
Double/pb: **$39**
Single/pb: **$33**

Guest Cottage: **$42; for 2**
Open: **All year**
Breakfast: **Continental**
Other Meals: **Available**
Credit Cards: **AMEX, DISC, MC, VISA**
Pets: **No**
Children: **Welcome**
Smoking: **Permitted**
Social Drinking: **Permitted**

Perched on a hill amid 140 acres and surrounded by the Kiamichi Mountains is this 50-year-old, two-story, stone and wood inn. It's furnished in a simple, traditional style with a beamed ceiling and fireplace. The on-premises restaurant is noted for its fine cooking. Bass fishing at Lake Sardis is two miles away, and an 18,000-acre game preserve is just across the highway. Feel free to bring your horse and enjoy trail rides under the vast Western skies.

Cedar Green Bed & Breakfast ✪
909 SOUTH 4, DAVIS, OKLAHOMA 73030

Tel: **(405) 369-2396**
Best Time to Call: **Evenings**
Hosts: **Pat and Miles Judkins**
Location: **75 mi. S of Oklahoma City**
No. of Rooms: **3**
No. of Private Baths: **3**
Double/pb: **$55**
Single/pb: **$40**
Suites: **$60**

Open: **All year**
Breakfast: **Full**
Pets: **No**
Children: **Welcome, over 10**
Smoking: **No**
Social Drinking: **No**
Minimum Stay: **2 nights holiday weekends**

Cedar Green Bed & Breakfast is located in the heart of the Arbuckle Mountains. Enjoy the large front porch, deck, and shade trees in this quiet residential area. Turner Falls Park, Arbuckle Wilderness Animal Theme Park, Chickasaw National Recreational Area, and Lake of the Arbuckles are located within ten minutes. Pat works part-time for the Chamber of Commerce and enjoys collectibles and crafts. Miles likes woodworking and do-it-yourself projects.

Cutting Garden Bed & Breakfast ✪
927 WEST BOYD, NORMAN, OKLAHOMA 73069

Tel: **(405) 329-4522**; fax: **(405) 321-7326**	Reduced Rates: **10% seniors**
Host: **Connie Byrum**	Breakfast: **Full**
Location: **10 mi. S of Oklahoma City**	Credit Cards: **AMEX, DISC, MC, VISA**
No. of Rooms: **3**	Pets: **No**
No. of Private Baths: **3**	Children: **Welcome, over 12**
Double/pb: **$55–$75**	Smoking: **No**
Open: **All year**	Social Drinking: **Permitted**

Connie's little place provides wide open spaces and a cozy relaxed atmosphere, yet there's nothing laid-back about the service. The lovely guest rooms overlook more than an acre of gardens and trees, all have queen-size beds, fresh flowers daily and, upon request, cable TV and phones. Breakfasts are made from healthy ingredients, with elegant touches of fresh herbs and edible flowers. Cutting Garden Bed & Breakfast is close to restaurants and near the University of Oklahoma, Campus Corner and downtown shopping.

Holmberg House Bed & Breakfast ✪
766 DEBARR, NORMAN, OKLAHOMA 73069

Tel: **(405) 321-6221**	Open: **All year**
Hosts: **Jo Meacham and Richard Divelbiss**	Reduced Rates: **$10 less Sun.–Thurs.**
	Breakfast: **Full**
Location: **17 mi. S of Oklahoma City**	Credit Cards: **AMEX, DISC, MC, VISA**
No. of Rooms: **4**	Pets: **No**
No. of Private Baths: **4**	Children: **Welcome, over 12**
Double/pb: **$55–$85**	Smoking: **No**
Single/pb: **$55–$75**	Social Drinking: **Permitted**

Located in Norman's National Register Historic District and across the street from the University of Oklahoma's campus, this handsome 1914 Craftsman house was built by Professor Frederick Holmberg and his wife Signy. Jo and Richard bought the house in 1993 and it now accommodates many of the university's visiting scholars and parents. Guest rooms are individually decorated with antiques, private baths with claw-footed tubs and color cable TVs. A parlor with a fireplace and porches with rockers and gardens are for your pleasure. A hearty breakfast is served in the dining room.

Country House ✪

10101 OAKVIEW ROAD, OKLAHOMA CITY, OKLAHOMA 73165

Tel: (405) 794-4008
Best Time to Call: **8 AM–10 PM**
Hosts: **Dee and Nancy Ann Curnutt**
Location: **10 mi. SE of center of Oklahoma City**
No. of Rooms: **2**
No. of Private Baths: **2**
Double/pb: **$60–$85**

Single/pb: **$50–$75**
Open: **All year**
Breakfast: **Full**
Pets: **Sometimes**
Children: **Welcome**
Smoking: **Restricted**
Social Drinking: **Permitted**

At Country House you will find genuine, old-fashioned hospitality in a warm romantic setting. The house rests on five beautiful acres; the interior is tastefully furnished with 19th-century antiques and country collectibles. Nancy offers in-room color TV on request, as well as a scrumptious breakfast served on the balcony if you wish. For fishing, water sports, and horseback riding go to nearby Lake Draper, where Captain Dee, Nancy's husband, runs a charter boat service. Ask about the large red heart-shaped whirlpool suite.

The Grandison ✪

1841 NORTHWEST FIFTEENTH STREET, OKLAHOMA CITY, OKLAHOMA 73106

Tel: (405) 521-0011; (800) 240-INNS [4667]
Hosts: **Claudia and Bob Wright**
Location: **2 mi. off I-44, Tenth St. exit**
No. of Rooms: **5**
No. of Private Baths: **5**
Double/pb: **$45–$85**
Suites: **$90–$125**
Open: **All year**

Breakfast: **Continental, plus**
Other Meals: **Available**
Credit Cards: **AMEX, DISC, MC, VISA**
Pets: **Sometimes**
Children: **Welcome, over 12**
Smoking: **Permitted**
Social Drinking: **Permitted**
Airport/Station Pickup: **Yes**

Named for its first owner and resident, Grandison Crawford, this turn-of-the-century brick Colonial was expanded in 1914, and again in the 1930s. It is furnished with antiques from many eras, so each bedroom has a distinctive look. The closest attractions—Civic Center Music Hall, the Convention Center, and Oklahoma City's fairgrounds—are just five minutes away. Breakfast consists of a meat and egg dish, fresh fruit, home-baked pastries, and beverage. For snacking, you'll find fruit, nuts, cookies, and mints in your bedroom.

Davarnathey Inn ✪
1001 WEST GRAND, PONCA CITY, OKLAHOMA 74601

Tel: **(405) 765-9922; (800) 763-9922**	Breakfast: **Full**
Hosts: **David and Shirley Zimmerman**	Credit Cards: **AMEX, CB, DC, DISC,**
Location: **80 mi. S of Wichita, Kans.**	**MC, VISA**
No. of Rooms: **3**	Pets: **No**
No. of Private Baths: **3**	Children: **Welcome**
Double/pb: **$69**	Smoking: **No**
Single/pb: **$59**	Social Drinking: **Permitted**
Open: **All year**	Airport/Station Pickup: **Yes**

Built in 1906 by an Oklahoma oilman, Davarnathey Inn has its original fretwork stairway, ornate mirrored mantel, and stained-glass windows. Period furnishings and floral wallpapers sustain the Victorian mood. Guests are encouraged to browse in the library; the musically inclined have both a piano and an organ to play. Other amenities include a hot tub. Snacks are served, but after a full breakfast of fresh baked Scandinavian breads, fruit crêpes, soufflés, and quiche, it may be a while before you're hungry again.

Artesian Bed and Breakfast ✪
1022 WEST 12TH STREET, SULPHUR, OKLAHOMA 73086

Tel: **(405) 622-5254**	Open: **All year**
Hosts: **Karen and Tom Byrd**	Reduced Rates: **15% Dec.–Mar.**
Location: **71 mi. S of Oklahoma City**	Breakfast: **Full**
No. of Rooms: **2**	Pets: **No**
No. of Private Baths: **2**	Children: **Welcome, over 10**
Double/pb: **$60**	Smoking: **No**
Single/pb: **$50**	Social Drinking: **No**
Suites: **$70**	

A quiet, homey atmosphere prevails at this 1904 Sears, Roebuck Victorian, where the L-shaped front porch is furnished with swing and willow chairs. Inside, you'll admire the wooden staircase, the tiled parlor fireplace, and the bay windows overlooking the backyard. There's natural beauty at every turn. For hiking, swimming, or just picnicking, Chickasaw Recreation Area is only half a mile away. For fishing, boating, and water skiing, take the ten-mile drive to Arbuckle Lake. Your hosts, a retired veterinarian and a homemaker, can help you make the most of your stay.

SOUTH CAROLINA

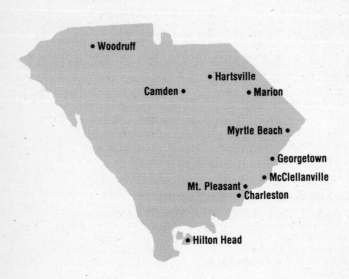

- Woodruff
- Hartsville
- Camden •
- Marion
- Myrtle Beach •
- Georgetown
- McClellanville
- Mt. Pleasant •
- Charleston
- Hilton Head

Candlelight Inn
1904 BROAD STREET, CAMDEN, SOUTH CAROLINA 29020

Tel: **(803) 424-1057**
Hosts: **George and JoAnn Celani**
Location: **30 mi. N of Columbia**
No. of Rooms: **3**
No. of Private Baths: **3**
Double/pb: **$65**
Open: **All year**
Breakfast: **Full**

Credit Cards: **MC, VISA**
Pets: **No**
Children: **Welcome, over 12**
Smoking: **No**
Social Drinking: **Permitted**
Minimum Stay: **2 nights Carolina and Colonial Cup Steeplechase**

Located in Camden's Historic District, Candlelight Inn stands on two acres, surrounded by azaleas and camellias and shaded by a canopy of grand old oaks. A brick drive will guide you to the inn where the glow of candles illuminates the windows. The warm and inviting interior reflects George and JoAnn's interest in needlework, quilts, and antiques. Nearby, guests can enjoy antique shops, Steeplechase facilities, golf courses and fine restaurants. One description by a guest says it all: "Candlelight, comfort, camellias, charm, cookies, conversation, and cooking all add up to the Candlelight Inn."

The Carriage House ✪
1413 LYTTLETON STREET, CAMDEN, SOUTH CAROLINA 29020

Tel: **(803) 432-2430**
Best Time to Call: **9 AM–7 PM**
Hosts: **Appie and Bob Watkins**
Location: **30 mi. N of Columbia**
No. of Rooms: **2**
No. of Private Baths: **1½**
Double/pb: **$65**

Open: **All year**
Breakfast: **Full**
Pets: **No**
Children: **Welcome, over 6**
Smoking: **Permitted**
Social Drinking: **Permitted**

The Carriage House is an antebellum cottage with window boxes and a picket fence. Located in the center of historic Camden, it is within walking distance of tennis, parks, and shops. The guest rooms have twin- or queen-size beds and are decorated with colorful fabrics and lovely antiques. Visitors are welcomed to their quarters with complimentary sherry. Your hosts serve a Southern-style breakfast.

Historic Charleston Bed & Breakfast
60 BROAD STREET, CHARLESTON, SOUTH CAROLINA 29401

Tel: **(803) 722-6606; (800) 743-3583**
Best Time to Call: **9:30 AM–6 PM**
 Mon.–Fri.

Coordinator: **Douglas B. Lee**
States/Regions Covered: **South Carolina**

Descriptive Directory: **Free**
Rates (Single/Double):
  Modest: **$65 / $75**
  Average: **$80 / $95**

Luxury: **$120 / $225**
Credit Cards: **AMEX, MC, VISA**
Minimum Stay: **2 nights Mar. 15—June 15, Oct.**

This port city is one of the most historic in the United States. Through the auspices of this service, you will enjoy your stay in a private home, carriage house, or mansion in a neighborhood of enchanting walled gardens, cobblestoned streets, and moss-draped oak trees. Each home is unique, yet each has a warm and friendly atmosphere provided by a host who sincerely enjoys making guests welcome. All are historic properties dating from 1720 to 1890, yet all are up to date with air-conditioning, phones, and television. Reduced rates may be available for weekly stays. There is a one-time $15 reservation fee charged with each reservation.

Ann Harper's Bed & Breakfast
56 SMITH STREET, CHARLESTON, SOUTH CAROLINA 29401

Tel: **(803) 723-3947**
Best Time to Call: **Before 10 AM; after 6 PM**
Host: **Ann D. Harper**
Location: **1 mi. from I-26**
No. of Rooms: **2**
Max. No. Sharing Bath: **3**
Double/pb: **$65—$75**

Single/pb: **$55—$65**
Open: **All year**
Breakfast: **Full**
Pets: **No**
Children: **Welcome, over 10**
Smoking: **Restricted**
Social Drinking: **Permitted**

This attractive home, circa 1870, is located in Charleston's historic district. The rooms, ideally suited for two friends traveling together, are decorated with wicker pieces and family treasures. Take a moment to relax on the porch or in the intimate walled garden out back. Ann serves a hot, Southern-style breakfast each morning featuring homemade bread and hominy grits. She will gladly direct you to the interesting sights of this historic area. There is a $5 surcharge for one-night stays; no single rates March 15 to June 15.

Country Victorian Bed and Breakfast ✪
105 TRADD STREET, CHARLESTON, SOUTH CAROLINA 29401

Tel: **(803) 577-0682**
Host: **Diane Deardurff Weed**
Location: **96 mi. S of Myrtle Beach**
No. of Rooms: **2**
No. of Private Baths: **2**
Double/pb: **$70—$95**
Single/pb: **$70—$95**

Suites: **$100—$140**
Open: **All year**
Breakfast: **Continental**
Pets: **No**
Children: **Welcome, over 8**
Smoking: **No**
Social Drinking: **Permitted**

As tourists pass in horse-drawn carriages, their eyes are drawn to the beautiful screen doors of this Victorianized house, built in 1820. Rooms have private entrances and are comfortably decorated with antique iron and brass beds, old quilts, and antique oak and wicker furniture. You'll find homemade cookies waiting for you when you arrive. Coffee and tea can be prepared in your room at any time, and snacks are served in the afternoon. Restaurants, churches, antique shops, museums, and art galleries are all within walking distance.

Johnson's Six Orange Street B&B
6 ORANGE STREET, CHARLESTON, SOUTH CAROLINA 29401

Tel: **(803) 722-6122**	Breakfast: **Continental**
Hosts: **Becky and Bill Johnson**	Credit Cards: **No**
Location: **Located in historic district of Charleston**	Pets: **No**
	Children: **Welcome (crib)**
No. of Rooms: **1**	Smoking: **No**
No. of Private Baths: **1**	Social Drinking: **Permitted**
Apartment: **$90**	Foreign Languages: **French, German**
Open: **All year**	

Within Charleston's historical district, Becky and Bill maintain an attached guest house complete with sitting room, efficiency kitchen, upstairs bedroom, and private bath and entrance. The bedroom sleeps three and features an antique sleigh bed plus an iron and brass single bed. A crib is also available for families with an infant. Enjoy scrumptious home-baked coffee cakes, pastries, and breads before you explore the numerous sights and attractions this city has to offer.

1790 House ✪
630 HIGHMARKET STREET, GEORGETOWN, SOUTH CAROLINA 29440

Tel: **(803) 546-4821; (800) 890-7432**	Reduced Rates: **Nov.–Feb. $10 less Sun.–Thurs., 10% seniors**
Best Time to Call: **9 AM–9 PM**	
Hosts: **Patricia and John Wiley**	Breakfast: **Full**
Location: **60 mi. N of Charleston**	Credit Cards: **AMEX, MC, VISA**
No. of Rooms: **6**	Pets: **No**
No. of Private Baths: **6**	Children: **Welcome, over 12**
Double/pb: **$75–$80**	Smoking: **No**
Guest Cottage: **$115**	Social Drinking: **Permitted**
Suites: **$95**	Minimum Stay: **Holiday weekends**
Open: **All year**	

This meticulously restored, 200-year-old Colonial plantation-style inn in Georgetown's historic district has spacious, luxurious rooms, 11-foot ceilings, and seven fireplaces. Slaves once slept in the Slave Quarters, while the elegant Rice Planters and Indigo Rooms have four-poster beds, sitting areas, and fireplaces. Your other options include the Prince George Suite, a hideaway under the eaves; Gabriella's

Library, with built-in bookcases and a fireplace; and the Dependency Cottage, with its private entrance, patio, and spacious bath with a Jacuzzi. Whichever you pick, you can walk to shops, restaurants, and historic sites. Or take a short drive to Myrtle Beach, golfing at the Grand Strand, the Brookgreen Gardens, Pawleys Island, and downtown Charleston.

Shaw House ✪
613 CYPRESS COURT, GEORGETOWN, SOUTH CAROLINA 29440

Tel: **(803) 546-9663**	Open: **All year**
Best Time to Call: **Anytime**	Reduced Rates: **10% after 4th night**
Host: **Mary Shaw**	Breakfast: **Full**
Location: **1 block off Hwy. 17**	Pets: **No**
No. of Rooms: **3**	Children: **Welcome**
No. of Private Baths: **3**	Smoking: **Permitted**
Double/pb: **$45–$60**	Social Drinking: **Permitted**
Single/pb: **$45**	Airport/Station Pickup: **Yes**

Shaw House is a two-story Colonial with a beautiful view of the Willowbank Marsh. Your host is knowledgeable about antiques and has filled the rooms with them. The rocking chairs and cool breeze will tempt you to the porch. Each morning a pot of coffee and Southern-style casserole await you. Fresh fruit and homemade snacks are available all day. The house is within walking distance of the historic district and is near Myrtle Beach, Pawleys Island, golf, tennis, and restaurants.

Missouri Inn B&B ✪
314 EAST HOME AVENUE, HARTSVILLE, SOUTH CAROLINA 29550

Tel: **(803) 383-9553**	Open: **All year**
Best Time to Call: **Noon–9 PM**	Reduced Rates: **Corporate**
Hosts: **Kyle and Kenny Segars, and Lucy Brown**	Breakfast: **Full**
	Credit Cards: **AMEX, MC, VISA**
Location: **28 mi. NW of Florence**	Pets: **No**
No. of Rooms: **5**	Children: **Welcome, over 10**
No. of Private Baths: **5**	Smoking: **Permitted**
Double/pb: **$85**	Social Drinking: **Permitted**
Single/pb: **$75**	

An elegant Southern mansion built around the turn of the century and completely renovated in 1990, the Missouri Inn offers discriminating guests exceptional peace, quiet, and privacy in a small, luxurious setting. Located in Hartsville's official historic district, the inn stands opposite the lovely Coker College campus, on about five acres landscaped with stately trees and flowering shrubs. The distinctively furnished rooms not only have telephones and TVs, but terry robes, bath sheets, towel warmers, hair dryers, and fresh floral arrangements. Amenities include afternoon tea and complimentary beverages at all times.

Ambiance Bed & Breakfast
8 WREN DRIVE, HILTON HEAD, SOUTH CAROLINA 29928

Tel: **(803) 671-4981**
Host: **Marny Kridel Daubenspeck**
Location: **40 mi. from I-95, Exit 28**
No. of Rooms: **2**
No. of Private Baths: **2**
Double/pb: **$75**
Single/pb: **$70**

Open: **All year**
Breakfast: **Continental**
Pets: **No**
Children: **Welcome, over 12**
Smoking: **No**
Social Drinking: **Permitted**

Marny welcomes guests to sunny Hilton Head Island. This cypress home, nestled in subtropical surroundings, is in Sea Pines Plantation. Ambiance reflects the hostess's interior decorating business by the same name. All the amenities of Hilton Head are offered in a contemporary, congenial atmosphere. The climate is favorable year-round for all sports. Ambiance is across the street from a beautiful beach and the Atlantic Ocean.

Montgomery's Grove ✪
408 HARLEE STREET, MARION, SOUTH CAROLINA 29571

Tel: **(803) 423-5220**
Hosts: **Coreen and Rick Roberts**

Location: **20 mi. E of Florence**
No. of Rooms: **4**

No. of Private Baths: **2**
Max. No. Sharing Bath: **4**
Double/pb: **$70**
Single/pb: **$60**
Double/sb: **$70**
Single/sb: **$60**
Open: **All year**
Reduced Rates: **10% weekly; 10% seniors**

Breakfast: **Full**
Other Meals: **Available**
Pets: **No**
Children: **Welcome**
Smoking: **No**
Social Drinking: **Permitted**

Nestled among five acres of century-old trees and gardens, Montgomery's Grove is a beautiful Victorian mansion known for its exceptional architectural features. Dramatic fourteen-foot archways and elaborate woodwork greet all guests. Yet it is easy to relax in the five beautifully decorated rooms, on the wraparound porches, or with a stroll through the woods. Walk beneath the Spanish moss to historic downtown Marion, or travel just thirty minutes to Myrtle Beach. Only 15 minutes from I-95, Montgomery's Grove is the perfect midway stopping point to and from Florida. Visit Marion, the pretty little town on the way to the beach. It'll be a visit you won't forget.

Laurel Hill Plantation ☉
8913 NORTH HIGHWAY 17, P.O. BOX 190, McCLELLANVILLE, SOUTH CAROLINA 29458

Tel: **(803) 887-3708**
Best Time to Call: **Before 9 PM**
Hosts: **Jackie and Lee Morrison**
Location: **30 mi. N of Charleston**
No. of Rooms: **4**
No. of Private Baths: **4**
Double/pb: **$75–$85**

Single/pb: **$65–$75**
Open: **All year**
Breakfast: **Full**
Pets: **No**
Children: **Welcome, over 6**
Smoking: **No**
Social Drinking: **Permitted**

The original Laurel Hill, an 1850s plantation house listed on the National Register of Historic Places, was destroyed by Hurricane Hugo in 1989. Nestled in a nook by a picturesque tidal creek, the spacious reconstruction retains the romance of the past while affording the convenience of the contemporary. Wraparound porches provide a sweeping panorama of the Atlantic Ocean and Cape Romain's salt marches, islands, and waterways. Four charming guest rooms feature fascinating views of the landscape and are furnished with carefully chosen primitives and antiques reflecting the renowned hospitality of South Carolina's low country.

Sunny Meadows
1459 VENNING ROAD, MT. PLEASANT, SOUTH CAROLINA 29464

Tel: **(803) 884-7062**
Best Time to Call: **Afternoons through 10 PM**
Hosts: **Charles and Agnes Houston**

Location: **5 mi. E of Charleston**
No. of Rooms: **2**
No. of Private Baths: **2**
Double/pb: **$65–$75**

Open: **All year**
Breakfast: **Full**
Pets: **No**

Children: **Welcome, infants, over 6**
Smoking: **No**
Social Drinking: **Permitted**

Situated on three acres of beautiful grounds, this two-story Southern Colonial is only fifteen minutes from historic Charleston and ten minutes from the beaches. Citadel College and the College of Charleston can be reached in twenty minutes and Southern University in thirty minutes. Guest rooms are located away from family living quarters and are beautifully decorated with antiques from the 18th century or reproductions. Each room has TV, private bath, and telephone. One room has a king four-poster bed and a double, the other room has a double four-poster bed. Strata and cheese-stuffed French toast with fruit topping are some of the breakfast specialties.

Brustman House
400 25TH AVENUE SOUTH, MYRTLE BEACH, SOUTH CAROLINA 29577

Tel: **(803) 448-7699**
Best Time to Call: **Early evening**
Host: **Dr. Wendell C. Brustman**
Location: **90 mi. N of Charleston**
No. of Rooms: **4**
No. of Private Baths: **4**
Double/pb: **$55–$85**
Single/pb: **$50–$80**
Suites: **$80–$120**

Open: **All year**
Reduced Rates: **Extended stay; Oct. 1–Mar. 31**
Breakfast: **Full**
Pets: **No**
Children: **Welcome, over 10**
Smoking: **No**
Social Drinking: **Permitted**
Airport/Station Pickup: **Yes**

Maybe you can't have it all, but Brustman House comes close. This Georgian-style home is two short blocks from the beach, and without leaving the almost two-acre, tree-studded property you can admire the fresh herb garden or have a tête-à-tête on the glider in the rose garden gazebo. Located nearby are golf courses, seafront restaurants, discount shops, and country music theaters. Afternoon tea includes wines, waters, and sweets served on exquisite Scandinavian dinnerware. Sleep late in your quiet room, its snug bed warmed by a down comforter. The Rosewood Room has a Jacuzzi tub for two. The breakfast menu includes healthful specialties, such as ten-grain buttermilk pancakes.

Serendipity, An Inn
407 71ST AVENUE NORTH, MYRTLE BEACH, SOUTH CAROLINA 29572

Tel: **(803) 449-5268; (800) 762-3229**
Best Time to Call: **8 AM–10 PM**
Hosts: **Terry and Sheila Johnson**
Location: **60 mi. from Rte. 95**

No. of Rooms: **14**
No. of Private Baths: **14**
Double/pb: **$67–$92**
Suites: **$78–$110**

Open: **Jan.–Nov.**
Breakfast: **Continental**
Credit Cards: **MC, VISA**
Pets: **No**

Children: **Welcome**
Smoking: **Permitted**
Social Drinking: **Permitted**

Serendipity is a Spanish Mission–style inn surrounded by lush tropical plants and flowers. The setting is peaceful, the street is quiet, and the ocean is less than 300 yards away. Bedrooms are highlighted with antiques drawing from Art Deco, Oriental, wicker, and pine motifs. The Garden Room is the place for a generous breakfast of homemade breads, fresh fruit, eggs, and cereal. Your hosts invite you to use the heated pool and spa, play shuffleboard, Ping-Pong, or just share a quiet moment beside the patio fountain. Myrtle Beach is known for its fine restaurants, but the Johnsons have a gas grill if you want to do your own cooking. Terry and Sheila will gladly direct you to nearby shops, fishing villages, golf courses, miles of beaches, and music theaters.

Nicholls-Crook Plantation House ✪
120 PLANTATION DRIVE, WOODRUFF, SOUTH CAROLINA 29388

Tel: **(803) 476-8820**
Best Time to Call: **9 AM–9 PM**
Host: **Suzanne Brown**
Location: **12 mi. S of Spartanburg**
No. of Rooms: **2**
No. of Private Baths: **2**
Max. No. Sharing Bath: **4**
Double/pb: **$85**
Single/pb: **$75**
Suites: **$150**
Open: **All year**

Reduced Rates: **Available**
Breakfast: **Continental**
Other Meals: **Available**
Credit Cards: **AMEX**
Pets: **Sometimes**
Children: **Welcome, over 8**
Smoking: **No**
Social Drinking: **Permitted**
Airport Pickup: **Yes**
Foreign Languages: **French, Spanish**

Surround yourself with the atmosphere of times gone by in this Georgian-style plantation house built in 1793, and listed on the National Register of Historic Places. Delight in the historical ambiance enhanced by antique period furnishings, charming gardens, and the white rock courtyard. A bountiful breakfast will add to the pleasures of your visit. Guest rooms are cozy and inviting. Relax in the parlor, play an old-fashioned board game in the tavern room, or spend your time exploring the many interesting attractions while in the area.

TENNESSEE

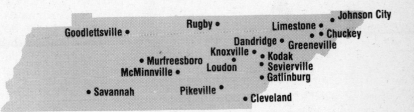

Goodlettsville •
Rugby •
Limestone •
Johnson City •
• Chuckey
Dandridge • • Greeneville
Knoxville •
• Kodak
• Murfreesboro
McMinnville •
Loudon
• Sevierville
• Gatlinburg
• Savannah
Pikeville •
• Cleveland

Harmony Hill Inn ✪
85 PLEASANT HILL ROAD, CHUCKEY, TENNESSEE 37641

Tel: (615) 257-3893
Best Time to Call: 8 AM–10 PM
Host: **Dodie Melton**
Location: **8 mi. NE of Greeneville, and 20 mi. from Jonesborough**
No. of Rooms: 2
No. of Private Baths: 2
Double/pb: **$55**

Single/pb: **$45**
Open: **All year**
Breakfast: **Full**
Pets: **Sometimes**
Children: **Welcome**
Smoking: **No**
Social Drinking: **No**

Located on Horse Creek in the foothills of the Appalachian Mountains, this two-story 1850 farmhouse has a soothing, country atmosphere. Dodie, a registered nurse, is also a skilled woodworker and has renovated much of the house herself. After a full breakfast featuring her homemade sourdough bread—special diets considered upon request—take an easy drive to some of the area's attractions, such as

Davy Crockett's birthplace, historic Jonesborough, Andrew Johnson's home and tailor shop, Bristol Caverns, Roan Mountain's rhododendron gardens, Smoky Mountain National Park, Dollywood, and North Carolina's Hot Springs Spa. For your greater relaxation, therapeutic massage is available by appointment.

Chadwick House ✪
2766 MICHIGAN AVENUE RD NORTH EAST, CLEVELAND, TENNESSEE 37312

Tel: **(615) 339-2407**	Open: **All year**
Host: **Winnie A. Chadwick**	Reduced Rates: **10% seniors**
Location: **35 mi. N of Chattanooga**	Breakfast: **Full**
No. of Rooms: **3**	Other Meals: **Available**
No. of Private Baths: **1**	Pets: **No**
Max. No. Sharing Bath: **4**	Children: **Welcome**
Double/pb: **$52**	Smoking: **Permitted**
Double/sb: **$43**	Social Drinking: **Permitted**
Single/sb: **$35**	Airport/Station Pickup: **Yes**

White shutters and trim accent the multicolored bricks of this handsome ranch home just a half hour from Chattanooga. White-water rafting, Red Clay's historic Indian meeting grounds, and Cherokee National Forest are close by, and golfing and tennis are available right in Cleveland. In their spare moments B&B guests can watch the squirrels and birds in the back garden or relax by the fireplace with a glass of locally made wine. Winnie's full country breakfasts include homemade rolls and muffins.

Sugarfork Bed & Breakfast ✪
743 GARRETT ROAD, DANDRIDGE, TENNESSEE 37725

Tel: (615) 397-7327; (800) 487-5634
Hosts: Mary and Sam Price
Location: 30 mi. E of Knoxville
No. of Rooms: 3
No. of Private Baths: 1
Max. No. Sharing Bath: 4
Double/pb: $65
Single/pb: $55
Double/sb: $55

Single/sb: $45
Open: All year
Reduced Rates: Available
Breakfast: Full
Credit Cards: MC, VISA
Pets: No
Children: Welcome, over 6
Smoking: Permitted
Social Drinking: Permitted

Guests will appreciate the tranquil setting of Sugarfork Bed & Break-fast, located on Douglas Lake in the foothills of the Great Smoky Mountains. Your hosts have private lake access and their own floating dock. Swimming, waterskiing, and boating are the main warm-weather activities here, while fishing is a year-round sport. On chilly mornings sit by the stone fireplace in the downstairs common room, or study the lake and mountains from the wall of windows upstairs. A hearty breakfast featuring homemade biscuits, country ham, and Mary's own special egg casseroles is served in the spacious dining room or, weather permitting, on the deck.

Butcher House in the Mountains ✪
1520 GARRETT LANE, GATLINBURG, TENNESSEE 37738

Tel: (615) 436-9457
Best Time to Call: 10 AM–9 PM
Hosts: Hugh and Gloria Butcher
Location: 50 mi. SE of Knoxville
No. of Rooms: 5
No. of Private Baths: 5
Double/pb: $79–$109
Open: All year
Reduced Rates: $10 less after 2nd
   night, Mon.–Thurs.

Breakfast: Full
Credit Cards: AMEX, MC, VISA
Pets: No
Children: Welcome, over 12
Smoking: No
Social Drinking: Permitted
Minimum Stay: Weekends
Foreign Languages: Italian

The ambiance at Butcher House is one of elegance, warmth, and beauty. Hugh and Gloria's years of collecting have resulted in a home filled with one-of-a-kind antique treasures. Guest rooms are decorated with unique linens and furniture from various eras. Nearby attractions include Pigeon Forge, Dollywood, and Smoky Mountains National Park. Guests can enjoy hiking, fishing, skiing, golfing, or visiting the many crafts shops. Your hosts will send you on your way after a gourmet breakfast that may consist of eggs Sebastian, Italian crêpes, or eggs cardamom.

Olde English Tudor Inn ○

135 WEST HOLLY RIDGE ROAD, GATLINBURG, TENNESSEE 37738

Tel: (615) 436-7760	Open: **All year**
Best Time to Call: **11 AM–9 PM**	Reduced Rates: **10% seniors**
Hosts: **Kathy and Larry Schuh**	Breakfast: **Full**
Location: **45 mi. SE of Knoxville**	Credit Cards: **MC, VISA**
No. of Rooms: **7**	Pets: **No**
No. of Private Baths: **7**	Children: **Welcome**
Double/pb: **$69–$79**	Smoking: **No**
Single/pb: **$65**	Social Drinking: **Permitted**
Suites: **$89–$99**	Airport Pickup: **Yes**

From the Olde English Tudor Inn's ideal downtown location, it's just a few minutes' walk to the attractions of Gatlinburg, and only a brief drive to Dollywood, Craft Community, outlet malls, and Great Smoky National Park. Handsomely decorated bedrooms have cable TV with HBO. Guests are invited to relax in the large, comfortably furnished community room with a TV/VCR and free-standing wood burning stove, or enjoy the peaceful seclusion of the rear patio. Generous breakfasts typically include fresh fruit, pancakes or French toast, and eggs, bacon, sausage, or ham. Make sure to save room for freshly baked breads with jams and jellies. Kathy and Larry want your visit to be memorable and will be happy to assist you with your touring, dining, and shopping questions.

The Drake Farm on Lumsley Creek

P.O. BOX 875, GOODLETTSVILLE, TENNESSEE 37070

Tel: (615) 859-2425; (800) 586-7539 reservations only	Open: **All year**
	Breakfast: **Full**
Best Time to Call: **10 AM–Noon**	Credit Cards: **AMEX, MC, VISA**
Host: **Rose Mary Drake**	Pets: **Sometimes**
Location: **15 mi. NE of Nashville**	Children: **Welcome, by arrangement**
No. of Rooms: **2**	Smoking: **No**
Max. No. Sharing Bath: **4**	Social Drinking: **Permitted**
Double/sb: **$55**	Minimum Stay: **Holiday weekends**
Single/sb: **$45**	Airport/Station Pickup: **Yes**

Guests frequently comment on the peaceful surroundings of this circa 1850 antebellum Greek Revival farmhouse. Since surviving a Civil War skirmish, the farmhouse has been maintained by the Drake family for five generations. The house is decorated with antiques and each guest room has a working fireplace. The location is perfect for the tourist or the business traveler. You can enjoy the seclusion of the farm, yet you are close enough to city attractions.

Woodshire B&B ✪
600 WOODSHIRE DRIVE, GOODLETTSVILLE, TENNESSEE 37072

Tel: **(615) 859-7369**
Best Time to Call: **Before 9 AM; after
  6 PM**
Hosts: **Beverly and John Grayson**
Location: **11 mi. N of Nashville**
No. of Rooms: **2**
No. of Private Baths: **2**
Double/pb: **$50**
Single/pb: **$40**

Guest Cabin: **$60–$70**
Open: **Feb. 1–Dec. 31**
Breakfast: **Continental**
Pets: **No**
Children: **Welcome**
Smoking: **No**
Social Drinking: **No**
Airport/Station Pickup: **Yes**

A blue clapboard house inspired by New England saltboxes, Woodshire B&B is 20 minutes from downtown Nashville and its attractions—Opryland Park, Andrew Jackson's Hermitage, and the homes and museums of country music stars. Beverly will gladly tell you the stories behind the antique family furniture. She's a retired art teacher, and as you look around you'll see her paintings and weavings, and John's woodcrafts. Continental breakfast features homemade preserves, breads, and waffles.

Hilltop House Bed and Breakfast Inn ✪
6 SANFORD CIRCLE, GREENEVILLE, TENNESSEE 37743

Tel: **(615) 639-8202**
Best Time to Call: **5 PM–7 PM**
Host: **Denise M. Ashworth**

Location: **7 mi. S. of Greeneville**
No. of Rooms: **3**
No. of Private Baths: **3**

Double/pb: **$75**
Single/pb: **$70**
Open: **All year**
Reduced Rates: **Available**
Breakfast: **Full**
Other Meals: **Available**

Credit Cards: **AMEX, MC, VISA**
Pets: **No**
Children: **Welcome, over 3 years**
Smoking: **No**
Social Drinking: **Permitted**
Airport/Station Pickup: **Yes**

Hilltop House is a 1920s manor house on a hillside above the Noli-chucky River Valley, with the Appalachian Mountains in the background. All the guest rooms, which are furnished in eighteenth-century English antiques and period reproductions, have mountain views; two have verandas. In keeping with her British birth, the innkeeper sets out a proper English tea every afternoon. The family-style breakfast consists of fruit, cereal, egg dishes, and homemade biscuits or muffins. Then it's time to explore the great outdoors: white-water rafting, hiking, biking, trout fishing, golfing, hunting, and bird-watching are among your options. Cherokee National Forest is within striking distance, as are the Great Smoky Mountains and the Blue Ridge Parkway.

Natchez Trace B&B Reservation Service ○
P.O. BOX 193, HAMPSHIRE, TENNESSEE 38461

Tel: **(800) 377-2770**
Best Time to Call: **Evening; weekends**
Coordinator: **Kay Jones**
States/Regions Covered:
   Alabama—Florence, Cherokee;
   Mississippi—Church Hill, Corinth,
   French Camp, Jackson, Kosciusko,
   Lorman, Natchez, Port Gibson,
   Vicksburg; Tennessee—Columbia,

Culleoka, Fairview, Franklin,
Hohenwald, Leiper's Fork, Nashville
Descriptive Directory of B&Bs: **Free**
Rates (Single/Double):
   Modest: **$55 / $65**
   Average: **$70 / $80**
   Luxury: **$90 / $115**
Credit Cards: **MC, VISA**

Kay's reservation service is unique in that the homes are all convenient to the Natchez Trace National Parkway, the historic Nashville-to-Natchez route that was first designated by President Thomas Jefferson. The parkway is known for both its natural beauty and the charming Southern towns along the way. Kay can help you plan your trip and give you access to homes ranging from rustic, woodsy sites to fine antebellum mansions. Call her for a free list of homes, as well as literature about the Natchez Trace.

Hart House Bed and Breakfast ○
207 EAST HOLSTON AVENUE, JOHNSON CITY, TENNESSEE 37601

Tel: **(615) 926-3147**
Hosts: **Francis and Vanessa Gingras**
Location: **90 mi. NE of Knoxville**
No. of Rooms: **3**

No. of Private Baths: **3**
Double/pb: **$60**
Single/pb: **$50**
Open: **All year**

Reduced Rates: **10% seniors**
Breakfast: **Full**
Credit Cards: **MC, VISA**
Pets: **Sometimes**

Children: **Welcome**
Smoking: **No**
Social Drinking: **Permitted**

Hart House is named after the original owner of this 1910 Dutch Colonial, which Francis and Vanessa have filled with antiques and collectibles. Johnson City is located in the heart of upper northeast Tennessee, an area brimming with both notable sites and scenic beauty. For history buffs, Jonesborough, the oldest town in the state, is five miles away, and those who love the great outdoors—camping, hiking, fishing, white-water rafting—will find plenty to do here. Each morning, guests wake up to an elegant breakfast of fresh fruit, homemade muffins, eggs, and fresh brewed coffee.

Windy Hill B&B ✪
1031 WEST PARK DRIVE, KNOXVILLE, TENNESSEE 37909

Tel: **(615) 690-1488**
Host: **Mary M. Mitchell**
Location: **1.6 mi. from I-75-40, Exit 380**
No. of Rooms: **1**
No. of Private Baths: **1**
Double/pb: **$40**
Single/pb: **$35**

Open: **All year**
Breakfast: **Continental**
Pets: **Sometimes**
Children: **Welcome**
Smoking: **Permitted**
Social Drinking: **Permitted**
Airport/Station Pickup: **Yes**

Located in a pleasant, quiet neighborhood with numerous shade trees, Mary's B&B is air-conditioned and has a private entrance with no steps to climb. There's a double bed and a rollaway is available. Breakfast features homemade muffins or cinnamon rolls with coffee. Windy Hill is convenient to the University of Tennessee; Oak Ridge is only a 15-minute drive while Great Smoky Mountains National Park is an hour away.

Grandma's House ✪
734 POLLARD ROAD, KODAK, TENNESSEE 37764

Tel: **(615) 933-3512; reservations:**
  (800) 676-3512
Best Time to Call: **Anytime**
Hosts: **Charlie and Hilda Hickman**
Location: **8 mi. N of Sevierville; 2 mi.**
  from I-40, Exit 407
No. of Rooms: **3**
No. of Private Baths: **3**
Double/pb: **$75**

Single/pb: **$50**
Open: **All year**
Breakfast: **Full**
Credit Cards: **MC, VISA**
Pets: **No**
Children: **Welcome, over 12**
Smoking: **No**
Social Drinking: **No**

Grandma's House is located on a quiet country lane in Dumplin Valley at the base of the Great Smoky Mountains. Nearby attractions include: Great Smoky Mountains National Park, Dollywood in Pigeon Forge, Museum of Science and Energy in Oak Ridge, and much more. The farm-style house is furnished with country antiques, handmade quilts, and interesting family heirlooms. The hearty farm breakfast features buttermilk biscuits, Hilda's own homemade jams and jellies, and the house specialty, Apple Stack Cake. Both hosts are native East Tennesseans with lots of down-home friendliness to share with their guests. Death by Design Murder Mystery weekends are available in November, January, February, and March.

Snapp Inn B&B ✪
1990 DAVY CROCKETT PARK ROAD, LIMESTONE, TENNESSEE 37681

Tel: **(423) 257-2482**	Single/pb: **$40**
Best Time to Call: **Before 10 AM; after**	Open: **All year**
7 PM	Breakfast: **Full**
Hosts: **Dan and Ruth Dorgan**	Pets: **Welcome**
Location: **4 mi. from Rte. 11 E**	Children: **Welcome (one at a time)**
No. of Rooms: **2**	Smoking: **No**
No. of Private Baths: **2**	Social Drinking: **Permitted**
Double/pb: **$50**	Airport/Station Pickup: **Yes**

Built in 1815 and situated in farm country, this Federal brick home has lovely mountain views. The house is decorated with antiques, including a Victorian reed organ. Now retired, Ruth and Dan have the time to pursue their interests in antiques restoration, history, needlework, and bluegrass music. It is an easy walk to Davy Crockett Birthplace State Park, and 15 minutes to historic Jonesboro or the Andrew Johnson Home in Greeneville. A swimming pool, golf, and fishing are close by. You are welcome to use the laundry facilities, television, and pool table.

The Mason Place ✪
600 COMMERCE STREET, LOUDON, TENNESSEE 37774

Tel: **(615) 458-3921**	Breakfast: **Full**
Hosts: **Bob and Donna Siewert**	Credit Cards: **MC, VISA**
Location: **25 mi. SW of Knoxville**	Pets: **No**
No. of Rooms: **5**	Children: **No**
No. of Private Baths: **5**	Smoking: **No**
Double/pb: **$96**	Social Drinking: **Permitted**
Open: **All year**	Airport/Station Pickup: **Yes**
Reduced Rates: **Long-term stays**	

This impeccably restored 1865 plantation home is nestled in a quaint Civil War town along the Tennessee River. Civil War bullets and artifacts are still being found on the property's three acres of lawns and gardens. Inside, Mason Place offers quality lodging and an opportunity to wander back to yesteryear. A grand entrance hall, ten working fireplaces, authentic feather beds, period antiques, a Grecian swimming pool, a gazebo, and a wisteria-covered arbor are only a few of the amenities at your disposal. Bountiful breakfasts are included. Cheese plates, local wine, and picnic lunches are available by prior arrangement.

Falcon Manor Bed and Breakfast ✪
2645 FAULKNER SPRINGS ROAD, McMINNVILLE, TENNESSEE 37110

Tel: **(615) 668-4444**	Hosts: **George and Charlien McGlothin**
Best Time to Call: **Anytime**	Location: **72 mi. SE of Nashville**

No. of Rooms: **5**
No. of Private Baths: **1**
Max. No. Sharing Bath: **4**
Double/pb: **$85**
Single/pb: **$85**
Double/sb: **$75**
Single/sb: **$75**
Open: **All year**

Reduced Rates: **$5 off per day, 3 days
  or more**
Breakfast: **Full**
Credit Cards: **MC, VISA**
Pets: **No**
Children: **Welcome, over 12**
Smoking: **No**
Social Drinking: **Permitted**

This historic Victorian mansion re-creates the romance of the 1890s.
Relax in the friendly warmth of this fine old house and savor the
luxury of its museum-quality antiques. The huge gingerbread veranda
is well stocked with rocking chairs and shaded by giant trees. Falcon
Manor is a favorite for couples celebrating anniversaries. It's also the
ideal base for a middle Tennessee vacation—halfway between Nashville and Chattanooga and just thirty minutes from four state parks.
McMinnville is "the nursery capital of the world" and the home of
America's second largest cave. George left a career in retail manage-
ment to spend four years restoring the house, while Charlien pitched
in during time off from her job as a NASA public affairs writer. They
love sharing stories about Falcon Manor's history and their adventures
bringing it back to life.

Clardy's Guest House ✪
435 EAST MAIN STREET, MURFREESBORO, TENNESSEE 37130

Tel: **(615) 893-6030**
Best Time to Call: **After 4 PM**

Hosts: **Robert and Barbara Deaton**
Location: **2 mi. from I-24**

No. of Rooms: **3**
No. of Private Baths: **2**
Max. No. Sharing Bath: **4**
Double/pb: **$48**
Single/pb: **$38**
Double/sb: **$38**
Single/sb: **$32**

Open: **All year**
Breakfast: **Continental**
Pets: **Sometimes**
Children: **Welcome (crib)**
Smoking: **Restricted**
Social Drinking: **Permitted**

This Romanesque-style Victorian dates back to 1898. The 20 rooms are filled with antiques; with 40 antiques dealers in town, you can guess what Murfreesboro is best known for. The world championship horse show at Shelbyville is 30 minutes away. Your hosts will be glad to advise on local tours and can direct you to the home of Grand Ole Opry, one hour away in Nashville, and fine eating places. Middle Tennessee State University is close by.

Quilts and Croissants
2231 RILEY ROAD, MURFREESBORO, TENNESSEE 37130

Tel: **(615) 893-2933**
Hosts: **Robert and Mary Jane Roose**
Location: **28 mi. S of Nashville**
No. of Rooms: **1**
No. of Private Baths: **1**
Double/pb: **$40**
Single/pb: **$35**

Open: **All year**
Reduced Rates: **Seniors**
Breakfast: **Continental**
Pets: **No**
Smoking: **No**
Social Drinking: **Permitted**

This unusual home, constructed out of logs hewn in 1834, combines old-fashioned country charm and modern efficiency. Stencils and folk art ornament the walls of the guest room, and patchwork quilts drape the twin beds. Don't be fooled by the appearance of the quaint ice-box in the kitchenette—it's really a refrigerator stocked with juice, breakfast foods, and soda. Quilts and Croissants is less than an hour's drive from Nashville, but your hosts can steer you to the notable sights of Murfreesboro, such as Oaklands Mansion (a mid-19th-century landmark) and Canonsburgh (a restored Civil War–era village). Breakfast here is a do-it-yourself affair; take whatever you want from the refrigerator.

Bed and Breakfast Adventures ✪
P.O. BOX 150586, NASHVILLE, TENNESSEE 37215

Tel: **(615) 383-6611; (800) 947-7404**
Best Time to Call: **9 AM–6 PM
Mon.–Sat.**
Coordinator: **Carol Montgomery**
States/Regions Covered:
   **Chattanooga, Clarksville, Franklin,
   Gatlinburg, Jackson, Knoxville,**

   **Memphis, Monteagle, Nashville,
   Townsend**
Descriptive Directory of B&Bs: **$1**
Rates (Single/Double):
   Modest: **$40–$50**
   Average: **$50–$85**
   Luxury: **$85–$135**

| Credit Cards: **AMEX, DC, DISC, MC, VISA** | Minimum Stay: **In some areas** |

Carol's worldwide travels, as well as her experience in hosting and entertaining business associates, relatives, and friends, has given her insight into people's needs and wants when traveling. The ambience of individual bed and breakfasts is very important, so Carol's policy is to see every bed and breakfast she represents, and to meet the owners/innkeepers. Her hosts are warm and gracious, knowledgeable of their area, and ready to help you have a memorable experience in Tennessee! Whether you're looking for that secluded hideaway, romantic weekend, or convenience to all the activities in a particular area, Carol will give you personalized service.

Fall Creek Falls Bed & Breakfast
ROUTE 3, BOX 298B, PIKEVILLE, TENNESSEE 37367

Tel: **(423) 881-5494**	Open: **All year (except Jan.)**
Hosts: **Doug and Rita Pruett**	Breakfast: **Full**
Location: **50 mi. N of Chattanooga**	Pets: **No**
No. of Rooms: **7**	Children: **Welcome, over 10**
No. of Private Baths: **7**	Smoking: **No**
Double/pb: **$68–$118**	Social Drinking: **Permitted**
Single/pb: **$65**	Minimum Stay: **2 nights, weekends**
Suite: **$125**	**and holidays**

Enjoy the relaxing atmosphere of a new country manor home on forty acres of rolling hillside one mile from the nationally acclaimed Fall Creek Falls State Resort Park. Beautiful guest rooms have pickled oak floors and antique furniture with two common sitting areas. Lodging includes a full breakfast served in a cozy country kitchen or an elegant dining room. Doug enjoys grouse hunting and trout fishing and is a licensed Tennessee building contractor. Rita is an insurance executive who enjoys bargain hunting and antique auctions. Touring, dining, and shopping information is always available.

Clear Fork Farm ✪
328 SHIRLEY FORD ROAD, RUGBY, TENNESSEE 37852

Tel: **(615) 628-2967**	Open: **All year**
Best Time to Call: **Anytime**	Breakfast: **Continental**
Hosts: **Ted and Barbara Lankford**	Pets: **No**
Location: **65 mi NW of Knoxville**	Children: **Welcome, over 12**
No. of Rooms: **3**	Smoking: **No**
No. of Private Baths: **3**	Social Drinking: **Permitted**
Double/pb: **$65**	

This large brick farmhouse, sitting high above the Clear Fork River on 200 acres, is furnished with antiques and period reproductions, with four fireplaces for guests to enjoy. Bedrooms contain locally-made quilts. A private sitting room is located off the bedrooms upstairs, and a large-screen television and VCR is available in the den. Admire the view from two large porches; one is screened with an adjacent hot tub. Continental breakfast is served on antique china in the dining room with its own fireplace. Hiking, biking, and horseback riding trails are on the property, as well as in the adjoining park, Big South Fork National Recreational Area. A four-stall horse barn is provided for your horse. Historical Rugby, an English settlement built in the 1880s by social reformer Thomas Hughes, is three miles away.

Ross House Bed and Breakfast ✪
504 MAIN STREET, P.O. BOX 398, SAVANNAH, TENNESSEE 38372

Tel: **(901) 925-3974; (800) 467-3174**	Credit Cards: **MC, VISA**
Best Time to Call: **9 AM–5 PM**	Pets: **No**
Hosts: **John and Harriet Ross**	Children: **Welcome, over 10**
Location: **110 mi. E of Memphis**	Smoking: **No**
Suites: **$65–$150**	Social Drinking: **Permitted**
Open: **All year**	Foreign Languages: **French, Spanish**
Breakfast: **Continental**	

Part of Savannah's National Register Historic District, which contains residences from the late 1860s to the 1920s, this B&B is a Neoclassical brick house built in 1908 by John's grandparents. Inside you'll see the original owners' furniture, books, paintings, and photographs. It is a short walk to the Cherry Mansion and Tennessee River and a short drive to Shiloh National Military Park and Pickwick Lake, for fishing and boating. If you'd rather paddle your canoe, take the 45-minute drive to the Buffalo River. John practices law next door where his grandfather once did, but when time permits, he accompanies guests on bicycle tours. Harriet is a full-time hostess.

Blue Mountain Mist Country Inn & Cottages
1811 PULLEN ROAD, SEVIERVILLE, TENNESSEE 37862

Tel: **(800) 497-2335; (615) 428-2335**	Suites: **$95–$115**
Best Time to Call: **10 AM–9 PM**	Open: **All year**
Hosts: **Norman and Sarah Ball**	Breakfast: **Full**
Location: **4 mi. E of Pigeon Forge**	Pets: **No**
No. of Rooms: **12**	Children: **Welcome (2 rooms)**
No. of Private Baths: **12**	Smoking: **No**
Double/pb: **$79**	Social Drinking: **Permitted**
Guest Cottage: **$125**	Minimum Stay: **2–3 nights**

This Victorian-style farmhouse inn with country cottages is located on 60 acres in the foothills of the Great Smoky Mountains. Away from the congestion you can enjoy beautiful views of rolling meadows and mountains while rocking on the huge front porch. The Inn is filled with country antiques, handmade quilts and local art. In the morning awake to a hearty Tennessee breakfast, in the evening indulge in a delicious homemade desert. Each cottage has a large Jacuzzi and a fireplace designed for a peaceful romantic getaway. Nearby attractions include Gatlinburg, the Crafts Community, Pigeon Forge and Dollywood.

Calico Inn ✪
757 RANCH WAY, SEVIERVILLE, TENNESSEE 37862

Tel: **(423) 428-3833**
Best Time to Call: **Evenings**
Hosts: **Lill and Jim Katzbeck**
Location: **35 mi. N of Knoxville**
No. of Rooms: **2**
No. of Private Baths: **2**
Double/pb: **$85–$89**
Open: **All year**
Reduced Rates: **10% Jan.–Feb., 15% weekly**

Breakfast: **Full**
Pets: **No**
Children: **Welcome, over 6**
Smoking: **No**
Social Drinking: **Permitted**
Minimum Stay: **2 nights holiday weekends**

Nestled among trees atop a peaceful ridge, Calico Inn offers guests a serene panoramic view of the Smoky Mountains. Lillian and Jim invite you to start your day with a delightful breakfast; quiche, egg strata, biscuits and gravy, homemade Amish bread and muffins may be served. Whether you choose to spend the day at Dollywood or go hiking in the mountains, you're only minutes from all the sightseeing, shopping, and entertainment the area has to offer. Best of all, you'll take pleasure in knowing the quiet Calico Inn awaits you each evening.

Little Greenbrier Lodge ✪
3685 LYON SPRINGS ROAD, SEVIERVILLE, TENNESSEE 37862

Tel: **(615) 429-2500**
Best Time to Call: **10 AM**
Hosts: **Barbara and David Matthews**
Location: **9 mi. W of Pigeon Forge**
No. of Rooms: **11**
No. of Private Baths: **8**
Max. No. Sharing Bath: **4**
Double/pb: **$95–$110**
Double/sb: **$75**
Single/sb: **$55**
Open: **All year, Jan. 1–Apr. 15th weekends only**

Reduced Rates: **Available**
Breakfast: **Full**
Credit Cards: **DISC, MC, VISA**
Pets: **No**
Children: **Welcome, over 12**
Smoking: **No**
Social Drinking: **Permitted**
Minimum Stay: **2 nights weekends**
Airport Pickup: **Yes**

Little Greenbrier Lodge is one of the oldest lodging facilities bordering the Great Smoky Mountains National Park. Built in 1939 and completely refurbished, the lodge still maintains its historic look. Rooms are furnished with oriental rugs, antique furniture, beautiful comforters and linens, and all have full access to relaxing decks that overlook tranquil Wears Valley. As you head to the dining room in the morning you will enjoy the aroma of hot pecan rolls; other breakfast specialties include fresh fruit, juices, cereals, Barb's famous French toast casseroles and her egg soufflés. You'll be left with feelings of friendship and welcome spending time with Barbara and David.

Von-Bryan Inn ✪
2402 HATCHER MOUNTAIN ROAD, SEVIERVILLE, TENNESSEE 37862

Tel: **(800) 633-1459**
Best Time to Call: **Anytime**

Hosts: **D. J. and Joann Vaughn**
Location: **9½ mi. S of Pigeon Forge**

No. of Rooms: **6**
No. of Private Baths: **6**
Double/pb: **$80–$125**
Single/pb: **$70–$115**
Guest Chalet: **160; sleeps 4**
Open: **All year**
Breakfast: **Full**
Other Meals: **Available**

Credit Cards: **AMEX, DISC, MC, VISA**
Pets: **No**
Children: **Welcome, over 10 in main house, any age in chalet**
Smoking: **No**
Social Drinking: **Permitted**
Minimum Stay: **2 nights in chalet**
Airport/Station Pickup: **Yes**

A curving, climbing gravel road leads to a mountaintop hideaway with sensational views of spectacular mountain ranges and peaceful valley farmland. The log structure has cathedral ceilings of warm wood, skylights, and big windows framing breathtaking views. There are six guest rooms, a two-bedroom chalet, and several common areas. Enjoy the pool, hot tub, rockers, telescope, Jacuzzis, books, music, and full breakfast in addition to hiking, bird-watching, or simply relaxing. Within minutes of Great Smoky National Park, Cades Cove, Gatlinburg, Pigeon Forge, and Townsend, which offer crafts, outlet shopping, and Dollywood.

TEXAS

The Bed & Breakfast Society of Texas ✪
1200 SOUTHMORE AVENUE, HOUSTON, TEXAS 77004

Tel: (713) 523-1114	Rates (Single/Double):
Best Time to Call: **10 AM–6 PM**	Modest: **$40 / $55**
Coordinator: **Pat Thomas**	Average: **$50 / $65**
States/Regions Covered: **Statewide**	Luxury: **$75 / $125**

Whether you're traveling for business or pleasure, Pat's hosts offer the kind of friendliness and individualized care that will make your stay pleasant. The area is known for the Astrodome, Galveston Bay, NASA, and the Texas Medical Center. There are wonderful restaurants, shops, museums, and historic sights, and Baylor, Rice, and the University of Houston are nearby. Many are conveniently located urban homes, serene country houses, historic inns, and waterfront cottages.

Bed & Breakfast Texas Style ✪
4224 WEST RED BIRD LANE, DALLAS, TEXAS 75237

Tel: (214) 298-8586
Best Time to Call: 9 AM–4:30 PM CST
Coordinator: **Ruth Wilson**
States/Regions Covered: **Austin, Dallas, Houston, Lake Travis, San Antonio, Tyler**

Descriptive Directory: **$6**
Rates (Single/Double):
  Modest: **$60 / $70**
  Average: **$70 / $90**
  Luxury: **$100 / $150**
Credit Cards: **MC, VISA**

The above cities are only a small sample of the locations of hosts waiting to give you plenty of warm hospitality. Ruth's register includes comfortable accommodations in condos, restored Victorians, lakeside cottages, and ranches. Texas University, Southern Methodist University, Baylor University, Rice University, and Texas Christian University are convenient to many B&Bs.

Bolin's Prairie House Bed & Breakfast ✪
508 MULBERRY, ABILENE, TEXAS 79601

Tel: (915) 675-5855; (800) 673-5855
Best Time to Call: 8AM–8 PM Mon.–Sat.
Hosts: **Sam and Ginny Bolin**
Location: **180 mi. W of Dallas**
No. of Rooms: **4**
No. of Private Baths: **2**
Max. No. Sharing Bath: **4**

Double/pb: $60–$65
Double/sb: $50–$55
Open: **All year**
Breakfast: **Full**
Credit Cards: **AMEX, MC, VISA**
Children: **Welcome, over 12**
Smoking: **No**

Tucked into the heart of this famous frontier town is Bolin's Prairie House, a 1902 house furnished with antiques and modern luxuries. The warm, homey atmosphere puts guests at their ease. Relax in the living room with its wood-burning stove, or settle in the den for a little TV. Each of the four bedrooms—named Love, Joy, Peace, and Patience—has its own special charm. Breakfast features Ginny's delicious baked egg dishes, fresh fruit, and homemade bread, all lovingly served in the dining room, where fine china and cobalt Depression glass are displayed.

Parkview House ✪
1311 SOUTH JEFFERSON, AMARILLO, TEXAS 79101

Tel: (806) 373-9464
Best Time to Call: **Before 10 AM, after 4 PM**
Hosts: **Nabil and Carol Dia**
Location: **½ mi. from I-40**
No. of Rooms: **5**
No. of Private Baths: **3**

Max. No. Sharing Bath: **4**
Double/pb: **$75**
Double/sb: **$65**
Suite: **$85**
Open: **All year**
Breakfast: **Continental**
Credit Cards: **MC, VISA**

Pets: **No**
Children: **No**
Smoking: **No**

Social Drinking: **Permitted**
Foreign Languages: **Arabic**
Airport/Station Pickup: **Yes**

Carol is a full-time host; Nabil a civil engineer. Both share interests in restoration and antiques, which is evident in their charming Prairie Victorian located in the historic district. The guest rooms are furnished with selected antiques, lace, and luxurious linens. The large columned porch is a fine place to start the day with breakfast or to relax. Carol will lend you a bike and be glad to prepare a picnic basket to take to nearby Palo Duro Canyon State Park or Lake Meredith. West Texas A and M University is nearby. They enjoy having guests join them for a "social hour" before dinner.

Austin's Wildflower Inn ✪
1200 WEST 22½ STREET, AUSTIN, TEXAS 78705

Tel: **(512) 477-9639**
Best Time to Call: **Anytime**
Hosts: **Kay Jackson and Claudean Schultz**
Location: **2 mi. from Rte. IH35, Exit MLK**
No. of Rooms: **4**
No. of Private Baths: **2**
Max. No. Sharing Bath: **4**
Double/pb: **$69–$75**
Single/pb: **$60–$65**

Double/sb: **$59**
Single/sb: **$50**
Open: **All year**
Reduced Rates: **10% seniors**
Breakfast: **Full**
Credit Cards: **AMEX, MC, VISA**
Pets: **No**
Smoking: **No**
Social Drinking: **Permitted**
Airport/Station Pickup: **Yes**

Nestled on a quiet, tree-lined street, this fifty-year-old central Austin home is within a few blocks of the University of Texas and within minutes of the State Capitol complex. Outdoor enthusiasts will love the hike and bike trails at Shoal Creek or tennis at Caswell Courts. Kay and Claudean pride themselves on their warm Texas hospitality and delight in serving you their hearty gourmet specialties each morning.

Carrington's Bluff B&B ✪
1900 DAVID STREET, AUSTIN, TEXAS 78705

Tel: **(512) 479-0638**
Best Time to Call: **8 AM–9 PM**
Hosts: **Gwen and David Fullbrook**
No. of Rooms: **8**
No. of Private Baths: **6**
Max. No. Sharing Bath: **4**
Double/pb: **$69–$89**
Single/pb: **$65–$80**
Double/sb: **$60–$65**
Single/sb: **$55–$60**

Open: **All year**
Reduced Rates: **Midweek business rate $10 less**
Breakfast: **Full**
Credit Cards: **AMEX, DC, MC, VISA**
Pets: **No**
Children: **Welcome, over 10**
Smoking: **No**
Social Drinking: **Permitted**

After operating other B&Bs in Vermont and Texas, Gwen and David are experienced innkeepers who know how to pamper their guests. Their 1877 farmhouse has an enviable downtown Austin location seven blocks from the University of Texas and nine blocks from the State Capitol. Still, you'll feel like you're in the country, since the 35-foot front porch faces a tree-covered bluff. The interior is decorated in an English country style, with English and American antiques. Full breakfasts feature homemade muffins or breads, egg dishes, and homemade granola.

The McCallum House
613 WEST 32ND, AUSTIN, TEXAS 78705

Tel: **(512) 451-6744;** fax: **(512) 451-6744**
Best Time to Call: **10 AM–9 PM**
Hosts: **Roger and Nancy Danley**
Location: **2 mi. W of I-35**
No. of Rooms: **5**
No. of Private Baths: **5**
Double/pb: **$80**
Single/pb: **$70**
Suites: **$95–$99**

Open: **All year**
Reduced Rates: **Weeknights, $15 nightly with 2 nights or more**
Breakfast: **Full**
Credit Cards: **MC, VISA**
Pets: **No**
Children: **Welcome, over 11**
Smoking: **No**
Social Drinking: **Permitted**

This late Victorian home is just 10 blocks north of the University of Texas and 20 blocks north of the capitol and downtown. Air-conditioned and furnished with antiques, all four guest rooms have private verandas. All facilities have phones, color TVs, sitting areas, and kitchens or mini-kitchens, irons, ironing boards, lighted mirrors, hair dryers. The garden apartment suite has a whirlpool tub and shower. McCallum House has a Texas historic marker, an Austin landmark designation and a preservation award from the Austin Heritage Society. Guests breakfast daily on fresh fruits and homemade egg dishes, muffins, and coffee cakes.

Peaceful Hill Bed & Breakfast ✪
6401 RIVER PLACE BOULEVARD, AUSTIN, TEXAS 78730-1102

Tel: **(512) 338-1817**	Open: **All year**
Best Time to Call: **Anytime**	Reduced Rates: **$50, 7 nights**
Host: **Peninnah Thurmond**	Breakfast: **Full**
Location: **15 min. W of Austin**	Credit Cards: **MC, VISA**
No. of Rooms: **2**	Pets: **No**
No. of Private Baths: **2**	Children: **Welcome**
Double/pb: **$60**	Smoking: **No**
Single/pb: **$60**	Social Drinking: **Permitted**

Deer watch you come to a small country inn located on ranchland high in the beautiful rolling hills fifteen minutes from Austin and ten minutes from Lake Travis and the Oasis. In springtime, settle on the porch with a cup of coffee and admire the countryside and the city below. Laze away the summer in a hammock built for two, or hike and bicycle; golf, swimming, and tennis are only two miles away. In the winter, warm up by a crackling fire in the grand stone fireplace in the living room, where a glass wall looks over both the country and the city. All this and a home-cooked breakfast. Peaceful is the name and peaceful is the game. Deer watch you go.

Mystic Cove Bed & Breakfast ✪
RR 1, BOX 309B, BUCHANAN DAM, TEXAS 78609

Tel: **(512) 793-6642**	Reduced Rates: **10% seniors**
Best Time to Call: **8 AM–8 PM**	Breakfast: **Full**
Hosts: **Ralph and Loretta Dueweke**	Other Meals: **Available**
Location: **73 mi. NW of Austin**	Pets: **No**
No. of Rooms: **3**	Children: **Welcome, over 10**
No. of Private Baths: **3**	Smoking: **No**
Double/pb: **$65–$75**	Social Drinking: **Permitted**
Single/pb: **$50**	Minimum Stay: **2 nights, summer**
Guest Cottage: **$75–$145, sleeps 2–6**	**weekends**
Open: **All year**	

Here's the perfect spot for artists, writers, mystics, and anyone else to relax and enjoy nature. Choose a room in the main house with either a king- or queen-size bed, or reserve the private guest house that can accommodate six. All rooms have beautiful lake views. Awaken to the smell of the best breakfast in the Texas hills. Afterwards, relax on the beach, fish from the dock, or enjoy a yoga class or a massage. You'll still have plenty of time to take a Texas River cruise or visit sights such as Longhorn Caverns, the LBJ ranch, and Fall Creek Vineyard.

Aunt Nora's Bed and Breakfast ✪

120 NAKED INDIAN TRAIL (NEW BRAUNFELS), CANYON LAKE, TEXAS 78132-1865

Tel: **(210) 905-3989; (800) 687-2887**
Best Time to Call: **9 AM–5 PM**
Hosts: **Iralee and Alton Haley**
Location: **15 mi. NW of New Braunfels**
No. of Rooms: **3**
No. of Private Baths: **2**
Max. No. Sharing Bath: **4**
Double/sb: **$65–$75**
Guest Cottage: **$95–$125**

Open: **All year**
Reduced Rates: **Available**
Breakfast: **Full, Continental**
Pets: **Sometimes**
Children: **Welcome, over 14**
Smoking: **No**
Social Drinking: **Permitted**
Airport Pickup: **Yes**

In the Texas hill country at Canyon Lake, just minutes from New Braunfels and Guadalupe River, is a country house with old-time Victorian charm, nestled on four tree-covered acres with a meadow. Walk to the top of the hill to view Canyon Lake, or breathe the fresh country air from the front porch swing. Relax amid handmade furnishings, antiques, a woodstove, and natural wood floors. Tastefully decorated Queen rooms have ruffled curtains, handmade quilts, private or semi-private baths and views. The cottages have private decks, sofa sleepers, kitchens, beautiful decor, private baths, and a view.

Magnolia Oaks ✪

634 SPRING STREET, COLUMBUS, TEXAS 78934

Tel: **(409) 732-2726**
Best Time to Call: **Evenings**
Hosts: **Bob and Nancy Stiles**
Location: **70 mi. W of Houston**
No. of Rooms: **5**
No. of Private Baths: **5**
Efficiency Apt.: **$80–$120**
Open: **All year**

Reduced Rates: **Available**
Breakfast: **Full**
Pets: **No**
Children: **No**
Smoking: **No**
Social Drinking: **Permitted**
Minimum Stay: **Homes Tour Weekend**
Airport Pickup: **Yes**

Magnolia Oaks is an Eastlake Victorian jewel two blocks from the historic square in Columbus. This landmark home was built in 1890 by Senator Marcus Townsend. Bob and Nancy Stiles restored the house and furnished it with Victorian Texana; they opened the B&B in 1990. Featured are two fireplaces, stained-glass windows, carved woodwork, gingerbread porches, a summer room, generous breakfasts, private baths, horseshoes, croquet, and a tandem bike. Columbus, on Interstate 10, is in the heart of wildflower country. It has museums, antique shops, and Stafford Opera House.

Bay Breeze Bed & Breakfast ✪
201 LOUISIANA, CORPUS CHRISTI, TEXAS 78404

Tel: (512) 882-4123
Best Time to Call: Anytime
Hosts: Perry and Frank Tompkins
Location: 145 mi. S of San Antonio
No. of Rooms: 4
No. of Private Baths: 4
Double/pb: $60–$75
Single/pb: $72

Treehouse: $85
Open: All year
Reduced Rates: Available
Breakfast: Full
Pets: No
Children: Welcome, over 13
Smoking: No
Social Drinking: Permitted

Standing within view of the sparkling bay waters, this fine older home radiates the charm and ambiance of days gone by. It's only a stroll to the city's finest park and fishing pier; nearby is Oleander Point, one of the world's premier sailboarding sites, with windsurfers flitting like butterflies on the waves. A five-minute drive takes you to the business district and city marinas, where sea vessels of every description are berthed and shrimp are sold directly from the net. Then travel the short distance to the Bayfront Convention Center, art and science museums, and the Harbor Playhouse Community Theater. Cross the High Bridge to the Texas State Aquarium and the U.S.S. *Lexington* Floating Museum. After experiencing Bay Breeze's many pleasures, you will want to return again and again.

B & G's ✪
15869 NEDRA WAY, DALLAS, TEXAS 75248

Tel: (214) 386-4323
Best Time to Call: Before 8 AM
Hosts: George and Betty Hyde
No. of Rooms: 2
No. of Private Baths: 2
Double/pb: $50
Single/pb: $45
Open: All year

Reduced Rates: Available
Breakfast: Full
Other Meals: Available
Pets: No
Children: Welcome
Smoking: No
Social Drinking: Permitted
Airport/Station Pickup: Yes

Betty and George are retirees who have had visitors from around the world since 1980. They want you to think of their home—furnished with "an eclectic collection of family heirlooms and junk"—as your own. Upon your arrival, they'll pour you something to drink, ascertain your interests, and direct you to appropriate activities in the Dallas–Fort Worth area. This B&B is close to prestigious shopping malls, the University of Texas at Dallas, Southern Methodist University, and the sights of downtown Dallas, such as the Kennedy Assassination Museum and the new Arts District. You'll start the day with conversation and a three-course breakfast at a lovely table set with grandma's antique silver and good crystal.

Bergmann Inn ✪

10009 TRINIDAD DRIVE, EL PASO, TEXAS 79925

Tel: (915) 599-1398	Breakfast: **Continental**
Host: **David Bergmann**	Other Meals: **Available**
No. of Rooms: 2	Pets: **No**
Max. No. Sharing Bath: 4	Smoking: **No**
Double/sb: $50	Social Drinking: **Permitted**
Single/sb: $35	Airport Pickup: **Yes**
Open: **All year**	

David has a spacious, two-story home with two large bedrooms, a sizable living room, a den with a fireplace, and air-conditioning. Guests will enjoy the back patio overlooking a yard with flower beds and fruit trees that provide shade in the summertime. Bergmann Inn offers easy access to the east–west freeway and the northbound highways leaving El Paso.

The Texas White House ✪

1417 8TH AVENUE, FORT WORTH, TEXAS 76104

Tel: (817) 923-3597	Reduced Rates: **Available**
Best Time to Call: 7 AM–10:30 PM	Breakfast: **Full**
Host: **Jamie Sexton**	Other Meals: **Available**
Location: **2 mi. SW of downtown**	Credit Cards: **AMEX, MC, VISA**
Fort Worth	Pets: **No**
No. of Rooms: 3	Children: **Welcome**
No. of Private Baths: 3	Smoking: **Restricted**
Double/pb: $85	Social Drinking: **Permitted**
Open: **All year**	Airport/Station Pickup: **Yes**

Texas White House is a 1910 Colonial Revival home with a large wraparound porch on the first floor. The parlor, living room with a fireplace, and formal dining room may be rented for business conferences and luncheons. Secretarial and notary services can also be arranged. Each guest room features a queen-size bed, desk, and chair, and sitting area. You'll receive keys both to your room and the front door, so you can come and go at your leisure. Full breakfasts are served; you may eat either in your bedroom or in the dining room. Architecture buffs will want to tour the area's historical districts and landmark homes, while flora and fauna fans may prefer the Botanical Gardens and the Fort Worth Zoo.

Jackson Street Inn ✪

901 JACKSON STREET, FRIONA, TEXAS 79035

Tel: (806) 247-2146; (800) 687-0013	No. of Rooms: 4
Hosts: **Leland and Geneva Gustin**	No. of Private Baths: 2
Location: **72 mi. SW of Amarillo**	Max. No. Sharing Bath: 4

Double/pb: **$55**
Double/sb: **$55–$65**
Open: **All year**
Reduced Rates: **10% seniors, weekly**
Breakfast: **Full**
Other Meals: **Available**

Credit Cards: **AMEX, MC, VISA**
Pets: **Sometimes**
Children: **Welcome**
Smoking: **Restricted**
Social Drinking: **Permitted**
Airport Pickup: **Yes**

Warm, down-home Texas hospitality awaits you at this comfortable hideaway full of recreational extras. Enjoy a rejuvenating swim in the indoor heated swimming pool, then relax in the adjacent lounging area. Select a movie from the video library and watch it on a big-screen TV, or engage in a stimulating game of snooker or eight-ball on the antique pool table. All of this can be enjoyed around a glowing fireplace in the spacious family room, sure to please everyone wanting a quiet getaway weekend. One of the novelties at the Jackson Street Inn is an antique phone booth that is in mint working condition. The Gustins offer off-street parking, ceiling fans and central heat. Food is the taste of the Texas Specialties gourmet line. The region has 16 days of pheasant season in December.

The Lovett Inn ✪
501 LOVETT BOULEVARD, HOUSTON, TEXAS 77006

Tel: **(713) 522-5224; (800) 779-5224;**
  fax: **(713) 528-6708**
Best Time to Call: **10 AM–6 PM**
Host: **Tom Fricke**
Location: **Downtown Houston**
No. of Rooms: **8**
No. of Private Baths: **8**
Double/pb: **$55–$85**
Single/pb: **$55–$80**
Townhouse: **$75–$150**

Suites: **$65–$125**
Open: **All year**
Reduced Rates: **Weekly**
Breakfast: **Continental**
Credit Cards: **AMEX, MC, VISA**
Pets: **Sometimes**
Children: **By arrangement**
Smoking: **Restricted**
Social Drinking: **Permitted**

It's easy to be fooled by the Lovett Inn: although it looks far older, this stately Federalist-style mansion, attractively furnished with 19th-century reproductions, was actually built in 1924. Its convenient museum-district location puts visitors within easy striking distance of downtown Houston, the Galleria, and the Houston Medical Center. After spending the day in the city, guests are sure to appreciate a dip in the pool. Each room has a color TV.

Sara's Bed & Breakfast Inn ✪
941 HEIGHTS BOULEVARD, HOUSTON, TEXAS 77008

Tel: **(713) 868-1130; (800) 593-1130**
Best Time to Call: **Anytime**
Hosts: **Donna and Tillman Arledge**
Location: **6 blocks from I-10**

No. of Rooms: **13**
No. of Private Baths: **11**
Max. No. Sharing Bath: **4**
Double/pb: **$55–95**

Double/sb: **$60**
Suites: **$150 for 4**
Open: **All year**
Breakfast: **Continental, plus**
Credit Cards: **AMEX, CB, DC, MC, VISA**

Pets: **No**
Children: **Welcome**
Smoking: **Restricted**
Social Drinking: **Permitted**

This Queen Anne Victorian, with its turret and widow's walk, is located in Houston Heights, a neighborhood of historic homes, many of which are on the National Historic Register. Each bedroom is uniquely furnished, having either single, double, queen- or king-size beds. The Balcony Suite consists of two bedrooms, two baths, full kitchen and living area. Cool drinks or hot coffee are graciously offered in the afternoon. The sights and sounds of downtown Houston are four miles away.

Blue Bonnet Bed & Breakfast ✪
1215 AVENUE G #4, HUNTSVILLE, TEXAS 77340

Tel: **(409) 295-2072**
Hosts: **John and Bette Nelson**
Location: **70 mi. N of Houston**
No. of Rooms: **4**
No. of Private Baths: **3**
Max. No. Sharing Bath: **4**
Double/sb: **$38**

Suite: **$48**
Open: **All year**
Breakfast: **Continental**
Pets: **Sometimes**
Children: **Welcome**
Smoking: **No**
Social Drinking: **Permitted**

Seven tree-shaded acres frame this appealing blue Victorian-style house, with its white trim and wraparound porch. Try your luck fishing in the pond, sit on the porch, or play horseshoes and croquet on the lawn. The house is less than five minutes from Sam Houston State University and the adjacent Sam Houston Grave and Museum complex. Antique-lovers will find plenty of shops in the neighborhood; Bette, who owns and manages two antique malls, can give you some good suggestions. Continental breakfast may include apple fritters, poppyseed muffins, filled croissants, and fruit compote.

Parker Ranch Bed & Breakfast
P.O. BOX 1320, IRAAN, TEXAS 79744

Tel: **(915) 639-2850**	Open: **All year**
Best Time to Call: **8 AM–4 PM,**	Reduced Rates: **Available**
6–9 PM	Breakfast: **Full, Continental**
Host: **Dickie Dell Ferro**	Credit Cards: **MC**
Location: **300 mi. W of San Antonio**	Pets: **No**
No. of Rooms: **4**	Children: **Welcome, over 12**
No. of Private Baths: **2**	Smoking: **No**
Max. No. Sharing Bath: **4**	Social Drinking: **Permitted**
Double/pb: **$50**	Foreign Languages: **Spanish**
Double/sb: **$50**	

Parker Ranch sets nestled in the mountains of the Pecos River Valley, protected by the majestic mesas bordering this historically famous trickle of water. This palm bordered home is an oasis in a sea of desert foliage—you will see fossils, unusual plants, and animals, especially in the two gullies in front of the house. Built in 1929, the house is furnished according to era; some pieces are heavily-carved Spanish style, while others are 1930s modern. Artists in the family have collected many intriguing works sure to be of interest to visitors.

On the Bayou ○
321 BUFFALO TRAIL, LAKE JACKSON, TEXAS 77566

Tel: **(800) 409-8845; (409) 297-8845**	Open: **All year**
Best Time to Call: **After 4 PM**	Breakfast: **Full, Continental**
Hosts: **Jean and Roger Williams**	Credit Cards: **AMEX, MC, VISA**
Location: **50 mi. S of Houston**	Pets: **Sometimes**
No. of Rooms: **2**	Children: **Welcome, over 14**
No. of Private Baths: **2**	Smoking: **No**
Double/pb: **$85**	Social Drinking: **Permitted**
Single/pb: **$75**	Airport/Station Pickup: **Yes**

This 4000-square-foot home is located near the water's edge on two acres—its eight sliding glass doors overlook the bayou. Inside, the B&B is furnished with antiques, three-inch pine floors, antique windows and doors, a wood-burning earth stove and two fireplaces in the kitchen for your comfort in the winter months. Guests are invited to use the library and game room equipped with a Ping-Pong, pool, and game table. Or just relax in the carousel sunroom that has an eight-foot by eight-foot plant-filled open atrium under a large skylight.

Trails End Bed & Breakfast ✪
12223 TRAILS END ROAD #7, LEANDER, TEXAS 78641

Tel: **(512) 267-2901**
Best Time to Call: **10 AM–10 PM**
Hosts: **JoAnn and Tom Patty**
Location: **10 minutes from Austin and Lake Travis**
No. of Rooms: **2**
No. of Private Baths: **2**
Double/pb: **$68.90**
Single/pb: **$58.30**

Guest House: **$79.50–$180.20, sleeps 6**
Open: **All year**
Reduced Rates: **Over 2 nights**
Breakfast: **Full**
Pets: **No**
Children: **Welcome**
Smoking: **No**
Social Drinking: **Permitted**

JoAnn designed this Colonial Texas–style home with the intention of opening a B&B. The main house has two guest rooms furnished with mahogany pieces. For greater privacy, stay in the guest house and save money by preparing your own meals in the fully furnished kitchen. Banana pancakes and cheese-and-bacon biscuits are among the highlights of breakfast, served in the main house. After your morning meal, walk around the Pattys' six-acre property or visit local points of interest, such as Zilker Gardens, Texas Memorial Museum, and Erwin Special Events Center. Golfers are urged to go to Lago Vista, while fans of water sports can swim, ski, fish, or sail on Lake Travis. For your enjoyment a pool and bicycles are available.

River Haus Bed & Breakfast ✪
817 EAST ZIPP ROAD, NEW BRAUNFELS, TEXAS 78130

Tel: **(210) 625-6411**
Hosts: **Dick and Arlene Buhl**
Location: **25 mi. NE of San Antonio**
No. of Rooms: **1**
No. of Private Baths: **1**
Double/pb: **$75**
Single/pb: **$70**
Open: **All year**

Reduced Rates: **10% Sun.–Thurs.**
Breakfast: **Full**
Pets: **Sometimes**
Children: **No**
Smoking: **No**
Social Drinking: **No**
Foreign Languages: **German**

Historic New Braunfels, a major tourist destination, offers museums, antique shopping, and unparalleled canoeing and river sports, all in the charming setting of the German Hill Country. River Haus is a delightful hill country–style home located on the Guadalupe River at Lake Dunlap. Watch the sun set over the lake from your spacious bedroom or sitting room. On the enclosed porch, with its deck overlooking the lake, you can sip a cool drink or enjoy the warmth of a wood-stove fire. The complete gourmet breakfasts include local specialties and homemade bread and preserves.

The Rose Garden ✪
195 SOUTH ACADEMY, NEW BRAUNFELS, TEXAS 78130

Tel: **(210) 629-3296**
Best Time to Call: **Before 8 PM**
Host: **Dawn Mann**
Location: **1½ mi. from I-35, Exit 187**
No. of Rooms: **2**
Double/pb: **$65–$105**
Open: **All year**

Reduced Rates: **Available**
Breakfast: **Full**
Pets: **No**
Children: **No**
Smoking: **No**
Social Drinking: **Permitted**
Foreign Languages: **German**

This half-century-old white brick Colonial is located one block from historic downtown New Braunfels. Enjoy a movie, browse the antique shops, or stroll along the Comal Springs. Then relax by the fireplace in the parlor, or in the formal dining room with a flavored cup of coffee. The Royal Rose Room features a four-poster bed; you'll also find English and German books, pictures, and magazines concerning the royal family. The Romantic Country Rose Room has a Victorian wrought-iron and brass bed, an antique English dresser.

The White House
217 MITTMAN CIRCLE, NEW BRAUNFELS, TEXAS 78132

Tel: (210) 629-9354
Best Time to Call: 9 AM–9 PM
Hosts: Beverly and Jerry White
Location: 25 mi. N of San Antonio
No. of Rooms: 3
Max. No. Sharing Bath: 4
Double/pb: $70
Single/pb: $65
Double/sb: $45–$50

Single/sb: $40–$45
Open: All year, except Thanksgiving, and Christmas
Breakfast: Full
Pets: No
Children: Welcome (crib)
Smoking: No
Social Drinking: Permitted

This Spanish-style white-brick ranch home is nestled among cedar and oaks in Texas hill country. Guests are welcomed here with tea and pastries and shown to comfortable rooms with antique iron beds and oak dressers. A large fishing pond is located on the premises, and a few miles away you may enjoy a refreshing tube or raft ride down the Guadalupe River. Your hosts have giant inner tubes to lend. Other attractions include the Alamo, the Riverwalk, and the many old missions located in nearby San Antonio.

Beckmann Inn and Carriage House ✪
222 EAST GUENTHER STREET, SAN ANTONIO, TEXAS 78204

Tel: (210) 229-1449; (800) 945-1449
Best Time to Call: 8 AM–10 PM
Hosts: Betty Jo and Don Schwartz
Location: ¾ mi. S of San Antonio
No. of Rooms: 5
No. of Private Baths: 5
Double/pb: $80–$130
Single/pb: $70–$120
Open: All year

Reduced Rates: Available
Breakfast: Full
Credit Cards: AMEX, DC, MC, VISA
Pets: No
Children: Welcome, over 12
Smoking: No
Social Drinking: Permitted
Minimum Stay: 2 nights, weekends

Enjoy gracious hospitality in an elegant Victorian inn located in San Antonio's King William historic district. The beautiful wraparound porch welcomes guests. Inside, rooms are colorfully decorated, with high-back, queen-size, antique Victorian beds. Gourmet breakfast, complete with dessert, is served in the formal dining room on a table set with china, crystal, and silver. Then guests may stroll over to the Riverwalk or ride the trolley to the sights of San Antonio.

The Belle of Monte Vista ✪
505 BELKNAP PLACE, SAN ANTONIO, TEXAS 78212

Tel: (210) 732-4006
Hosts: Joann and David Bell
No. of Rooms: 5

No. of Private Baths: 3
Max. No. Sharing Bath: 4
Double/sb: $60

Single/sb: **$50**
Suite: **$75**
Open: **All year**
Breakfast: **Full**
Credit Cards: **AMEX, MC, VISA**

Pets: **No**
Children: **Welcome**
Smoking: **No**
Social Drinking: **Permitted**
Airport/Station Pickup: **Yes**

J. Riely Gordon designed this Queen Anne Victorian as a model house for a local developer. Built in 1890 with limestone that was quarried less than half a mile away, the house has been beautifully restored and is located in the elegant Monte Vista historic district. Inside, you'll find eight fireplaces, stained-glass windows, a hand-carved oak staircase, and Victorian furnishings. Joann serves a Southern breakfast with homemade muffins and jellies each morning. They are happy to help you plan your day and will direct you to nearby attractions such as Alamo Plaza, the Riverwalk, and El Mercado Market Place.

Falling Pines B&B ○

300 WEST FRENCH PLACE, SAN ANTONIO, TEXAS 78212

Tel: **(210) 733-1998; (800) 880-4580**
Best Time to Call: **9 AM–noon**
Hosts: **Grace and Bob Daubert**
No. of Rooms: **4**
No. of Private Baths: **4**
Double/pb: **$100**
Suite: **$150**
Open: **All year**

Reduced Rates: **15% families; weekly**
Breakfast: **Full**
Pets: **No**
Children: **Welcome, over 10**
Smoking: **No**
Social Drinking: **Permitted**
Minimum Stay: **2 nights**

When you enter Falling Pines through the magnificent front archway, you realize that they don't make estates like this anymore. Pines, oaks, and pecan trees shade the one-acre property. Inside, the brick-and-limestone mansion is sumptuously decorated with oak paneling, oriental rugs, and antique furnishings. Tennis courts, a swimming pool, and a zoo are all a short walk away, or you can ride over on the bikes Grace and Bob will lend you. A breakfast of fresh fruit, pastries, and hot and cold cereals is served in the tiled solarium.

VIRGINIA

Woodstock •
Flint Hill •
• Alexandria
New Market • • Luray
Harrisonburg •
Manassas •
Chincoteague
Island
Gordonsville • Fredericksburg •
Staunton • • Waynesboro
• Onancock
Goshen •
Richmond •
Madison Heights •
Rockville • • Urbanna
• Cape
Charles
Buchanan • • Lexington Lynchburg
Williamsburg •
Pulaski • Roanoke • Smith Mountain Lake
Smithfield •
Abingdon •
Capron •
• Virginia Beach

River Garden ✪
19080 NORTH FORK, RIVER ROAD, ABINGDON, VIRGINIA 24210

Tel: (703) 676-0335; (800) 952-4296
Best Time to Call: **Evenings and weekends**
Hosts: **Bill Crump and Carol Schoenherr-Crump**
Location: **9 mi. NE of Abingdon**
No. of Rooms: **4**
No. of Private Baths: **4**

Double/pb: **$60–$65**
Open: **All year**
Breakfast: **Full**
Pets: **No**
Children: **Welcome, infants, over 4**
Smoking: **No**
Social Drinking: **Permitted**

River Garden is tucked into the foothills of the Clinch Mountains, on the bank of the Holston River's North Fork. Each room has its own riverside deck, private entrance, and a king- or queen-size bed. Guests are encouraged to try their hand at weaving on the antique loom. More contemporary challenges can be had in the recreation room, which is equipped with a Ping-Pong table, board games, and exercise equipment. Fishing equipment, a picnic table, and inner tubes are also at your disposal. The center of Abingdon, fifteen minutes away, is home to the historic Barter Theater, as well as many eateries. Lovers of the outdoors will want to head for the Virginia Creeper Trail—34 miles of scenic mountain trails for hikers, bikers, and horseback riders.

Princely B&B Ltd. ✪
819 PRINCE STREET, ALEXANDRIA, VIRGINIA 22314

Tel: **(703) 683-2159**	States/Regions Covered: **Alexandria**
Best Time to Call: **10 AM–6 PM**	Rates (Single/Double):
Mon.–Fri.	Modest: **$75–$100**
Coordinator: **E. J. Mansmann**	Minimum Stay: **2 nights**

This reservation service lists more than thirty privately owned historic homes, circa 1750 to 1890, many furnished with fine antiques, located in the heart of the Old Town area of Alexandria. All are within eight miles of the White House or Mount Vernon and afford easy access to shopping, dining, and monuments in and around Washington, D.C.

The Berkley House ✪
ROUTE 2, BOX 220A, BUCHANAN, VIRGINIA 24066

Tel: **(703) 254-2548; (800) 466-1891**	Suites: **$95–$125**
Best Time to Call: **After 4 PM**	Open: **All year**
Hosts: **John and Sue Shotwell**	Reduced Rates: **Available**
Location: **13 mi. N of Roanoke**	Breakfast: **Full**
No. of Rooms: **4**	Credit Cards: **AMEX, MC, VISA**
No. of Private Baths: **1**	Pets: **No**
Max. No. Sharing Bath: **4**	Children: **Welcome, over 8**
Double/pb: **$65**	Smoking: **No**
Single/pb: **$55**	Social Drinking: **Permitted**
Double/sb: **$55–$65**	Airport/Station Pickup: **Yes**
Single/sb: **$45–$55**	

Farmland surrounds this 1887 Victorian country home, located within minutes of the Peaks of Otter on the Blue Ridge Parkway. Three porches, a guest kitchen, and a TV/VCR room are at your disposal. Golfers have a choice of several excellent courses in the immediate area. Sue's breakfast menu features homemade pancakes, waffles, and breads; complimentary refreshments, served from 4 to 5 PM, will tide visitors over until dinnertime.

Nottingham Ridge
28184 NOTTINGHAM RIDGE LANE, CAPE CHARLES, VIRGINIA 23310

Tel: **(804) 331-1010**	Double/pb: **$85**
Best Time to Call: **Anytime**	Single/pb: **$60**
Hosts: **Bonnie Nottingham and M.S.**	Open: **All year**
Scott	Breakfast: **Full**
Location: **20 mi. N of Norfolk**	Other Meals: **Available**
No. of Rooms: **4**	Pets: **No**
No. of Private Baths: **4**	Children: **Welcome, over 7**

Smoking: **No**
Social Drinking: **Permitted**

Airport/Station Pickup: **Yes**

Reflecting the beauty and charm of Virginia's historic Eastern Shore, this lovely home boasts a private secluded beach on the Chesapeake Bay, bordered by tall trees, sand dunes, and abundant wildlife. Guests can savor breakfast on the porch while watching boats and birds; at day's end, the sunsets are spectacular. Cooler times can be spent in the den by a crackling fire. Biking, fishing, tennis, golf, running, bird-watching, crabbing, swimming, and sightseeing are just a few pastimes guests can enjoy. Visitors to Nottingham Ridge can look forward to an informal, relaxed atmosphere with emphasis on the small details that create a memorable stay.

Picketts Harbor
BOX 97AA, CAPE CHARLES, VIRGINIA 23310

Tel: **(804) 331-2212**
Best Time to Call: **After 5 PM**
Hosts: **Sara and Cooke Goffigon**
Location: **21 mi. E of Virginia Beach**
No. of Rooms: **6**
Max. No. Sharing Bath: **4**
Double/pb: **$85–$125**
Single/pb: **$65–$85**
Double/sb: **$75–$85**
Single/sb: **$65–$75**

Suites: **$125**
Open: **All year**
Breakfast: **Full**
Other Meals: **Available**
Pets: **Sometimes**
Children: **Welcome**
Smoking: **No**
Social Drinking: **Permitted**
Airport/Station Pickup: **Yes**

Picketts Harbor is a real find on Virginia's Eastern Shore, with twenty-seven acres of private beach and views of the Chesapeake Bay from all rooms. Set amid pine trees, the home is built to an eighteenth-century design; central air-conditioning, fireplaces and antique pieces complement the two-hundred-year-old red heart-pine floors and cupboards. One wing of the house has a private entrance. A country breakfast is served on the porch, in the country kitchen, or in the dining room. Seasonal fruit, homemade breads with jam, and Virginia ham tempt guests. Things to do include fishing, bird-watching, and antiquing, and reasonable restaurants are nearby. Williamsburg and Chincoteague lie within a short drive.

Sunset Inn Bed & Breakfast ☉
108 BAY AVENUE, CAPE CHARLES, VIRGINIA 23310

Tel: **(804) 331-2424; (800) 331-3113**
   for reservations
Hosts: **Al Longo and Joyce Tribble**
Location: **35 mi. N of Norfolk**
No of Rooms: **4**
No. of Private Baths: **4**
Double/pb: **$65–$85**
Single/pb: **$60–$80**

Open: **All year**
Reduced Rates: **Available**
Breakfast: **Full**
Credit Cards: **MC, VISA**
Pets: **No**
Children: **Welcome, over 10**
Smoking: **Restricted**
Social Drinking: **Permitted**

Minimum Stay: **2 nights, holiday weekends**   Airport Pickup: **Yes**

Enjoy a waterfront getaway on the unspoiled Eastern Shore. Cape Charles is directly on the Chesapeake Bay, at the southernmost part of the Delmarva Peninsula; this picturesque town has no traffic lights or parking meters. You'll be able to watch spectacular unobstructed sunsets from the Inn's breezy porch or common area. Sun, swim, and relax—a hot tub is available. Then walk the beach, explore the historic district, or take a bike ride. Bird-watching and charter fishing are nearby. A hearty full breakfast features homemade baked goods and fresh fruit, and delicious hot entrees.

Sandy Hill Farm B&B ✪

11307 RIVERS MILL ROAD, CAPRON, VIRGINIA 23829

Tel: **(804) 658-4381**
Best Time to Call: **6:30–8 AM; 7:30–11:30 PM**
Host: **Anne Kitchen**
Location: **11 mi. from I-95**
No. of Rooms: **2**
Double/pb: **$50**
Single/pb: **$40**

Open: **Mar. 20–Dec. 5**
Reduced Rates: **Families; 5 nights**
Breakfast: **Full**
Other Meals: **Available**
Pets: **Welcome**
Children: **Welcome**
Smoking: **Permitted**
Social Drinking: **Permitted**

Experience the pleasures of an unspoiled rural setting at this ranch-style farmhouse. There are animals to visit, quiet places to stroll, and a lighted tennis court on the grounds. This is an ideal hub from which to tour southeastern and central Virginia. Day trips to Williamsburg, Norfolk, and Richmond are possibilities. Fresh fruits and homemade breads are served at breakfast.

Guesthouses Reservation Service ✪

P.O. BOX 5737, CHARLOTTESVILLE, VIRGINIA 22905

Tel: **(804) 979-7264**
Best Time to Call: **12–5 PM Mon.–Fri.**
Coordinator: **Mary Hill Caperton**
States/Regions Covered: **Albemarle County, Charlottesville**
Descriptive Directory: **$1**

Rates (Single/Double):
  Modest: **$48 / $60**
  Average: **$68 / $72**
  Luxury: **$80 / $150**
  Estate Cottages: **$100 up**
Credit Cards: **AMEX, MC, VISA**

Charlottesville is a gracious town. The hosts in Mary's hospitality file offer you a genuine taste of Southern hospitality. All places are close to Thomas Jefferson's Monticello and James Madison's Ash Lawn, as well as the University of Virginia. Unusual local activities include ballooning, steeplechasing, and wine festivals. Reduced rates are available for extended stays, and most hosts offer a full breakfast.

Miss Molly's Inn ✪
4141 MAIN STREET, CHINCOTEAGUE ISLAND, VIRGINIA 23336

Tel: **(804) 336-6686; (800) 221-5620**
Best Time to Call: **10 AM–10 PM**
Hosts: **Barbara and David Wiedenheft**
Location: **50 mi. S of Salisbury, Maryland**
No. of Rooms: **7**
No. of Private Baths: **5**
Max. No. Sharing Bath: **4**
Double/pb: **$69–$149**
Single/pb: **$59–$109**
Double/sb: **$75–$109**
Single/sb: **$65–$99**
Open: **Mar. 1–New Year's day**

Reduced Rates: **10% seniors; Oct. 1–Memorial Weekend**
Breakfast: **Full**
Other Meals: **Available**
Pets: **No**
Children: **Welcome, over 8**
Smoking: **No**
Social Drinking: **Permitted**
Minimum Stay: **2 days, weekends**
Airport/Station Pickup: **Yes**
Foreign Languages: **French, Dutch, German**

This bayside Victorian inn has been lovingly restored to its nineteenth-century charm; lace curtains, stained glass windows, and period pieces add to the ambience. While writing her book *Misty of Chincoteague*, Marguerite Henry stayed here. The ponies celebrated by that story roam wild at the nearby National Wildlife Refuge close to the unspoiled beaches of Assateague Island. You, too, may find Miss Molly's cool breezes, five porches, and traditional English tea—complete with superlative scones—worth writing about.

The Watson House ✪
4240 MAIN STREET, CHINCOTEAGUE, VIRGINIA 23336

Tel: **(804) 336-1564; (800) 336-6787**
Hosts: **Tom and Jacque Derrickson, David and Joanne Snead**
Location: **180 mi. SE of Washington, DC**

No. of Rooms: **6**
No. of Private Baths: **6**
Double/pb: **$59–$85**
Suites: **$79–$99**
Open: **Apr.–Nov.**

Reduced Rates: **Available**
Breakfast: **Full**
Credit Cards: **MC, VISA**
Pets: **No**
Children: **Welcome, over 10**

Smoking: **No**
Social Drinking: **Permitted**
Minimum Stay: **2 nights, weekends; 3 nights, holidays**

Friendly hosts and Southern hospitality await you at this newly restored country Victorian home. Guest rooms are tastefully decorated with antiques, wicker, and nostalgic pieces; each room has a ceiling fan and air-conditioning. Watson House is within biking distance of Assateague National Wildlife Refuge, where you can enjoy numerous nature trails, guided tours, crabbing, fishing, clamming, or swimming. Your hosts will equip you with bicycles, beach chairs, and towels. In the mornings, you can mingle with other guests over a hearty breakfast which includes fruit, eggs, breads, pastries, and aromatic coffee and tea.

Caledonia Farm–1812 ✪
ROUTE 1, BOX 2080, FLINT HILL, VIRGINIA 22627

Tel: **(703) 675-3693; (800) BNB-1812**
Best Time to Call: **10 AM–6 PM**
Host: **Phil Irwin**
Location: **68 mi. SW of Washington, D.C.; 4 mi. N of Washington, Va.**
No. of Rooms: **3**
Max. No. Sharing Bath: **4**
Double/sb: **$80**

Suite: **$140**
Open: **All year**
Breakfast: **Full**
Credit Cards: **DISC, MC, VISA**
Pets: **No**
Children: **Welcome, over 12**
Smoking: **No**
Social Drinking: **Permitted**

This charming 1812 stone manor house and its companion "summer kitchen" are located on a working beef cattle farm adjacent to Shenandoah National Park. Each accommodation has a fireplace, period furnishings, individual temperature controls for heat or air-conditioning, and spectacular views of the Blue Ridge Mountains. A candlelight breakfast is served from a menu that offers a choice of omelette, smoked salmon, or eggs. The Skyline Drive, fine dining, caves, wineries, hayrides, antiquing, historic sites, and sporting activities are a few of the possible diversions. Caledonia Farm is a Virginia Historic Landmark and on the National Register of Historic Places.

La Vista Plantation ✪
4420 GUINEA STATION ROAD, FREDERICKSBURG, VIRGINIA 22408

Tel: **(540) 898-8444**
Best Time to Call: **Before 9:30 PM**
Hosts: **Michele and Edward Schiesser**
Location: **60 mi. S of Washington, D.C.; 4.5 mi. from I-95**
No. of Rooms: **2**

No. of Private Baths: **2**
Double/pb: **$85**
Single/pb: **$65**
Guest Apartment: **$85; sleeps 6**
Open: **All year**
Reduced Rates: **7th night free; families**

Breakfast: **Full**
Credit Cards: **MC, VISA**
Pets: **No**

Children: **Welcome**
Smoking: **No**
Social Drinking: **Permitted**

Built in 1838, this Classical Revival country home is nestled amidst ancient tulip poplars, cedars, and hollies, and surrounded by pastures, woods and fields. The site is close to historic Fredericksburg, but in a quiet rural area. The house retains its original charm, with intricate acorn and oak leaf moldings, high ceilings, wide pine floors and a two-story front portico. Guest rooms have private baths, air-conditioning, working fireplaces, TV, radio and refrigerator. Enjoy brown egg breakfasts from resident hens. The Schiessers also have a stocked pond, rowboat, and bicycles.

Mary Josephine Ball B&B ⊙
1203 PRINCE EDWARD STREET, FREDERICKSBURG, VIRGINIA 22401

Tel: **(800) 376-4242**
Best Time to Call: **8 AM–12 noon, after 4 PM**
Hosts: **Bill and Mary Jo Bible**
Location: **50 mi. S of D.C.**
No. of Rooms: **3**
No. of Private Baths: **2**
Max. No. Sharing Bath: **4**
Double/pb: **$85**
Single/sb: **$65**
Suite: **$120; sleeps 2**

Open: **All year**
Reduced Rates: **10% seniors**
Breakfast: **Full**
Other Meals: **Available**
Credit Cards: **MC, VISA**
Pets: **No**
Children: **Welcome, over 10**
Smoking: **No**
Social Drinking: **Permitted**
Airport/Station Pickup: **Yes**

For a peaceful, romantic getaway, enjoy the exceptional warmth and hospitality that await you at this charming, circa 1879 Victorian town home in the historic district. This B&B is elegantly appointed with period and rare family antiques along with private fireplaces and central air-conditioning. Bathrooms are conveniently located across the hallway from guest rooms to provide a high degree of privacy. After a full day of touring, relax in its formal parlor or sunporch/scenic garden for afternoon tea or snacks. A delectable candlelight breakfast is served each morning.

Selby House Bed & Breakfast ⊙
226 PRINCESS ANNE STREET, FREDERICKSBURG, VIRGINIA 22401

Tel: **(540) 373-7037**
Hosts: **Jerry and Virginia Selby**
Location: **54 mi. S of Washington, D.C.**
No. of Rooms: **4**
No. of Private Baths: **4**
Double/pb: **$75**
Single/pb: **$65**
Open: **All year**

Reduced Rates: **Available**
Breakfast: **Full**
Credit Cards: **MC, VISA**
Pets: **No**
Children: **Welcome**
Smoking: **No**
Social Drinking: **Permitted**
Station Pickup: **Yes**

Warm Southern hospitality is the order every day at this restored, late 19th-century Colonial located in Fredericksburg's historic district. Selby House is decorated throughout with late American Empire furniture. Just two blocks from the railroad station and with off-street parking provided, this B&B assures easy access to good restaurants, museums, art galleries, fine antique shops, and the numerous historic attractions Fredericksburg offers. Civil War buffs will enjoy talking with Jerry and perhaps signing up for one of his Civil War seminars. Virginia, a Richmond local, will have you raving over her full Southern breakfasts with all the trimmings.

The Spooner House Bed and Breakfast
1300 CAROLINE STREET, FREDERICKSBURG, VIRGINIA 22401-3704

Tel: (540) 371-1267
Best Time to Call: After 6 PM
Hosts: Peggy and John Roethel
Location: 54 mi. S of Washington, D.C.
Suites: $95; sleeps 2, $20 each
   additional person
Open: All year

Reduced Rates: 10% weekly
Breakfast: Full
Pets: No
Children: Welcome
Smoking: No
Social Drinking: Permitted
Station Pickup: Yes

Built in 1793 on land once owned by George Washington's youngest brother, Charles, the Spooner House operated as a general store and later a tavern. Located in Fredericksburg's historic district, it is within walking distance of museums, restaurants, shops, and the Amtrak station. The lovely two-room suite has its own private entrance and private bath. Breakfast, along with the morning paper, is delivered to guests at their convenience. A complimentary guided tour of the Rising Sun Tavern, the National Historic Landmark that is adjacent to the Spooner House, is available to guests.

Sleepy Hollow Farm Bed & Breakfast ✪
16280 BLUE RIDGE TURNPIKE, ROUTE 231 N, GORDONSVILLE, VIRGINIA 22942

Tel: (703) 832-5555; (800) 215-4804
Best Time to Call: 8 AM–noon; 5–10
   PM
Hosts: Beverley Allison and Dorsey
   Allison Comer
Location: 25 mi. N of Charlottesville
No. of Rooms: 6
No. of Private Baths: 6
Double/pb: $65–$95
Single/pb: $50–$75
Guest Cottage: $95–$225; sleeps 4–8

Suites: $85–$125
Open: All year
Reduced Rates: Weekly
Breakfast: Full
Credit Cards: MC, VISA
Pets: Sometimes
Children: Welcome
Smoking: Permitted
Social Drinking: Permitted
Minimum Stay: 2 nights weekends
   Sept.–Nov. and May–June

Sleepy Hollow Farm lies in the heartland of American history, where evidence of Indians and the Revolutionary and Civil War periods still exists. The air-conditioned brick farmhouse evolved from an 18th-century structure, and today boasts terraces, porches, gazebo, pond, a croquet lawn, and rooms with fireplaces. Furnished with antiques and carefully chosen accessories, the decor is picture pretty. Beverley, a retired missionary and journalist, is a fine cook as evidenced by breakfast treats such as sausage pie, fried apples, apple cake, and fruit compote. While in the area, you may want to visit Montpelier, home of James and Dolley Madison, local wineries, and a church dating back to 1769, or fish at Lake Orange.

The Hummingbird Inn
WOOD LANE, P.O. BOX 147, GOSHEN, VIRGINIA 24439

Tel: (703) 997-9065; (800) 397-3214
Best Time to Call: 8 AM–5 PM
Hosts: Jeremy and Diana Robinson
Location: 23 mi. NW of Lexington
No. of Rooms: 5
No. of Private Baths: 5
Double/pb: $70–$95
Open: All year
Reduced Rates: 10% seniors;
  Nov. 1–Mar. 31

Breakfast: Full
Other Meals: Available
Credit Cards: AMEX, MC, VISA
Pets: Sometimes
Children: Welcome, over 12
Smoking: No
Social Drinking: Permitted

Located on an acre of landscaped grounds in the Shenandoah Valley, this Victorian Carpenter Gothic villa has accommodated Eleanor Roosevelt and Efrem Zimbalist, Sr. Wraparound verandas, original pine floors, a rustic den and a solarium give Hummingbird Inn an old-fashioned ambiance. In keeping with its architecture, the B&B is decorated in an early Victorian style and furnished with antiques. Nearby recreational facilities offer golf, swimming, hiking, skiing, canoeing, tubing, fishing, and hunting. Head out in your car for scenic routes like the Blue Ridge Parkway and Skyline Drive. Or visit the Garth Newell Music Center, historic Staunton, the Museum of American Frontier Culture, Virginia Military Institute, and Washington and Lee University. Rates for MAP double: $130–$155.

Kingsway Bed & Breakfast ✪
3581 SINGERS GLEN ROAD, HARRISONBURG, VIRGINIA 22801

Tel: (540) 867-9696
Hosts: Chester and Verna Leaman
Location: 2.5 mi. NW of Harrisonburg
No. of Rooms: 3
No. of Private Baths: 1
Max. No. Sharing Bath: 4
Double/pb: $50–$55
Single/pb: $45
Double/sb: $50

Single/sb: $40
Open: All year
Reduced Rates: Available
Breakfast: Continental, plus
Pets: Yes
Children: Welcome
Smoking: No
Social Drinking: No
Airport Pickup: Yes

This modern country home reveals the carpentry and decorating skills of Chester, a cabinet builder, and Verna, a full-time homemaker. Enjoy the gardens or take a dip in the pool. If you're up for an excursion, visit George Washington National Forest, Shenandoah National Park with picturesque Skyline Drive, Thomas Jefferson's home at Monticello, or New Market Battlefield and caverns. Local sports range from hiking, skiing, to pricing the wares at the antique shops, flea markets, and the Valley Mall.

Asherowe ⊘
314 SOUTH JEFFERSON STREET, LEXINGTON, VIRGINIA 24450

Tel: (703) 463-4219	Single/sb: $53.75
Best Time to Call: Early mornings, evenings	Open: Closed July
	Breakfast: Continental
Host: Yvonne Emerson	Pets: Sometimes
Location: 45 mi. N of Roanoke	Children: Welcome, over 15
No. of Rooms: 4	Smoking: No
Max. No. Sharing Bath: 4	Social Drinking: Permitted
Double/sb: $53.75	Foreign Languages: French, German

This comfortable 1911 wooden home lies only minutes from downtown, in the Golden Triangle section of Lexington's historic district. Sights include the Marshall Library, Washington and Lee University, the Virginia Horse Center, the Virginia Military Institute, and the home of Stonewall Jackson. Guests from both sides of the Atlantic will feel right at home here, since Yvonne speaks fluent French and German. With the Blue Ridge Parkway to the east, and the Allegheny Mountains to the west, the breathtaking scenery is sure to entice any outdoor enthusiast. Lady Calypso, the resident cat, greets all guests on arrival as any good Southern hostess would.

Brierley Hill
RT 6, BOX 21, LEXINGTON, VIRGINIA 24450

Tel: (540) 464-8421; (800) 422-4925	Reduced Rates: Available
Best Time to Call: 8 AM–8 PM	Breakfast: Full
Hosts: Barry and Carole Speton	Other Meals: Available
Location: 50 mi. N of Roanoke	Credit Cards: AMEX, MC, VISA
No. of Rooms: 6	Pets: No
No. of Private Baths: 6	Children: Welcome, over 14
Double/pb: $70–$95	Smoking: No
Single/pb: $60–$85	Social Drinking: Permitted
Open: All year	

This charming B&B sits on eight acres of farmland. Guests are sure to appreciate the spectacular views of the Blue Ridge Mountains and the Shenandoah Valley. Located nearby are Blue Ridge Parkway, the Natural Bridge area and historic Lexington. All rooms are furnished with antique brass or canopy beds, plus Laura Ashley wall coverings and linens. A TV room and a sitting room with a fireplace are at your disposal, and the dining room also has a fireplace. Barry, a retired Canadian lawyer, is interested in antique prints and refinishing furniture. Carole likes cooking, gardening, and quilting. Together, they offer relaxed comfort, wonderful food, and friendly hospitality.

Lavender Hill Farm B&B ✪
ROUTE 1, BOX 515, LEXINGTON, VIRGINIA 24450

Tel: (703) 464-5877; (800) 446-4240	Reduced Rates: **Available**
Best Time to Call: **9 AM–6 PM**	Breakfast: **Full**
Hosts: **Cindy and Colin Smith**	Other Meals: **Available**
Location: **50 mi. N of Roanoke**	Credit Cards: **MC, VISA**
No. of Rooms: **3**	Pets: **No**
No. of Private Baths: **3**	Children: **Welcome**
Double/pb: **$60–$75**	Smoking: **No**
Single/pb: **$50–$60**	Social Drinking: **Permitted**
Suites: **$110**	Minimum Stay: **2 nights, holidays,**
Open: **All year**	**special events**

Situated on a 20-acre working farm in the beautiful Shenandoah Valley, this restored farmhouse (circa 1790) is located five miles from historic Lexington. It has been carefully renovated to blend old and new for your comfort and relaxation. Enjoy the large front porch, fishing, hiking, bird-watching, panoramic mountain views, and lambs frolicking on the hillside. Breakfast specialties include homemade bread, stuffed French toast, fresh farm eggs, and much more. Dinner, served to guests by advance reservation, is highly recommended. Colin, the English half of the family, is the chef whose specialties involve fresh herbs and vegetables from the garden. Cindy will be glad to direct you to nearby attractions, give a spinning demonstration, or arrange a horseback riding package for you.

Llewellyn Lodge at Lexington ✪
603 SOUTH MAIN STREET, LEXINGTON, VIRGINIA 24450

Tel: (703) 463-3235; (800) 882-1145	Open: **All year**
Best Time to Call: **9:30 AM–7:30 PM**	Breakfast: **Full**
Hosts: **Ellen and John Roberts**	Credit Cards: **AMEX, MC, VISA**
Location: **50 mi. N of Roanoke**	Pets: **No**
No. of Rooms: **6**	Children: **Welcome, over 10**
No. of Private Baths: **6**	Smoking: **Restricted**
Double/pb: **$70–$85**	Social Drinking: **Permitted**
Single/pb: **$60–$75**	Airport/Station Pickup: **Yes**

A warm and friendly atmosphere, combining country charm with a touch of class, awaits you at this lovely brick Colonial furnished in traditional and antique pieces. Guests are welcomed with a cool drink on the deck in warm months, or with a refreshment by the fire in the winter. Ellen spent twenty years in the airline, travel, and hospitality business before moving to Lexington in 1985 to start her B&B. John, a native Lexingtonian, is acquainted with the hiking and biking trails and knows where the fish are hiding. A hearty gourmet breakfast is offered each morning, including omelettes, Belgian waffles, Virginia maple syrup, sausage, bacon, and Ellen's famous blueberry muffins. The lodge is an easy walk to the Robert E. Lee Chapel, the Stonewall Jackson House, Washington and Lee University, and the Virginia Military Institute.

The Woodruff House Bed & Breakfast ✪
330 MECHANIC STREET, LURAY, VIRGINIA 22835

Tel: **(540) 743-1494**
Hosts: **Lucas and Deborah Woodruff**
Location: 89 mi. W of Washington, D.C.
No. of Rooms: 3
No. of Private Baths: 3
Double/pb: **$98–$125**
Suites: **$115–$145**
Open: **All year**
Reduced Rates: **20% Mon.–Thurs., 5% after 3 nights**

Breakfast: **Full**
Other meals: **Dinner, included with room rate**
Credit Cards: **DISC, MC, VISA**
Pets: **No**
Children: **Welcome, Mon.–Thurs. only**
Smoking: **No**
Social Drinking: **Permitted**
Minimum Stay: **2 nights weekends**

This fairy-tale Victorian, beautifully appointed with period antiques, hallmarked silver and fine china, is chef-owned and -operated. Escape from reality and come into this fairy tale, where the ambiance never ends. Awaken to your choice of freshly-brewed coffees delivered to your door; a gourmet candlelit breakfast follows. A sumptuous candle-lit high-tea buffet dinner is also included. You may want to relax in the fireside candlelit garden spa, or enjoy the canoes and bicycles provided by your hosts. Each guest room has a working fireplace and a private bath. The Woodruff House is located in the beautiful Shenandoah Valley of Virginia.

Federal Crest Inn B&B ✪
1101 FEDERAL STREET, LYNCHBURG, VIRGINIA 24504

Tel: **(804) 845-6155**
Best Time to Call: **10 AM–10 PM**
Hosts: **Phil and Ann Ripley**
Location: **50 mi. E of Roanoke**
No. of Rooms: 5
No. of Private Baths: 4
Max. No. Sharing Bath: 4
Double/pb: **$85**
Single/pb: **$80**
Double/sb: **$55**
Suites: **$100–$115**
Open: **All year**

Reduced Rates: **$5 Sun.–Thurs., 5% business rates, seniors**
Breakfast: **Full**
Other Meals: **Available**
Credit Cards: **AMEX, MC, VISA**
Pets: **No**
Children: **Welcome, over 10**
Smoking: **No**
Social Drinking: **Permitted**
Minimum Stay: **May–Oct. 2 nights weekends**
Airport/Station Pickup: **Yes**

This elegant 1909 Georgian Revival home has over 7000 square feet in the Federal Hill Historic District. The original charm is seen in the woodwork and the interior columns that lead to the grand central staircase in the front foyer. Guests are invited to enjoy the antiques, the unique mantels of the seven fireplaces and the '50s cafe which offers delightful surprises. Perhaps there will be a special visitation on the third floor, where the original owner constructed a stage for his children to give plays. All rooms have queen beds, down comforters, plush robes and towels, snack baskets and clock radios. In one room, atmosphere is meant to be shared in the romantic Jacuzzi tub, as the lights dim on a painted mural of Virginia's Blue Ridge Mountains. Federal Crest lies within walking distance to many attractions.

Lynchburg Mansion Inn B&B ✪
405 MADISON STREET, LYNCHBURG, VIRGINIA 24504

Tel: **(804) 528-5400; (800) 352-1199**
Hosts: **Bob and Mauranna Sherman**
Location: **65 mi. S of Charlottesville**
No. of Rooms: **5**
No. of Private Baths: **5**
Double/pb: **$85**
Suites: **$119**
Open: **All year**

Reduced Rates: **Available**
Breakfast: **Full**
Credit Cards: **AMEX, DC, MC, VISA**
Pets: **No**
Children: **Welcome**
Smoking: **No**
Social Drinking: **Permitted**

Restored with your every comfort in mind, this Spanish Georgian mansion has pretty gardens, a spacious veranda, oak floors, tall ceilings, pocket doors, and cherry woodwork. Bedrooms are lavish, with either king- or queen-size beds, luxurious linens, fireplaces, TVs, and turndown service. Bob and Mauranna have also added an outdoor hot tub for guests to use. Fine china, silver, and crystal complement the sumptuous full breakfasts. The mansion surveys a half-acre in downtown Lynchburg's Garland Hill Historic District, which is listed on the National Register of Historic Places; impressive Federal and

Victorian homes line Madison Street, still paved in its turn-of-the-century brick. Plus there are Civil War sites, antique shops, art galleries, and countless programs offered by the city's colleges and universities.

Winridge Bed & Breakfast ○
ROUTE 1, BOX 362, WINRIDGE DRIVE, MADISON HEIGHTS, VIRGINIA 24572

Tel: **(804) 384-7220**
Best Time to Call: **10 AM–4 PM**
Hosts: **Lois Ann and Ed Pfister**
Location: **6 mi. N of Lynchburg**
No. of Rooms: **3**
No. of Private Baths: **1**
Max. No. Sharing Bath: **4**
Double/pb: **$79**
Double/sb: **$65**

Open: **All year**
Reduced Rates: **Available**
Breakfast: **Full**
Pets: **No**
Children: **Welcome**
Smoking: **No**
Social Drinking: **No**
Airport/Station Pickup: **Yes**

Enjoy wonderful mountain views while relaxing on the large porches of this grand Colonial Southern home. Swing under the shade trees and stroll through the gardens, where you'll admire the beauty of flowers, birds, and butterflies. Spacious rooms with high ceilings, large sunny windows, and a delightful mix of modern and antique furniture await you. Breakfasts are tempting, with offerings like oven baked pecan French toast and blueberry patch muffins. The Blue Ridge Parkway, Appomattox Courthouse, Poplar Forest, and much more are close by for your diversion.

Sunrise Hill Farm ○
5590 OLD FARM LANE, MANASSAS, VIRGINIA 22110

Tel: **(703) 754-8309**
Best Time to Call: **Anytime**

Hosts: **Frank and Sue Boberek**

Location: **35 minutes W of Washington, D.C.**
No. of Rooms: **2**
No. of Private Baths: **1**
Max. No. Sharing Bath: **4**
Double/pb: **$85**
Double/sb: **$75**
Open: **All year**

Reduced Rates: **15% families using both rooms**
Breakfast: **Full**
Credit Cards: **MC, VISA**
Pets: **Horses boarded**
Children: **Welcome, over 10**
Smoking: **No**
Social Drinking: **Permitted**

Standing in the heart of the 6000-acre Manassas National Battlefields, this Civil War treasure overlooks Bull Run Creek. Sunrise Hill Farm is an uncommonly charming, Federal-era country home furnished in period style. This B&B is a haven for Civil War buffs and guests visiting northern Virginia and the nation's capital. Situated within the renowned Virginia hunt country, it is just 35 minutes from Washington, D.C., and close to Harpers Ferry, Antietam, Skyline Drive, Luray Caverns, and numerous historic sites and antique-filled towns.

A Touch of Country Bed & Breakfast ✪
9329 CONGRESS STREET, NEW MARKET, VIRGINIA 22844

Tel: **(703) 740-8030**
Hosts: **Jean Schoellig and Dawn Kasow**
Location: **18 mi. N of Harrisonburg**
No. of Rooms: **6**
No. of Private Baths: **6**
Double/pb: **$60–$75**
Single/pb: **$50–$65**

Open: **All year**
Breakfast: **Full**
Credit Cards: **DISC, MC, VISA**
Pets: **No**
Children: **Welcome, over 12**
Smoking: **No**
Social Drinking: **Permitted**

This restored 1870s home is located in a historic town in the beautiful Shenandoah Valley. It displays the original hardwood floors and is decorated with antiques and collectibles in a country motif. You'll start your day with a hearty breakfast of pancakes, meats, gravy, and biscuits. Daydream on the porch swings or stroll through town with its charming shops, dine at a variety of restaurants or visit the legendary New Market Battlefield and Park. Close by are Skyline Drive, George Washington National Forest, caverns, and vineyards.

The Spinning Wheel Bed & Breakfast ✪
31 NORTH STREET, ONANCOCK, VIRGINIA 23417

Tel: **(804) 787-7311; Nov. 1–March 31 (703) 684-0067**
Hosts: **David and Karen Tweedie**
Location: **60 mi. N of Virginia Beach**
No. of Rooms: **5**
No. of Private Baths: **5**
Double/pb: **$85–$95**
Open: **Apr. 1–Oct. 31**

Reduced Rates: **Over 4 nights**
Breakfast: **Full**
Credit Cards: **MC, VISA**
Pets: **No**
Children: **Welcome, over 12**
Smoking: **No**
Social Drinking: **Permitted**
Minimum Stay: **2 nights, weekends**

This 1890s folk Victorian home is in the historic waterfront town of Onancock, on the Eastern Shore peninsula separating the Chesapeake

Bay from the Atlantic Ocean. The B&B is decorated with antiques and, true to its name, spinning wheels. Guest rooms have queen-size beds and air-conditioning. Kerr Place (a 1799 museum), restaurants, shops, the town wharf, and the ferry to Tangier Island are all within walking distance. David is a college professor and Karen is a teacher of the deaf. Their guests are greeted by Nelly, the resident old English sheepdog.

Count Pulaski Bed & Breakfast and Gardens ✪
821 NORTH JEFFERSON AVENUE, PULASKI, VIRGINIA 24301

Tel: (703) 980-1163
Host: **Dr. Flo Stevenson**
Location: **55 mi S of Roanoke**
No. of Rooms: 3
No. of Private Baths: 3
Double/pb: $75
Single/pb: $60

Open: **All year**
Breakfast: **Full**
Credit Cards: **MC, VISA**
Pets: **Sometimes**
Children: **Welcome, over 15**
Smoking: **No**
Social Drinking: **No**

In a mountain village in southwest Virginia, you'll find this spacious eighty-year-old house furnished with family antiques, paintings, and pieces your host collected around the world. Guest rooms have carpeting, air-conditioning, and king- or queen-size beds; one room has a fireplace. A television, beverage center, and games and books are inside, while garden sitting areas beckon you outside. Breakfast is served by candlelight on a one-hundred-fifty-year-old table set with china, crystal, and silver. From its quiet hillside perch, this B&B overlooks the town and mountains below, yet Main Street's restaurants and antique shops are only a few blocks away. A fifty-mile bike trail originates in Pulaski; other recreational options include rafting, canoeing, and golf.

The Emmanuel Hutzler House
2036 MONUMENT AVENUE, RICHMOND, VIRGINIA 23220

Tel: (804) 353-6900, 355-4885
Best Time to Call: **11AM–6 PM**
Host: **John E. Richardson**
Location: **1½ mi. from Rte. I-95/64**
No. of Rooms: 4
No. of Private Baths: 1
Double/pb: $85–$135
Open: **All year**

Reduced Rates: **Corporate, 5%, seniors**
Breakfast: **Full**
Credit Cards: **AMEX, MC, VISA**
Pets: **No**
Children: **Welcome, over 12**
Smoking: **No**
Social Drinking: **Permitted**

This spacious Italian Renaissance inn, built in 1914, recently received a total renovation. The classical interior has raised mahogany paneling, lavish wainscoting, leaded glass windows, and, on the first floor, coffered ceilings with dropped beams. Mahogany bookcases flank the marble fireplace in the living room, where guests can relax and converse. The generously sized guest rooms, all on the second floor, are furnished with antiques and handsome draperies; two rooms have fireplaces. The central location makes this an ideal location for either a midweek business trip or a weekend getaway.

The Mary Bladon House ✪
381 WASHINGTON AVENUE SOUTH WEST, ROANOKE, VIRGINIA 24016

Tel: (540) 344-5361	Reduced Rates: **Available**
Hosts: **Mr. and Mrs. W. D. Bestpitch**	Breakfast: **Full**
Location: **220 mi. S of Washington, D.C.**	Credit Cards: **MC, VISA**
	Pets: **No**
No. of Rooms: **3**	Children: **Welcome**
No. of Private Baths: **3**	Smoking: **No**
Double/pb: **$80**	Social Drinking: **Permitted**
Single/pb: **$62.50**	Airport/Station Pickup: **Yes**
Open: **All year**	Foreign Languages: **German**

The Mary Bladon House is located in the old southwest neighborhood, just five minutes away from the Blue Ridge Parkway. This Victorian dates back to the late 1800s and has four porches. Although the original brass light fixtures are still in place, the decor in the public rooms is constantly changing, with works by local artists and craftsmen. All the rooms are elegantly appointed with antiques, and guest rooms feature fresh flowers in season.

Woodlawn ✪
2211 WILTSHIRE ROAD, ROCKVILLE, VIRGINIA 23146

Tel: (804) 749-3759	Open: **All year**
Best Time to Call: **3–10 PM**	Breakfast: **Full**
Host: **Ann Nuckols**	Pets: **No**
Location: **20 mi. W of Richmond**	Children: **No**
No. of Rooms: **2**	Smoking: **No**
No. of Private Baths: **2**	Social Drinking: **Permitted**
Double/pb: **$75**	

An ideal hub from which to tour many historic points of interest in the area, this circa 1813 farmhouse is set on 40 acres of peaceful, grassy slopes, just 3 miles from the interstate. The interior has been completely restored, tastefully decorated, and furnished with antiques. The house has central air-conditioning for summer comfort. Each of the two guest rooms has its own fireplace. Both guest rooms are furnished with majestic hand-carved double beds and down pillows and comforters. Breakfasts with sourdough rolls, bran muffins, homemade jellies, and juice are served on the screened porch or in the dining area in the English basement.

Isle of Wight Inn ✪
1607 SOUTH CHURCH STREET, SMITHFIELD, VIRGINIA 23430

Tel: **(804) 357-3176**
Best Time to Call: **3–9 PM**
Hosts: **The Earls and The Harts**
Location: **27 mi. W of Norfolk**
No. of Rooms: **9**
No. of Private Baths: **9**
Double/pb: **$59**
Single/pb: **$49**

Suites: **$79–$99**
Open: **All year**
Breakfast: **Full**
Credit Cards: **AMEX, MC, VISA**
Pets: **No**
Children: **Welcome**
Smoking: **Restricted**
Social Drinking: **Permitted**

The Isle of Wight Inn is a sprawling brick Colonial, one mile from downtown Smithfield. Inside you will find antiques, reproductions, and motifs of glass, wood, and wicker. Wake up to fresh coffee and Smithfield's own ham rolls. This riverport town has numerous historic homes that will surely delight you. Williamsburg, Norfolk, and Virginia Beach are less than an hour's drive from the house. An antique shop is on the premises.

The Manor at Taylor's Store B&B Country Inn ✪
ROUTE 1, BOX 533, SMITH MOUNTAIN LAKE, VIRGINIA 24184

Tel: **(703) 721-3951; (800) 248-6267**
Hosts: **Lee and Mary Lynn Tucker**
Location: **20 mi. E of Roanoke**
No. of Rooms: **6**
No. of Private Baths: **4**
Double/pb: **$90–$145**
Guest Cottage: **$100–$150; sleeps 2–6**
Open: **All year**

Reduced Rates: **$300–up weekly for cottage**
Breakfast: **Full**
Credit Cards: **MC, VISA**
Pets: **No**
Children: **Welcome in cottage**
Smoking: **Cottage only**
Social Drinking: **Permitted**
Airport/Station Pickup: **Yes**

Situated on 120 acres in the foothills of the Blue Ridge Mountains, this elegant manor house, circa 1799, was the focus of a prosperous tobacco plantation. It has been restored and refurbished, and you'll experience the elegance of the past combined with the comfort of tasteful modernization. The estate invites hiking, swimming, and fishing. The sunroom, parlor, and hot tub are special spots for relaxing. Smith Mountain Lake, with its seasonal sporting activity, is five miles away. Breakfast, designed for the health-conscious, features a variety of fresh gourmet selections.

Frederick House ✪
28 NORTH NEW STREET, STAUNTON, VIRGINIA 24401

Tel: **(703) 885-4220; (800) 334-5575**
Best Time to Call: **7 AM–10 PM**
Hosts: **Joe and Evy Harman**
Location: **2.7 mi. from Route I-81 exit 222**

No. of Rooms: **14**
No. of Private Baths: **14**
Double/pb: **$65–$150**
Single/pb: **$65–$135**
Suites: **$95–$150**

Open: **All year**
Reduced Rates: **Available**
Breakfast: **Full**
Credit Cards: **AMEX, DC, DISC, MC, VISA**

Pets: **No**
Children: **Welcome**
Smoking: **No**
Social Drinking: **Permitted**
Station Pickup: **Yes**

Frederick House is located across from Mary Baldwin College in downtown Staunton, the oldest city in the Shenandoah Valley. The five separate buildings that are listed in the National Register of Historic Places have been tastefully restored and furnished with antiques. The large rooms and suites feature oversize beds, modern baths, remote cable TV, air-conditioning, ceiling fans, robes, telephones, and private entrances. Some have fireplaces or balconies. A full breakfast, prepared by the owners, is served in Chumley's Tearoom between 7:30 and 10:30 AM. Breakfast choices include ham and cheese pie, apple raisin quiche, waffles, stratta, fresh fruit, juice, coffee, tea, warm bread and hot or cold cereal. Joe and Evy Harman previously worked in banking and insurance. Since 1984 they have enjoyed informing guests about the area and suggesting trips to many nearby interesting sights.

Kenwood ○
235 EAST BEVERLEY STREET, STAUNTON, VIRGINIA 24401

Tel: **(703) 886-0524**
Hosts: **Liz and Ed Kennedy**
Location: **30 mi. W of Charlottesville**
No. of Rooms: **3**
No. of Private Baths: **3**
Double/pb: **$70–$75**
Single/pb: **$60–$65**
Open: **All year**

Breakfast: **Full**
Credit Cards: **MC, VISA**
Pets: **No**
Children: **Welcome**
Smoking: **No**
Social Drinking: **Permitted**
Airport/Station Pickup: **Yes**

Kenwood, a stately brick Colonial revival home built in 1910, has been restored and decorated with floral wallpapers and antique furniture. The Woodrow Wilson Birthplace—and its museum and research library—are next door. Staunton boasts several other museums and numerous antique shops, and it's only a half-hour drive to attractions like Monticello and the Virginia Horse Center. Select your destinations over such breakfast fare as fresh seasonal fruit and homemade baked goods.

The Sampson Eagon Inn ✪
238 EAST BEVERLEY STREET, STAUNTON, VIRGINIA 24401

Tel: (540) 886-8200; (800) 597-9722
Best Time to Call: 10 AM–9 PM
Hosts: Laura and Frank Mattingly
Location: 35 mi. W of Charlottesville
No. of Rooms: 5
No. of Private Baths: 5
Double/pb: $80–$85
Suites: $99

Open: All year
Breakfast: Full
Pets: No
Children: Welcome, over 12
Smoking: No
Social Drinking: Permitted
Minimum Stay: Weekends in Oct. and May

This circa 1840 in-town Greek Revival mansion provides affordable luxury accommodations in a preservation award-winning setting. Comfort and hospitality are key. Guest rooms are spacious, air-conditioned, and have modern ensuite baths. Canopied beds and antique furnishings reflect various periods of this elegant building's past. Scrumptious, gourmet breakfasts are served daily. Within two blocks of shops and restaurants, the Inn is adjacent to the Woodrow Wilson Birthplace and Mary Baldwin College. Nearby, guests can enjoy the natural and historic attractions and recreational activities of the central Shenandoah Valley. Charlottesville and Lexington are within a 40-minute drive.

Thornrose House at Gypsy Hill ✪
531 THORNROSE AVENUE, STAUNTON, VIRGINIA 24401

Tel: (540) 885-7026; (800) 861-4338
Best Time to Call: 9 AM–9 PM
Hosts: Suzanne and Otis Huston
Location: 3½ mi. from Rte. I-81, Exit 222
No. of Rooms: 5
No. of Private Baths: 5
Double/pb: $55–$75
Single/pb: $45–$65
Open: All year

Reduced Rates: Available
Breakfast: Full
Pets: No
Children: Welcome
Smoking: No
Social Drinking: Permitted
Minimum Stay: 3 days over July 4th; 2 days October weekends
Airport/Station Pickup: Yes

This 1912 Georgian Revival home is six blocks from the center of Victorian Staunton and adjacent to 300-acre Gypsy Hill Park, which has facilities for golf, tennis, swimming, and summer concerts. A wraparound veranda and Greek colonnades grace the exterior of the house. Inside, there's a cozy parlor with a fireplace and a grand piano. A relaxed, leisurely breakfast is set out in the dining room, which offers the comfort of a fireplace on chilly mornings. Local attractions include Blue Ridge National Park, Natural Chimneys, Skyline Drive,

Woodrow Wilson's birthplace, and the Museum of American Frontier Culture.

The Duck Farm Inn ✪
P.O. BOX 787, RTES. 227 AND 639, URBANNA, VIRGINIA 23175

Tel: **(804) 758-5685; (800) 447-1369**
Host: **Fleming Godden**
Location: **55 mi. E of Richmond**
No. of Rooms: **6**
No. of Private Baths: **2**
Max. No. Sharing Bath: **4**
Double/pb: **$85**
Single/pb: **$60**
Double/sb: **$75**

Single/sb: **$60**
Open: **All year**
Reduced Rates: **After first visit**
Breakfast: **Full**
Pets: **No**
Children: **Welcome**
Smoking: **No**
Social Drinking: **Permitted**
Airport/Station Pickup: **Yes**

This elegant, contemporary inn is situated on Virginia's middle peninsula, surrounded by 800 secluded acres and bordered by the Rappahannock River. Guests are welcome to hike along the shore or through the woods, fish in the river, sunbathe on the private beach, lounge on the deck, or retire to the cozy library with a good book. Fleming has traveled all over the world and thoroughly enjoys her role as full-time innkeeper. One of her breakfast menus consists of seasonal fresh fruit, jumbo blueberry muffins, cheese-and-egg scramble served with spiced sausage, and a variety of hot beverages.

Hewick Plantation ✪
VSH 602/VSH 615 BOX 82, URBANNA, VIRGINIA 23175-0082

Tel: **(804) 758-4214; (800) 484-7514**
  code 1678
Hosts: **Helen and Ed Battleson**
Location: **60 mi. E. of Richmond**
No. of Rooms: **2**
No. of Private Baths: **2**
Double/pb: **$85**
Single/pb: **$75**
Open: **All year**
Reduced Rates: **10% less Jan. & Feb.,**
  seniors 10%

Breakfast: **Continental**
Credit Cards: **MC, VISA**
Pets: **No**
Children: **Welcome, over 2**
Smoking: **No**
Social Drinking: **Permitted**
Station Pickup: **Yes**
Foreign Languages: **Spanish**

Hewick Plantation was the home of an English family that immigrated in 1670; the sixty-acre site includes an old family cemetery and an archaeological dig being conducted by the College of William and Mary. The manor house's spacious bedrooms are decorated with antiques and heirlooms, such as four-poster beds. To accommodate little ones, the twin beds come equipped with trundle beds. Among the local attractions is Christ Church and Cemetery, where General Lewis Puller, the most decorated soldier in American history, is buried. Helen runs a nearby antique shop and Ed is retired from the DEA/US Customs. Their daughter Rachel is a sixth-grader who loves horses, while her little sister Regina, a third-grader, is partial to all animals, especially her dog and cat.

Angie's Guest Cottage ✪
302 24TH STREET, VIRGINIA BEACH, VIRGINIA 23451

Tel: **(804) 428-4690**
Best Time to Call: **10 AM–10 PM**
Host: **Barbara G. Yates**
Location: **20 mi. E of Norfolk**
No. of Rooms: **6**
No. of Private Baths: **1**
Max. No. Sharing Bath: **4**
Double/pb: **$78**
Single/pb: **$68**
Double/sb: **$52–$72**
Single/sb: **$44–$62**

Guest Cottage: **$425–$550 weekly; sleeps 2–6**
Open: **Apr. 1–Oct. 1**
Reduced Rates: **Off-season**
Breakfast: **Continental, plus**
Pets: **Sometimes**
Children: **Welcome**
Smoking: **No**
Social Drinking: **Permitted**
Minimum Stay: **2 nights**

Just a block from the beach, shops, and restaurants is this bright and comfortable beach house. Former guests describe it as "cozy, cute, and clean." Deep-sea fishing, nature trails, and harbor tours are but a few things to keep you busy. Freshly-baked croissants in various flavors are a breakfast delight. You are welcome to use the sundeck, barbecue, and picnic tables.

Barclay Cottage ✪
400 16TH STREET, VIRGINIA BEACH, VIRGINIA 23451

Tel: **(804) 422-1956**
Hosts: **Peter and Claire**
Location: **20 mi. E of Norfolk**
No. of Rooms: **6**
No. of Private Baths: **2**

Max. No. Sharing Bath: **2**
Double/pb: **$80**
Double/sb: **$65–$70**
Open: **Apr.–Oct.; Special holidays**
Reduced Rates: **10% seniors**

Breakfast: **Full**
Credit Cards: **AMEX, MC, VISA**
Pets: **No**
Children: **No**

Smoking: **No**
Social Drinking: **Permitted**
Minimum Stay: **2 nights**

The Barclay is a historic building designed in turn-of-the-century, Southern Colonial style. Your hosts bring you casual sophistication in a warm, inn-like atmosphere two blocks from the beach and fishing pier. The inn has been completely restored to add the feeling of yesterday to the comfort of today. Peter and Claire look forward to welcoming you to their B&B, where the theme is, "We go where our dreams lead us."

The Iris Inn ✪
191 CHINQUAPIN DRIVE, WAYNESBORO, VIRGINIA 22980

Tel: **(540) 943-1991**
Best Time to Call: **10 AM–8 PM**
Hosts: **Wayne and Iris Karl**
Location: **25 mi. W of Charlottesville**
No. of Rooms: **6**
No. of Private Baths: **6**
Double/pb: **$75–$95**
Single/pb: **$65**
Open: **All year**
Reduced Rates: **Corporate, Sun.–Thurs.**

Breakfast: **Full**
Credit Cards: **MC, VISA**
Pets: **No**
Children: **Welcome, by arrangement**
Smoking: **No**
Social Drinking: **Permitted**
Minimum Stay: **2 nights weekends**
Airport: **Yes**

The charm and grace of southern living in a totally modern facility, nestled in a wooded tract on the western slope of the Blue Ridge overlooking the historic Shenandoah Valley—that's what awaits you at the Iris Inn in Waynesboro. It's ideal for a weekend retreat, a refreshing change for the business traveler, and a tranquil spot for the tourist to spend a night or a week. Guest rooms are spacious, comfortably furnished, and delightfully decorated in nature and wildlife motifs. Each room has private bath and individual temperature control.

The Travel Tree ✪
P.O. BOX 838, WILLIAMSBURG, VIRGINIA 23187

Tel: **(800) 989-1571**
Best Time to Call: **6–9 PM, weekdays**
Coordinator: **Joann Proper**
States/Regions Covered:
  Williamsburg, Jamestown, Yorktown
Descriptive Directory of B&Bs: **Free**

Rates (Single/Double):
  Modest: **$50–$70**
  Average: **$75–$95**
  Luxury: **$100–$125**
Credit Cards: **No**

This complimentary service offers you a broad view—a variety of choices among the B&B accommodations available in the Williamsburg area. Searching for lodgings in a historic estate, small inn, or private home becomes a one-step process when you make your reservations through The Travel Tree. Gift certificates are also available.

Applewood Colonial Bed & Breakfast ○
605 RICHMOND ROAD, WILLIAMSBURG, VIRGINIA 23185

Tel: **(800) 899-APLE (2753)**
Best Time to Call: **9:30 AM–12:30 PM;**
 3–10 PM
Hosts: **Fred Strout and Martha R. Jones**
Location: **5 mi. from Rte. I-64, Exit 238**
No. of Rooms: **4**
No. of Private Baths: **4**
Double/pb: **$75–$85**
Suites: **$125**
Open: **All year**

Reduced Rates: **Available**
Breakfast: **Full**
Credit Cards: **MC, VISA**
Pets: **No**
Children: **Welcome, in suite**
Smoking: **No**
Social Drinking: **Permitted**
Minimum Stay: **2 nights holiday**
 weekends
Airport/Station Pickup: **Yes**

The owner's apple collection is evident throughout this restored elegant Colonial home built in 1929 by the construction manager for Colonial Williamsburg. The house is located four short blocks from Colonial Williamsburg. Three guest rooms have queen canopy or poster beds, antique chests, and oriental rugs. The suite, on the first floor, has a queen poster bed with a fishnet canopy, a sitting area in front of a fireplace banked by bookcases, and a sunny breakfast room. Breakfast and afternoon refreshments are served in the formal dining room.

Blue Bird Haven B&B ○
**8691 BARHAMSVILLE ROAD, WILLIAMSBURG-TOANO,
VIRGINIA 23168**

Tel: **(804) 566-0177**
Best Time to Call: **Early mornings**
Host: **June Cottle**
Location: **9 mi. N of Williamsburg**
No. of Rooms: **3**
No. of Private Baths: **2**
Max. No. Sharing Bath: **4**
Double/pb: **$65**

Suites: **$76**
Open: **All year**
Breakfast: **Full**
Pets: **Sometimes**
Children: **Welcome**
Smoking: **No**
Social Drinking: **Permitted**

June welcomes you to her ranch-style home, located 20 minutes from Colonial Williamsburg. Guest accommodations, located in a private wing, feature traditional furnishings. June is interested in many kinds of handcrafts and has decorated the rooms with one-of-a-kind quilts, spreads, rugs, and pictures. Breakfast includes a Southern-style assortment of Virginia ham, spoon bread, red-eye gravy, blueberry pancakes, fresh fruits, home-baked biscuits, and granola. Blue Bird Haven is convenient to Busch Gardens, James River Plantations, and Civil War battlefields. After a full day of seeing the sights, you are welcome to enjoy some of June's evening desserts.

Candlewick Inn B&B ✪
800 JAMESTOWN ROAD, WILLIAMSBURG, VIRGINIA 23185

Tel: (804) 253-8693; (800) 418-4949	Reduced Rates: Available
Best Time to Call: Anytime	Breakfast: Full
Host: Mary L. Peters	Credit Cards: MC, VISA
Location: 2 miles from Route 64, Exit 242A	Pets: No
	Children: Welcome, over 12
No. of Rooms: 2	Smoking: No
No. of Private Baths: 2	Social Drinking: Permitted
Double/pb: $85	Minimum Stay: 2 nights
Single/pb: $75	Station Pickup: Yes
Open: All year	Foreign Languages: German

Mary restored and redecorated this 1946 two-story frame house so that it looks like a farmhouse from the previous century, with beam ceilings, chair rails, and beautiful canopy beds. She also sets out wonderful country breakfasts featuring home-baked bread and muffins. Then it's an easy four-block walk or bike ride to the historic area; first stop is William and Mary College, just across the way.

Colonial Capital Bed & Breakfast ✪
501 RICHMOND ROAD, WILLIAMSBURG, VIRGINIA 23185

Tel: (800) 776-0570; fax (804) 253-7667	Open: All year
	Breakfast: Full
Hosts: Barbara and Phil Craig	Credit Cards: AMEX, DISC, MC, VISA
Location: 2.5 mi. from I-64, Exit 238	Pets: No
No. of Rooms: 5	Children: Welcome, over 6
No. of Private Baths: 5	Smoking: Restricted
Double/pb: $76–$115	Social Drinking: Permitted
Suites: $100–$135	Airport/Station Pickup: Yes

Barbara and Phil offer a warm welcome to guests in their three-story Colonial revival (c.1926) home only three blocks from the historic area. The B&B is decorated with period antiques, oriental rugs, and many of the original lighting and plumbing fixtures, all guest rooms feature four-poster beds crowned with charming canopies. In the morning you can look forward to such treats as a soufflé, French toast, fluffy omelette, or yeast waffles complemented with a choice of juices, fresh fruits, and specially blended coffees and tea. The sunny solarium or formal dining room invite guests to linger over breakfast and get to know one another as does the plantation parlor where tea and wine are served during afternoons and evenings. Games, books, and puzzles are provided for your pleasure. Jamestown, Yorktown, some of the state's finest plantations, Busch Gardens, and Water Country USA are only a few minutes away. Personalized gift certificates are available.

For Cant Hill Guest Home
4 CANTERBURY LANE, WILLIAMSBURG, VIRGINIA 23185

Tel: **(804) 229-6623**
Best Time to Call: **Anytime**
Hosts: **Martha and Hugh Easler**
No. of Rooms: **2**
No. of Private Baths: **2**
Double/pb: **$65–$75**

Open: **All year**
Breakfast: **Continental**
Pets: **No**
Children: **Welcome, over 10**
Smoking: **No**
Social Drinking: **Permitted**

Situated in the heart of town, overlooking Lake Matoaka, a part of the campus of the College of William and Mary, the home is only a few blocks from the restored area of Colonial Williamsburg, yet very secluded and quiet in a lovely wooded setting. Both rooms are tastefully decorated, accented in winter with homemade quilts. Each room has a TV and a hearty Continental breakfast is served in the room. The hosts are happy to make dinner reservations for guests and provide very helpful information on the many attractions in the entire area.

Fox Grape Bed & Breakfast ☉
701 MONUMENTAL AVENUE, WILLIAMSBURG, VIRGINIA 23185

Tel: **(804) 229-6914; (800) 292-3699**
Best Time to Call: **9 AM–9 PM**
Hosts: **Bob and Pat Orendorff**
Location: **2 mi. from I-64, Exit 238**
No. of Rooms: **4**
No. of Private Baths: **4**
Double/pb: **$78–$84**
Single/pb: **$78–$84**

Open: **All year**
Reduced Rates: **10% seniors**
Breakfast: **Continental**
Pets: **No**
Children: **Welcome**
Smoking: **No**
Social Drinking: **Permitted**
Station Pickup: **Yes**

Warm hospitality awaits you just a seven-minute walk north of Virginia's restored Colonial capital. Furnishings include counted cross-stitch pieces, antiques, stained glass, stenciled walls, duck decoys, and a cup-plate collection. Pat enjoys doing counted cross-stitch. Bob carves walking sticks and makes stained-glass windows.

Governor's Trace ☺
303 CAPITOL LANDING ROAD, WILLIAMSBURG, VIRGINIA 23185

Tel: **(804) 229-7552; (800) 303-7552**	Open: **All year**
Best Time to Call: **9 AM–10 PM**	Breakfast: **Continental, plus**
Hosts: **Sue and Dick Lake**	Credit Cards: **MC, VISA**
Location: **2 mi. from I-64, exit 238**	Pets: **No**
No. of Rooms: **3**	Children: **No**
No. of Private Baths: **3**	Smoking: **No**
Double/pb: **$85**	Social Drinking: **Permitted**
Suites: **$95–$115**	

This Georgian brick home featured on the back cover of the 1992 edition of *Bed & Breakfast U.S.A.* is Colonial Williamsburg's closest B&B neighbor, just one door away. Hardy patriot, loyal royalist or plantation gentry travelers would have found the rooms here comfortably familiar but with modern exceptions, king- and queen-size beds and private baths. Special amenities include a fireplace in one bedroom and a screened-in porch off another. Private romantic candlelit breakfast is served in each room. Sue and Dick provide refuge from the modern world's hectic pace to let you discover unexpected treasures in an 18th-century atmosphere. Make "take away" memories at the Governor's Trace.

The Greenwoode Inn
104 WOODMONT PLACE, WILLIAMSBURG, VIRGINIA 23188

Tel: **(804) 566-8800**	Open: **All year**
Best Time to Call: **8 AM–10 PM**	Breakfast: **Full**
Hosts: **Dr. and Mrs. James Stam**	Pets: **No**
Location: **40 mi. E of Richmond**	Children: **Welcome, over 12**
No. of Rooms: **4**	Smoking: **No**
No. of Private Baths: **4**	Social Drinking: **Permitted**
Suites: **$95–$105**	

This B&B, in a three-story Georgian home, is especially noted for warm hospitality, good conversation, interesting antiques, beautiful accommodations, and a delicious breakfast—all the things one looks for in a bed and breakfast. Your hosts, Jim and Priscilla, who have retired from academia, love travel and people. They previously owned Miss Malley's Inn and The Little Traveller Inn, both on Chincoteague Island.

The Homestay Bed & Breakfast ❂
517 RICHMOND ROAD, WILLIAMSBURG, VIRGINIA 23185

Tel: (804) 229-7468; (800) 836-7468
Best Time to Call: 10 AM–9 PM
Hosts: Barbara and Jim Thomassen
Location: 3 mi. from Rte. I-64, Exit 238
No. of Rooms: 3
No. of Private Baths: 3
Double/pb: $75–$85
Single/pb: $65–$75
Open: All year
Reduced Rates: 20% less Jan. 2–
Mar. 15

Breakfast: Full
Credit Cards: MC, VISA
Pets: No
Children: Welcome, over 10
Smoking: No
Social Drinking: Permitted
Minimum Stay: 2 nights, weekends,
holidays, and special events
Airport/Station Pickup: Yes

Cozy and convenient! Enjoy the comfort of a lovely Colonial Revival home furnished with turn-of-the-century family antiques and country charm. Rooms with a Victorian double bed, king-size bed, or twin beds are available. The rooms are accented with an attention to detail. You may relax in the second floor sitting room or by the fire in the living room. A full breakfast, served in the formal dining room, features homemade breads, herb jellies (made with herbs from the garden), and delicious hot dishes. You are just four blocks from Williamsburg's famed historic area, adjacent to the College of William and Mary campus, alumni house and football stadium, and minutes away from Jamestown, Yorktown, and Busch Gardens.

Legacy of Williamsburg Tavern ❂
930 JAMESTOWN ROAD, WILIAMSBURG, VIRGINIA 23185-3917

Tel: (800) 962-4722; (804) 220-0524
Best Time to Call: 7 AM–9 PM
Hosts: Mary Ann and Ed Lutkewich
Location: 2 mi. from Rte. 64, exit 59
No. of Rooms: 4
No. of Private Baths: 4
Double/pb: $90
Suites: $135

Open: All year
Breakfast: Full
Credit Cards: MC, VISA
Pets: No
Children: No
Smoking: No
Social Drinking: Permitted

The Legacy of Williamsburg Tavern is furnished in true 18th-century tradition. Once you cross the brick entryway you begin your journey into another place and time. The suites have living rooms with fireplaces and decks for the ultimate romantic setting. Suites and rooms all feature beautiful canopy beds. Mary Ann and Ed like to share their experience of extensive travels and their vast knowledge of Colonial Williamsburg. In residence is a manager from China with five-star experience and service. In the morning, mouth-watering smells will awake you as your "all-day breakfast" is being prepared.

Liberty Rose B&B Inn ✪

1022 JAMESTOWN ROAD, WILLIAMSBURG, VIRGINIA 23185

Tel: **(804) 253-1260**	Reduced Rates: **5% after 3rd night**
Best Time to Call: **9 AM–9 PM**	Breakfast: **Full**
Hosts: **Brad and Sandi Hirz**	Credit Cards: **MC, VISA**
Location: **1 mi. from historic area**	Pets: **No**
No. of Rooms: **4**	Children: **No**
No. of Private Baths: **4**	Smoking: **No**
Double/pb: **$105–$115**	Social Drinking: **No**
3 Suites: **$145–$185**	Minimum Stay: **2 nights**
Open: **All year**	

This enchanting old home is one of Williamsburg's most romantic—Brad and Sandi created their B&B as a honeymoon project! Antiques from all periods fill the Liberty Rose. In the guest rooms, comfortable queen-size poster beds are draped with fringed reproduction damasks and topped with silk-covered goose-down duvets. Alongside the bed, in an old-fashioned armoire, you'll find a TV/VCR. The luxurious baths have claw-footed tubs, marble showers, and ample supplies of robes, towels, and bubble bath. And everywhere you'll notice little extras, such as a dish full of chocolates, complimentary soft drinks, freshly baked chocolate chip cookies, and a long-stemmed silk rose that's yours to keep.

War Hill ✪

4560 LONG HILL ROAD, WILLIAMSBURG, VIRGINIA 23188

Tel: **(804) 565-0248; (800) 743-0248**	Cottage: **$110–$155; sleeps 2–5**
Best Time to Call: **9 AM–9 PM**	Open: **All year**
Hosts: **Shirley, Bill, and Will Lee**	Breakfast: **Full**
Location: **2 mi. from Williamsburg**	Credit Cards: **MC, VISA**
No. of Rooms: **5**	Pets: **No**
No. of Private Baths: **5**	Children: **Welcome**
Double/pb: **$70–$90**	Smoking: **No**
Suite: **$95–$140; sleeps 2–5**	Social Drinking: **Permitted**

War Hill is situated in the center of a 32-acre working farm, just three miles from the tourist attractions. Built in 1968, this Colonial replica couples the charm of yesteryear with today's contemporary conveniences. The suite is composed of two bedrooms and a bath. The wide heart-pine floors came from an old school, the stairs from a church, the overhead beams from a barn; the oak mantel is over 200 years old. Fruits from a variety of trees in the orchard are yours to pick in season. In autumn, Shirley and Bill serve delicious homemade applesauce and cider. Angus show cattle graze in the pasture, and the sounds you'll hear are crickets, frogs, owls, and the morning crowing of the rooster.

Williamsburg Sampler Bed and Breakfast ✪
922 JAMESTOWN ROAD, WILLIAMSBURG, VIRGINIA 23185

Tel: (800) 722-1169; (804) 253-0398
Best Time to Call: 7:30 AM–10:30 PM
Hosts: Helen and Ike Sisane
Location: Heart of Williamsburg
No. of Rooms: 4
No. of Private Baths: 4
Double/pb: $90–$140

Open: All year
Breakfast: Full
Pets: No
Children: Welcome, over 12
Smoking: No
Social Drinking: Permitted
Airport/Station Pickup: Yes

Welcome to one of Williamsburg's finest 18th-century plantation-style homes. The three-story, brick Colonial B&B is richly furnished throughout with antiques, pewter, and samplers. This elegant home complements those located in the restored area and is within walking distance to historic Colonial Williamsburg. Lovely accommodations include two suites, four-poster beds in king and queen sizes, television, fireplaces, and your hosts' famous "skip lunch" breakfast. Personalized gift certificates are available.

Azalea House ✪
551 SOUTH MAIN STREET, WOODSTOCK, VIRGINIA 22664

Tel: (703) 459-3500
Hosts: Margaret and Price McDonald
Location: 35 mi. N of Harrisonburg
No. of Rooms: 3
No. of Private Baths: 3
Double/pb: $50–$70
Open: All year

Breakfast: Full
Credit Cards: AMEX, MC, VISA
Pets: No
Children: Welcome, over 6
Smoking: No
Social Drinking: Permitted

This spacious home, built in the early 1890s, served as a parsonage for 70 years. It has been restored following its Victorian tradition and has porches, bay windows, and a white picket fence—in spring, one hundred blooming azaleas enhance its beauty. The interior is made particularly lovely with family heirlooms and pretty color schemes. Azalea House is within walking distance of fine restaurants, antique shops, and an art gallery. It is convenient to wineries, orchards, trails, horseback riding, and fishing. Air-conditioning assures your summer comfort.

The Country Fare ✪
402 NORTH MAIN STREET, WOODSTOCK, VIRGINIA 22664

Tel: (703) 459-4828
Best Time to Call: 7–11 AM; 6–10 PM
Host: Bette Hallgren
Location: 35 mi. S of Winchester
No. of Rooms: 3

No. of Private Baths: 1
Max. No. Sharing Bath: 3
Double/pb: $65
Double/sb: $45–$55
Single/sb: $35

Open: **All year**
Breakfast: **Continental**
Pets: **No**

Children: **Welcome, by arrangement**
Smoking: No
Social Drinking: **Permitted**

A small cozy inn, circa 1772, The Country Fare is one of Shenandoah County's oldest homes. It is restored and carefully preserved and has wide pine floorboards upstairs, original doors and hardware, and walls hand-stenciled with original designs. Nana's Room boasts hand-painted furniture and a private bath. Two other bedrooms—one with a queen-size, the other with a full-size bed—share an old-fashioned bathroom with a claw-footed tub. Expanded Continental breakfast, served before the dining room's wood-burning stove, consists of seasonal fruits, juices, home-baked breads and muffins, and some of Nana's surprises. Your host will share information on the interesting sights and attractions of the valley.

For key to listings, see inside front or back cover.

✪ This star means that rates are guaranteed through December 31, 1996, to any guest making a reservation as a result of reading about the B&B in *Bed & Breakfast U.S.A.*—1996 edition.

Important! To avoid misunderstandings, always ask about cancellation policies when booking.

Please enclose a self-addressed, stamped, business-size envelope when contacting reservation services.

For more details on what you can expect in a B&B, see Chapter 1.

Always mention *Bed & Breakfast U.S.A.* when making reservations!

If no B&B is listed in the area you'll be visiting, use the form on page 249 to order a copy of our "List of New B&Bs."

We want to hear from you! Use the form on page 251.

WEST VIRGINIA

Gerrardstown •   • Martinsburg

Romney •   •
                   Charles Town

Elkins •

Huttonsville •   Mathias •

• Charleston

• White Sulphur Springs

Historic Charleston Bed & Breakfast ✪
114 ELIZABETH STREET, CHARLESTON, WEST VIRGINIA 25311

Tel: **(304) 345-8156; (800) CALL-WVA**
Best Time to Call: **8 AM–11 PM**
Hosts: **Bob and Jean Lambert**
Location: **½ mi. from I-77, I-64, Exit 99**
No. of Rooms: **3**
No. of Private Baths: **3**
Double/pb: **$70**
Single/pb: **$65**

Open: **All year**
Reduced Rates: **6% seniors, families**
Breakfast: **Full**
Credit Cards: **AMEX, MC, VISA**
Children: **Welcome**
Smoking: **No**
Airport Pickup: **Yes**

The exterior of this 1905 American Foursquare home is painted gray clapboard with white trim. Most of the interior woodwork is the original natural oak. Guest accommodations are spacious—each room has a fireplace, private sitting area, and central heating and air-conditioning. The entrance hall is furnished with a Victorian loveseat, candle table, and a claw-footed desk, setting the tone for the rest of the house, which is decorated with antiques, collectibles, and handicrafts. Breakfast is served in the dining room, on an early 1930s dining suite. Then you can explore the area, starting with the state capitol and cultural center one block away.

Washington House Inn ✪
216 SOUTH GEORGE STREET, CHARLES TOWN, WEST VIRGINIA 25414

Tel: **(304) 725-7923; (800) 297-6957**	Reduced Rates: **Available**
Best Time to Call: **Anytime**	Breakfast: **Full**
Hosts: **Nina and Mel Vogel**	Credit Cards: **AMEX, MC, VISA**
Location: **60 mi. NW of Washington, D.C.**	Pets: **No**
	Children: **Welcome, over 6**
No. of Rooms: **6**	Smoking: **No**
No. of Private Baths: **6**	Social Drinking: **Permitted**
Double/pb: **$70–$95**	Airport/Station Pickup: **Yes**
Open: **All year**	

George Washington didn't sleep here—but his relatives did. Built in 1899 by descendants of the president's brothers, John Augustine and Samuel, Washington House Inn is a wonderful example of Late Victorian architecture. From the three-story turret and wraparound porch to the carved oak mantels, this home echoes a bygone era. As you enter the main foyer, period antiques help you step back in time. In the morning, a hearty full breakfast is served in the dining room. Located in West Virginia's eastern gateway, the Inn is convenient to a host of activities. Within a ten-minute drive you will find Harpers Ferry National Park, white-water rafting, biking, and hiking on the restored C&O Canal towpath, thoroughbred horse racing, and Grand Prix–style sports car racing.

The Retreat at Buffalo Run ✪
214 HARPERTOWN ROAD, ELKINS, WEST VIRGINIA 26241

Tel: **(304) 636-2960**	Open: **All year**
Best Time to Call: **8 AM–9 PM**	Reduced Rates: **Weekly**
Hosts: **Kathleen Rhoad and Leslie Gordon**	Breakfast: **Full**
	Pets: **No**
Location: **160 mi. S of Pittsburgh**	Children: **Welcome**
No. of Rooms: **6**	Smoking: **No**
Max. No. Sharing Bath: **4**	Social Drinking: **Permitted**
Double/sb: **$64**	Airport Pickup: **Yes**
Single/sb: **$54**	

This gracious turn-of-the-century home on five acres is located at the gateway to the 840,000-acre Monongahela National Forest, within walking distance of downtown Elkins and Davis and Elkins College. The home is warmly decorated with antiques, art, and contemporary

furnishings. Wide porches, tall shade trees, evergreens, and rhododendron groves surround the house. Close by are wilderness areas
for hiking, biking, fishing, cross-country skiing; country auctions; and
the Augusta Heritage Arts Festival. Breakfasts receive rave reviews.
Leslie Gordon has been a forester and is a basket maker and weaver
on small looms.

Gerrardstown's Prospect Hill
BOX 135, GERRARDSTOWN, WEST VIRGINIA 25420

Tel: **(304) 229-3346**
Best Time to Call: **Evenings**
Hosts: **Hazel and Charles Hudock**
Location: **4 miles from Route 81**
No. of Rooms: **3**
No. of Private Baths: **3**
Double/pb: **$85–$95**
Single/pb: **$75–$85**

Guest Cottage: **$95 for 2; $135 for 4**
Open: **All year**
Breakfast: **Full**
Pets: **No**
Children: **Welcome in cottage**
Smoking: **Permitted**
Social Drinking: **Permitted**

Prospect Hill is a Georgian mansion set on 225 acres. The house dates
back to the 1790s, and is listed on the National Register of Historic
Places. One can see that this was a well-to-do gentleman's home, with
permanent Franklin fireplaces, antiques, and a half mural depicting
life in the days of the early Republic. Guests may choose one of the
beautifully appointed rooms in the main house or the former servants'
quarters, complete with country kitchen and a fireplace in the living
room. There is much to do on this working farm, including visiting
the antebellum outbuildings, fishing, biking, and exploring the vast

grounds. Near historic Harpers Ferry, Martinsburg, and Winchester, the area offers fine sightseeing and splendid restaurants.

The Hutton House ✪

ROUTES 219 AND 250, HUTTONSVILLE, WEST VIRGINIA 26273

Tel: **(304) 335-6701**	Reduced Rates: **Available**
Best Time to Call: **Anytime**	Breakfast: **Full**
Hosts: **Dean and Loretta Murray**	Other Meals: **Available**
Location: **17 mi. S of Elkins**	Credit Cards: **MC, VISA**
No. of Rooms: **6**	Pets: **No**
No. of Private Baths: **6**	Children: **Welcome**
Double/pb: **$65–$70**	Smoking: **No**
Single/pb: **$55–$65**	Social Drinking: **Permitted**
Open: **All year**	Airport/Station Pickup: **Yes**

Built in 1899 by a scion of Huttonsville's founder, Hutton House commands a broad view of the Tygart Valley and Laurel Mountain ridges. This ornate Queen Anne mansion, with its extraordinary woodwork and windows, is listed on the National Register of Historic Places. Travelers come here to ski at Snowshoe, visit Cass Railroad, and hike in the Monongahela National Forest. Civil War buffs will find plenty of battle sites to study, and the Augusta Heritage Arts Festival, in nearby Elkins, also merits a detour. For breakfast, your hosts dish out cantaloupe sorbet and whole wheat pancakes drizzled with maple syrup made from their own trees.

Mr. Richard's Olde Country Inn ✪

U.S. 219, ROUTE 1, BOX 11-A1, HUTTONSVILLE, WEST VIRGINIA 26273

Tel: **(304) 335-6659**	Open: **All year**
Best Time to Call: **AM**	Reduced Rates: **10% seniors**
Host: **Richard S. Brown**	Breakfast: **Full**
Location: **21 mi. S of Elkins**	Other Meals: **Available**
No. of Rooms: **13**	Credit Cards: **MC, VISA**
No. of Private Baths: **8**	Pets: **Sometimes**
Max. No. Sharing Bath: **4**	Children: **Welcome**
Double/pb: **$75**	Smoking: **Permitted**
Single/pb: **$35**	Social Drinking: **Permitted**
Double/sb: **$50**	Minimum Stay: **2 nights on 3-day**
Single/sb: **$35**	**weekends**
Guest Cottage: **$135; sleeps 6**	

Built in 1835, this antebellum mansion has been restored to its original splendor, with a full-service bar and restaurant. Some rooms have fireplaces, some have verandas. Guests dine on a robust West Virginia breakfast with specialties like stuffed French toast, omelettes, and fresh fruit. The restaurant is open daily for light lunches and dinners of seafood, charbroiled steaks, and family meals. The great outdoors is the big attraction here; local activities run the gamut from white-water rafting, hiking, mountain biking, skiing, hunting, and fishing, to the tamer sports of golfing and antiquing. Amateur astonomers will want to pull up at Greenbank Observatory, the largest telescope in the U.S.

Pulpit & Palette Inn ✪
516 WEST JOHN STREET, MARTINSBURG, WEST VIRGINIA 25401

Tel: **(304) 263-7012**
Hosts: **Bill and Janet Starr**
Location: **20 mi. S of Hagerstown**
No. of Rooms: **2**
Max. No. Sharing Bath: **4**
Double/sb: **$75**
Single/sb: **$60**
Open: **Mar.—Dec.**

Breakfast: **Full**
Credit Cards: **DISC, MC, VISA**
Pets: **No**
Children: **Welcome, over 12**
Smoking: **No**
Social Drinking: **Permitted**
Station Pickup: **Yes**

Built in 1870, this Italianate Victorian is furnished with American antiques, Oriental objets d'art, Tibetan rugs, paintings, and stained glass work done by the hostess. Bill and Janet's objective is to give personalized attention to guests with afternoon tea, complimentary evening drinks and hors d'oeuvres, a morning bed tray, and a full gourmet breakfast. Bill and Janet are retired educators; their interests include drama production, stained glass work, art appreciation, travel, and community service. The Pulpit & Palette Inn is located 30 minutes from Harpers Ferry National Park and the Antietam National Battlefield, and 80 minutes from historic Gettysburg.

Valley View Farm ✪
ROUTE 1, BOX 467, MATHIAS, WEST VIRGINIA 26812

Tel: **(304) 897-5229**
Best Time to Call: **Evenings, 8–10PM**
Host: **Edna Shipe**
Location: **130 mi. SW of D.C.**
No. of Rooms: **4**
Max. No. Sharing Bath: **4**
Double/sb: **$40**
Single/sb: **$20**
Open: **All year**

Reduced Rates: **Weekly**
Breakfast: **Full**
Other Meals: **Available**
Pets: **Welcome**
Children: **Welcome (crib)**
Smoking: **Permitted**
Social Drinking: **Permitted**
Airport/Station Pickup: **Yes**

This 1920s farmhouse is decorated with comfortable Early American–style furniture and family mementos, and there's a nice porch for relaxed visiting. This is no place to diet because Edna is a good cook. Seasonal recreational activities are available in nearby Lost River State Park and on Rock Cliff Lake. You are certain to enjoy the local festivals, house tours, and interesting crafts shops. Bryces Ski Resort is less than an hour away.

Hampshire House 1884 ○

165 NORTH GRAFTON STREET, ROMNEY, WEST VIRGINIA 26757

Tel: **(304) 822-7171**
Hosts: **Jane and Scott Simmons**
Location: **35 mi. W of Winchester, Va.**
No. of Rooms: **5**
No. of Private Baths: **5**
Double/pb: **$65–$85**
Single/pb: **$50–$60**
Open: **All year**
Reduced Rates: **Available**

Breakfast: **Full**
Credit Cards: **AMEX, DC, DISC, MC, VISA**
Pets: **No**
Children: **Welcome**
Smoking: **No**
Social Drinking: **Permitted**
Airport/Station Pickup: **Yes**

Only two and one half hours west of Washington, D.C., via Route 50, lies Romney, the oldest town in West Virginia. Surrounded by beautiful rolling hills, Hampshire House is conveniently located to the downtown area. Bicycles are ready for touring the town, with its quaint shops and historic buildings. Trail rides and hayrides are available at the local equestrian center, and winery tours are nearby. The bedrooms are attractively furnished with old-fashioned furniture and wallpapers and kept comfortable with central heating and air-conditioning. Jane and Scott graciously offer complimentary snacks and invite you to enjoy the old pump organ, television, VCR, or a variety of games.

The James Wylie House

208 EAST MAIN STREET, WHITE SULPHUR SPRINGS, WEST VIRGINIA 24986

Tel: **(304) 536-9444; (800) 870-1613**
Hosts: **Cheryl and Joe Griffith**
Location: **100 mi. SE of Charleston**
No. of Rooms: **4**
No. of Private Baths: **4**
Double/pb: **$55–$65**
Single/pb: **$50–$55**
Open: **All year**

Reduced Rates: **10% after 3rd night**
Breakfast: **Full or Continental**
Credit Cards: **AMEX, MC, VISA**
Pets: **No**
Children: **Welcome**
Smoking: **No**
Social Drinking: **Permitted**
Airport/Station Pickup: **Yes**

This three-story Georgian Colonial-style dwelling dating back to 1819 features large, airy rooms that are comfortably furnished and accented with antiques. Pretty quilts, iron beds, old toys, and select period pieces enhance the bedrooms' decor. Specialties such as apple pudding, homemade coffee cake, and a delicious egg-and-sausage casserole are often part of the breakfast fare. The world-famous Greenbrier Resort is less than one mile away and historic Lewisburg is less than nine miles away. Recreational opportunities abound in the nearby state parks and ski resorts.

Appendix:
UNITED STATES AND CANADIAN TOURIST OFFICES

Listed here are the addresses and telephone numbers for the tourist offices of every U.S. state and Canadian province. When you write or call one of these offices, be sure to request a map of the state and a calendar of events. If you will be visiting a particular city or region, or if you have any special interests, be sure to specify them as well.

State Tourist Offices

Alabama Bureau of Tourism and
  Travel
401 Adams Ave.
Montgomery, Alabama 36103
(205) 242-4169; (800) ALABAMA [252-2262]

Alaska Division of Tourism
P.O. Box 110801
Juneau, Alaska 99811-0801
(907) 465-2010

Arizona Office of Tourism
1100 W. Washington Street
Phoenix, Arizona 85007
(602) 542-8687 or (800) 842-8257

Arkansas Department of Park and
  Tourism
1 Capitol Mall
Little Rock, Arkansas 72201
(501) 682-7777 or (800) 643-8383 or
  (800) 828-8974

California Office of Tourism
801 K Street, Suite 1600
Sacramento, California 95814
(800) 862-2543 or (916) 322-2881

Colorado Dept. of Tourism
1625 Broadway
Suite 1700
Denver, Colorado 80202
(303) 592-5510 or (800) 255-5550

Connecticut Department of Economic
  Development—Vacations
865 Brook Street
Rocky Hill, Connecticut 06067-3405
(203) 258-4355 or (800) CT-BOUND
  [282-6863]

Delaware Tourism Office
99 Kings Highway, P.O. Box 1401
Dover, Delaware 19903
(302) 739-4271 or (800) 441-8846

Washington, D.C. Convention and
  Visitors' Association
1212 New York Avenue N.W.
Suite 600
Washington, D.C. 20005
(202) 789-7000

Florida Division of Tourism
126 W. Van Buren Street
Tallahassee, Florida 32399-2000
(904) 487-1462

Georgia Tourist Division
Box 1776
Atlanta, Georgia 30301
(404) 656-3590 or (800) 847-4842

Hawaii Visitors Bureau
2270 Kalakaua Avenue
Suite 801
Honolulu, Hawaii 96815
(808) 923-1811

Idaho Travel Council
700 W. State Street
P.O. Box 83720
Hall of Mirrors, 2nd floor
Boise, Idaho 83720-0093
(800) 635-7820 or (208) 334-2470

Illinois Office of Tourism
310 South Michigan Avenue
Suite 108
Chicago, Illinois 60604
(312) 744-2400 or (312) 814-4732 or
  (800) 822-0292 or
  (800) 223-0121 (out of state)

Indiana Tourism Development
  Division
1 North Capitol, Suite 100
Indianapolis, Indiana 46204-2288
(317) 232-8860 or (800) 759-9191

Iowa Tourism Office
200 East Grand Ave.
Des Moines, Iowa 50309
(515) 242-4705 or (800) 345-IOWA
  [4692]

Kansas Travel and Tourism Division
700 SW Harrison Street, Suite 1300
Topeka, Kansas 66603-3712
(913) 296-2009 or (800) 252-6727

Kentucky Department of Travel
  Development
Capitol Plaza Tower, 22nd floor
500 Mero Street
Frankfort, Kentucky 40601-1974
(502) 564-4930 or (800) 225-8747
  (out of state)

Louisiana Office of Tourism
P.O. Box 94291
Baton Rouge, Louisiana 70804-9291
(504) 342-8119 (within Louisiana) or
  (800) 633-6970 (out of state)

Maine Publicity Bureau
P.O. Box 2300
97 Winthrop Street
Hallwell, Maine 04347
(207) 582-9300 or (800) 533-9595

Maryland Office of Tourist
  Development
217 E. Redwood Street
Baltimore, Maryland 21202
(410) 333-6611 or (800) 719-5900

Massachusetts Office of Tourism
100 Cambridge Street—13th Floor
Boston, Massachusetts 02202
(617) 727-3201 or (800) 447-MASS
  [6277] (out of state)

Michigan Travel Bureau
Department of Commerce
P.O. Box 30226
Lansing, Michigan 48909
(517) 373-0670 or (800) 543-2YES [2937]

Minnesota Tourist Information Center
121 7th Place East
#100 Metro Square
St. Paul, Minnesota 55101-2112
(612) 296-5029 or (800) 657-3700
  (out of state)

Mississippi Division of Tourism
P.O. Box 1705
Ocean Springs, Mississippi 39566-1705
(601) 359-3297 or (800) 927-6378

Missouri Division of Tourism
P.O. Box 1055
Jefferson City, Missouri 65102
(314) 751-4133 or (800) 877-1234

Travel Montana
1424 9th Avenue
Helena, Montana 59620
(406) 444-2654 or (800) 548-3390

Nebraska Division of Travel and
  Tourism
P.O. Box 94666
Lincoln, Nebraska 68509
(402) 471-3791 or (800) 228-4307 (out of
  state) or (800) 742-7595 (within
  Nebraska)

Nevada Commission on Tourism
Capitol Complex
Carson City, Nevada 89710
(702) 687-4322 or (800) NEVADA 8
[638-2328]

New Hampshire Office of Travel and
  Tourism Development
P.O. Box 1856
Concord, New Hampshire 03302-1856
(800) FUN-IN-NH [386-4664] or (603)
  271-2666

New Jersey Division of Travel and
  Tourism
C.N. 826
Trenton, New Jersey 08625
(609) 292-2470 or (800) 537-7397

New Mexico Department of Tourism
491 Old Santa Fe Trail
Santa Fe, New Mexico 87503
(505) 827-7400, (800) 545-2040, or (800)
    545-2040 (out of state), (505) 827-
    7402 (FAX)

New York State Division of Tourism
1 Commerce Plaza
Albany, New York 12245
(518) 474-4116 or (800) 225-5697
    (in the Northeast except Maine)

North Carolina Travel and Tourism
    Division
430 North Salisbury Street
Raleigh, North Carolina 27611
(919) 733-4171 or (800) VISIT NC
    [847-4862]

North Dakota Tourism Promotion
Liberty Memorial Building
604 E. Boulevard
Bismarck, North Dakota 58505
(701) 224-2525 or (800) HELLO ND
    [435-5663]

Ohio Division of Travel and Tourism
77 South High Street, 29th Floor
P.O. Box 1001
Columbus, Ohio 43266
(800) 282-5393

Oklahoma Division of Tourism
P.O. Box 60,000
Oklahoma City, Oklahoma 73146
(405) 521-2406 or (800) 522-8565
    (within Oklahoma)

Oregon Economic Development
    Tourism Division
775 Summer Street N.E.
Salem, Oregon 97310
(503) 378-3451 or (800) 547-7842

Pennsylvania Bureau of Travel
    Marketing
Department of Commerce
453 Forum Building
Harrisburg, Pennsylvania 17120
(717) 787-5453 or (800) 847-4872

Puerto Rico Tourism Company
23rd Floor
575 Fifth Avenue
New York, New York 10017
(212) 599-6262 or (800) 223-6530
    or (800) 866-STAR [7827]

Rhode Island Department of
    Economic Development
Tourism and Promotion Division
7 Jackson Walkway
Providence, Rhode Island 02903
(401) 277-2601 or (800) 556-2484
    (East Coast from Maine to Virginia,
    also West Virginia and Ohio)

South Carolina Division of Tourism
1205 Pendleton St.
Columbia, South Carolina 29201
(803) 734-0122

South Dakota Division of Tourism
Capitol Lake Plaza
711 East Wells Avenue
Pierre, South Dakota 57501
(605) 773-3301 or (800) 732-5682
    (out of state) or (800) 952-2217
    (within South Dakota)

Tennessee Tourist Development
P.O. Box 23170
Nashville, Tennessee 37202-3170
(615) 741-2158

Texas Dept. of Commerce
Division of Tourism
P.O. Box 12728
Austin, Texas 78711-2728
(512) 462-9191 or (800) 452-9292

Utah Travel Council
Council Hall
Capitol Hill
Salt Lake City, Utah 84114
(801) 538-1030 or (800) 200-1160

Vermont Department of Travel and
    Tourism
134 State Street
Montpelier, Vermont 05602
(802) 828-3236 or (800) VERMONT
    [837-6668]

Virginia Division of Tourism
901 E. Byrd St.
Richmond, Virginia 23219
(804) 786-4484 or (800) 932-5827

Washington State Tourism
    Development Division
P.O. Box 42500
101 General Administration Building
Olympia, Washington 98504
(206) 586-2088 or (800) 544-1800 (out
    of state)

Travel West Virginia
2101 E. Washington Street
Charleston, West Virginia 25305
(800) CALL WVA [225-5982] or
(304) 558-2286

Wisconsin Division of Tourism
P.O. Box 7606
Madison, Wisconsin 53707-7606
(608) 266-2161 or (800) 372-2737
(within Wisconsin and neighboring
states) or (800) 432-8747 (out of
state)

Wyoming Travel Commission
I-25 and College Drive
Cheyenne, Wyoming 82002
(307) 777-7777 or (800) 225-5996
(out of state)

Canadian Province Tourist Offices

Alberta Tourism, Parks, and
Recreation
City Center Building
10155 102 Street
Edmonton, Alberta, Canada T5J 4L6
(403) 427-4321 (from Edmonton area)
or (800) 661-8888 (from the U.S. and
Canada)

Tourism British Columbia
1117 Wharf Street
Victoria, British Columbia, Canada
V8W 2Z2
(604) 663-6000 or (800) 663-6000

Travel Manitoba
Department 6020
7th Floor
155 Carlton Street
Winnipeg, Manitoba, Canada
R3C 3H8
(204) 945-3777 or (800) 665-0040 (from
mainland U.S. and Canada)

New Brunswick Tourism
P.O. Box 12345
Fredericton, New Brunswick, Canada
E3B 5C3
(506) 453-8745 or (800) 561-0123 (from
mainland U.S. and Canada)

Newfoundland/Labrador Tourism
Branch
Department of Tourism & Culture
P.O. Box 8730
St. John's, Newfoundland, Canada
A1B 4K2
(709) 729-2830 (from St. John's area)
or (800) 563-6353 (from mainland
U.S. and Canada)

Northwest Territories Tourism
(403) 873-7200 or (800) 661-0788

Tourisme Quebec
C.P. 979
Montreal, Quebec H3C QW3
(800) 363-7777 (from 26 eastern states)
or (514) 873-2015 (collect from all
other U.S. locations)

Tourism Saskatchewan
1919 Saskatchewan Drive
Regina, Saskatchewan, Canada
S4P 3V7
(306) 787-2300 or (800) 667-7191
(from Canada and mainland U.S.,
except Alaska)

Tourism Yukon
P.O. Box 2703
Whitehorse, Yukon, Canada Y1A 2C6
(403) 667-5340

BED AND BREAKFAST RESERVATION REQUEST FORM

Dear _____
   Host's Name

I read about your home in *Bed & Breakfast U.S.A., Southeast 1996*, and would be interested in making reservations to stay with you.

My name: _____

Address: _____
   street
_____
   city   state   zip

Telephone: _____
   area code

Business address/telephone: _____
_____

Number of adult guests: _____

Number and ages of children: _____

Desired date and time of arrival: _____

Desired length of stay: _____

Mode of transportation: _____
(car, bus, train, plane)

Additional information/special requests/allergies:

_____
_____
_____
_____
_____
_____

I look forward to hearing from you soon.

                              Sincerely,

APPLICATION FOR MEMBERSHIP
(Please type or print)
(Please refer to Preface, pages xvii–xviii for our membership criteria.)

Name of Bed & Breakfast: _____

Address: _____

City: _____ State: _____ Zip: _____ Phone: (   ) _____

Best Time to Call: _____

Host(s): _____

Located: No. of miles _____ compass direction _____ of Major

City _____ Geographic region _____

No. of miles _____ from major route _____ Exit: _____

No. of guest bedrooms with private bath: _____

No. of guest bedrooms that share a bath: _____

How many people (including *your* family) must use the shared
bath? _____

How many bedrooms, if any, have a sink in them? _____

Room Rates:
$ _____ Double—private bath $ _____ Double—shared bath
$ _____ Single—private bath $ _____ Single—shared bath
$ _____ Suites
Separate Guest Cottage $ _____ Sleeps _____

Are you open year-round? ☐ Yes   ☐ No
If "No," specify when you are open: _____

How many rooms are wheelchair-accessible? _____

Do you require a minimum stay? _____

Do you discount rates at any time? ☐ No   ☐ Yes

Do you offer a discount to senior citizens? ☐ No   ☐ Yes: _____ %

Do you offer a discount for families? ☐ No   ☐ Yes: _____ %

Breakfast: Type of breakfast included in rate:
☐ Full ☐ Continental

Describe breakfast specialties: _____
_____

Are any other meals provided? ☐ No   ☐ Yes
   Lunch ☐ cost: $ _____   Dinner ☐ cost: $ _____

Do you accept credit cards? ☐ No   ☐ Yes:
☐ AMEX ☐ DINERS ☐ DISCOVER ☐ MASTERCARD ☐ VISA

Will you GUARANTEE your rates from January through December
   1997? ☐ Yes   ☐ No

Note: This Guarantee applies only to those guests making reservations having read about you in *Bed & Breakfast U.S.A., Southeast
   1997.*

If you have household pets, specify how many:
   ☐ Dog(s)   ☐ Cat(s)   ☐ Other

Can you accommodate a guest's pet?
   ☐ No   ☐ Yes   ☐ Sometimes

Are children welcome? ☐ No   ☐ Yes   If "Yes," specify age
   restriction _____

Do you permit smoking somewhere inside your house?
   ☐ No ☐ Yes

Do you permit social drinking? ☐ No   ☐ Yes

Guests can be met at ☐ Airport ____ ☐ Train ____   ☐ Bus ____

Can you speak a foreign language fluently? ☐ No   ☐ Yes
Describe: _____

GENERAL AREA OF YOUR B&B (e.g., Boston historic district; 20 minutes from Chicago Loop):

GENERAL DESCRIPTION OF YOUR B&B (e.g., brick Colonial with white shutters; Victorian mansion with stained-glass windows):

AMBIENCE OF YOUR B&B (e.g., furnished with rare antiques; lots of wood and glass):

THE QUALITIES THAT MAKE YOUR B&B SPECIAL ARE:

THINGS OF HISTORIC, SCENIC, CULTURAL, OR GENERAL INTEREST NEARBY (e.g., one mile from the San Diego Zoo; walking distance to the Lincoln Memorial):

YOUR OCCUPATION and SPECIAL INTERESTS (e.g., a retired teacher of Latin interested in woodworking; full-time host interested in quilting):

If you do welcome children, are there any special provisions for them (e.g., crib, playpen, high-chair, play area, baby-sitter)?

Do you offer snacks (e.g., complimentary wine and cheese; pretzels and chips but BYOB)?

Can guests use your kitchen for light snacks? ☐ No ☐ Yes

Do you offer the following amenities? ☐ Guest refrigerator
   ☐ Air-conditioning ☐ TV ☐ Piano ☐ Washing machine
   ☐ Dryer ☐ Hot tub ☐ Pool ☐ Tennis court
   Other _____

What major college or university is within 10 miles?
_____

Please supply the name, address, and phone number of three personal references from people not related to you (please use a separate sheet).

Please enclose a copy of your brochure along with color photos including exterior, guest bedrooms, baths, and breakfast area. Bedroom photos should include view of the headboard(s), bedside lamps and night tables. Please show us a typical breakfast setting. Use a label to identify the name of your B&B *on each*. If you have a black-and-white line drawing, send it along. If you have an original breakfast recipe that you'd like to share, send it along, too. (Of course, credit will be given to your B&B.) **Nobody can describe your B&B better than you. Limit your description to 100 words and submit it typed, double-spaced, on a separate sheet of paper. We will of course reserve the right to edit.** As a member of the Tourist House Association of America, your B&B will be described in the next edition of our book, *Bed & Breakfast U.S.A., Southeast*, published by Plume, an imprint of Dutton Signet, a division of Penguin USA, and distributed to bookstores and libraries throughout the U.S. The book is also used as a reference for B&Bs in our country by major offices of tourism throughout the world.

Note: The following will NOT be considered for inclusion in *Bed & Breakfast U.S.A., Southeast:* B&Bs having more than 15 guest rooms. Rental properties or properties where the host doesn't reside on the premises. Rates over $85 for double occupancy. (This does not include reservation services, suites, cottages, apartments; or qualified B&Bs.) Rates exceeding $35 where 6 people share a bath. Rates exceeding $40 where 5 people share a bath, or rooms are without night tables or adequate bedside reading lamps. Applications that are incomplete, no photos, write up etc. Applications received in states that are overcrowded; this is due to space limitations.

Note: If the publisher or authors receive negative reports from your guests regarding a deficiency in our standards of CLEANLINESS, COMFORT, and CORDIALITY, and/or failure to honor the rate guarantee, we reserve the right to cancel your membership.

This membership application has been prepared by:

_____
(Signature)

Please enclose your $45 membership dues.   Date: _____

Yes! ☐ I'm interested in Group Liability Insurance.
No ☐ I am insured by _____ .

Return to:
Tourist House Association of America
RD 1, Box 12A
Greentown, Pennsylvania 18426

To assure that your listing will be considered for the 1997 edition of
Bed & Breakfast U.S.A., Southeast, we MUST receive your completed
application by March 31, 1996. Thereafter, listings will be considered only for the semiannual supplement. (See page 249.)

APPLICATION FOR MEMBERSHIP FOR A
BED & BREAKFAST RESERVATION SERVICE

NAME OF BED & BREAKFAST SERVICE: _____

ADDRESS: _____

CITY: _____ STATE: _____ ZIP: _____ PHONE:(   ) _____

COORDINATOR: _____

BEST TIME TO CALL: _____

Do you have a telephone answering ☐ machine?   ☐ service?

Names of state(s), cities, and towns where you have hosts (in alphabetical order, please, and limit to 10):

Number of hosts on your roster: _____

THINGS OF HISTORIC, SCENIC, CULTURAL, OR GENERAL INTEREST IN THE AREA(S) YOU SERVE:

Range of Rates:
    Modest: Single $ _____   Double $ _____
    Average: Single $ _____   Double $ _____
    Luxury: Single $ _____   Double $ _____

Will you GUARANTEE your rates through December 1997?
☐ Yes ☐ No

How often do you reinspect listings? _____
Do you require a minimum stay? _____
Surcharges for one-night stay? _____
Do you accept credit cards? ☐ No ☐ Yes:
☐ AMEX ☐ DINERS ☐ DISCOVER ☐ MASTERCARD
☐ VISA

Is the guest required to pay a fee to use your service?
☐ No ☐ Yes—The fee is $ _____

Do you publish a directory of your B&B listings?
☐ No ☐ Yes—The fee is $ _____

Are any of your B&Bs within 10 miles of a university? Which? ____

Briefly describe a sample host home in each of the previous categories: e.g., a cozy farmhouse where the host weaves rugs; a restored 1800 Victorian where the host is a retired general; a contemporary mansion with a sauna and swimming pool.

Please supply the name, address, and phone number of three personal references from people not related to you (please use a separate sheet of paper). Please enclose a copy of your brochure.

This membership application has been prepared by:

_____
(Signature)

Please enclose your $45 membership dues.   Date: _____

If you have a special breakfast recipe that you'd like to share, send it along. (Of course, credit will be given to your B&B agency.) As a member of the Tourist House Association of America, your B&B agency will be described in the next edition of our book, *Bed & Breakfast U.S.A., Southeast*, published by Plume, an imprint of Dutton Signet, a division of Penguin USA. Return to: Tourist House Association, RD 1, Box 12A, Greentown, PA 18426.

To ensure that your listing will be considered for the 1997 edition, we must receive your completed application by March 31, 1996. Thereafter, listings will be considered only for the semiannual supplement. (See next page.)

INFORMATION ORDER FORM

We are constantly expanding our roster to include new members in the Tourist House Association of America. Their facilities will be fully described in the next edition of *Bed & Breakfast U.S.A., Southeast*. In the meantime, we will be happy to send you a list including the name, address, telephone number, etc.

For those of you who would like to order additional copies of the book, and perhaps send one to a friend as a gift, we will be happy to fill mail orders. If it is a gift, let us know and we'll enclose a special gift card from you.

ORDER FORM

To:
Tourist House
Association—
Book Dept.
RD 1, Box 12A
Greentown, PA
18426

From: _____
(Print your name)
Address: _____

City   State   Zip

Date: _____

Please send:

☐ List of new B&Bs ($3.00), available July to December.

☐ _____ copies of *Bed & Breakfast U.S.A., Southeast* @ $14.00 each (includes 4th class mail)

Send to: _____

Address: _____

City   State   Zip

☐ Enclose a gift card from:

Please make check or money order payable to Tourist House Association.

WE WANT TO HEAR FROM YOU!

The Tourist House Association of America is looking for Bed & Breakfasts completely set up to accommodate disabled guests.

A special section of wheelchair accessible B&B listings has been incorporated in *Bed & Breakfast U.S.A., Southeast*.

Requirements are comfort, cordiality, and cleanliness at a fair price. Ramps for wheelchairs, reach bars for bathtubs and toilets, doorways wide enough and breakfast table high enough so a wheelchair can fit comfortably. Also activities that are accessible to disabled participants.

If you or someone you know meets these requirements, please fill out the enclosed form. If you need more information as to whether you qualify, contact Tourist House Association of America at (717) 676-3222.

Name of B&B: _____

Address: _____
       Street

_____
       City   State   Zip

Please contact the following B&Bs; I think that they would be great additions to the next edition of *Bed & Breakfast U.S.A., Southeast*.

Name of B&B: _____

Address: _____
       Street

_____
       City   State   Zip

Comments:

As a member of the Tourist House Association, there is no charge for this listing.

Just tear out this page and mail it to us. It won't ruin your book!

Return to:
Tourist House Association of America
RD 1, Box 12A
Greentown, Pennsylvania 18426